EDUCATIONAL TECHNOLOGY
Concept and Technique

EDUCATIONAL TECHNOLOGY

Concept and Technique

B.D. BHATT
S.R. SHARMA

KANISHKA PUBLISHERS, DISTRIBUTORS
NEW DELHI-110 002

KANISHKA PUBLISHERS, DISTRIBUTORS
4697/5-21A, Ansari Road, Daryaganj
New Delhi -110 002
Phones : 2327 0497, 2328 8285
Fax : 011-2328 8285
E-mail : kanishka_publishing@yahoo.co.in

Educational Technology: Concept and Technique
First Published 1993
Edition 2020

ISBN: 978-81-85475-52-0

PRINTED IN INDIA

Published by Madan Sachdeva for Kanishka Publishers, Distributors, 4697/5-21A, Ansari Road, Daryaganj, New Delhi-110 002, Typeset by Sunshine Graphics, Delhi, and Printed at Rajdhani Printers, Delhi.

PREFACE

With the advancement in industrial and technological fields the process of education has become more complex and technical. The industrialized countries of the West have tried to adjust their educational systems according to the needs of the technological and scientific developments and have invested huge sums of money in research. The new findings in the field of psychology also have led to changes in the techniques and methodology of teaching.

The concerns for getting a regular supply of scientific and technological manpower, the societies of West have modified the methods of teaching. This new concern is reflected by the newer methodology popularly called as educational technology.

For a new education new methods of teaching are needed. The best use of audio-visual aids mechines radio, television and computer is the broader area of educational technology. This use is for improving the quality of education. Some rudimentary efforts have been made in India in the field of educational technology. All these issues have been discussed in the coming parts of this book.

AUTHORS

PREFACE

CONTENTS

1

INTRODUCTION

In a recent article titled, 'U.S. Schools lack Academic Focus', Philip G. Altbach has observed that yet another international survey of educational achievement conducted a while ago has ranked the United States near the bottom of the academic heirarchy*. He has observed that the first step to school improvement is to figure out what we really want from our schools and then perhaps to look abroad for some useful models to follow. Simply he moaning the modest academic achievement of many of America's children will not get us far.

But this is equally true that while as America is the only super power in the world at the moment, it is providing leadership in the academic field also.

The American Government, Foundåtions and social scientists and the university academics are putting in lot of efforts in research in the field of education.

A.N. Whitehead had rightly said, "In the conditions of modern life the rule is absolute, the race which does not value trained intelligence is doomed."

*Times of India, New Delhi 31st March 1992. In America sufficient amount of money is invested in research and for the training of man power. In the contemporary period American education is passing through a revolutionary phase. The American findings have a relevance for India in the field of educational technology also.

Frontiers of Education

Revolutions always look impossible before the fact, inevitable afterward. So it is with the current revolution in American education. New ideas are routing traditional ideas and are beginning to transform every aspect of school practice from curriculum to architecture from the structure of the grades to the purpose of learning, from the training of teachers to the motivating of students. Yet a decade ago the "conventional wisdom" about teaching and learning was so entrenched that it seemed impossible for new ideas to sweep through the schools with such speed.

In 1955 the Progressive Education Association closed its doors, marking the end of an era. Progressive education was clearly dead as a reform movement—the slogans it promulgated had been accepted verbally by most American educators, but at the cost of its basic principles. Started as a movement to use education to reform society, it had degenerated into a parody of itself, a kind of quasi-vocational training designed to adjust the student to the status quo. The springs of creativity and experimentation in American education seemed to have run dry.

In retrospect, however, it is clear that powerful forces in American society and in education were generating another spurt of innovation and reform, along quite different lines. On the one hand, Americans increasingly realized the importance of education. For the individual, it meant a chance for college and, beyond that, an opportunity to fit into the new occupational world of managers, experts, and skilled workers which was being shaped by automation. For the nation, education was clearly the key to strength in a scientific and technological age. Sputnik, that superb visual aid, riveted home the relevance of Whitehead's dictum: "In the conditions of modern life the rule is absolute, the race which does not value trained intelligence is doomed."

On the other hand, new ideas were sprouting within education itself They had four chief sources: university scholars, educational foundations (governmental and private), experimental psychologists and other social scientists, and imaginative schoolmen. From these sources, singly and in combination, came notions leading to bold experimentation.

The university scholars, after years of merely sniping at the public schools from their ivory towers, came down to help revise the curricula in physics, mathematics, biology, and other subjects. Their contribution was a profound understanding of the basic structure of their subjects: what the latest developments were, what was really important, what should be learned first.

The foundations, such as Ford and Carnegie and the National Science Foundation, contributed several things besides money, that necessary but not sufficient cause of improvement in education. They encouraged a break with tradition through their receptivity to new ideas; they instilled a sense of urgency and relevance through their national viewpoint and their public responsibility; and they assisted the spread of new ideas, once these were formulated and tested, by such means as the government-sponsored summer institutes in foreign languages, mathematics, and science.

The experimental psychologists tended to make their impact as individuals rather than as a group. B.F. Skinner sparked the whole teaching-machine movement with his notions of operant conditioning; Jerome S. Bruner synthesized and extended the new ideas of structure, intuition, and discovery in learning; Omar Khayyam Moore led the way in autotelic learning. Men such as these exercised far—reaching influence as they continued the Copernican revolution in education begun by Comenius in the seventeenth century—to put the learner, rather than the teacher, at the heart of the educational enterprise.

Finally, the front-line, battle-scarred veterans—the practicing schoolmen—deserve the most credit if our schools today contain at least the seeds of a new kind of education. For through them the experiments supported by the foundations and the notions about teaching and learning suggested by the psychologists and other social scientists found their way into schools. Schoolmen joined with the university scholars in framing and constantly revising the new curricula. It is they —the school administrators and, even more, the practicing teachers—who adjusted to radical changes in what, how, and why they were teaching, bringing their own experience and insights to bear on powerful new techniques such as team teaching and nongraded schools.

American education has a long way to go before it is caught up in thoroughgoing revolution, innovation, and change. A frontier is, by definition, a thin line, which few inhabitants of a country ever see. Still fewer live there. The overwhelming majority of our teachers, administrators, and school systems are still wedded to the status quo. The subjects that dominate the agendas of local school boards in our typical towns and cities are not the learning, process, teaching machines, team teaching, or autotelic learning. More likely they are the immemorial problems of school bond issues, plumbing contracts, and the bus routes—and this is all but inevitable.

Yet surely there is more than this to the educational enterprise of a great nation. In every other field we are committed to do more than merely sustain the status quo. We see, to surpass ourselves, to devise more potent means to more civilized ends, to give our children more than we had, whether that was much or little. Surely we seek no less in education, which is the single most important provision we can make for our children.

It is in this realm that we must turn for guidance and inspiration to the pioneers on the frontiers of education. They will not help us with bond issues, plumbing, or bus routes. But they will show us what lies beyond those problems. Dealing as they do with the basic questions of educational substance, instructional technique, and human potential, the pioneers indicate how our schools can be significantly improved for every child, rather than merely sustained for the mythical average. The new ideas reported in this book have by no means captured the American educational establishment, but they do constitute the vital growing edge of education. Without such creative ideas, the vast hinterland would eventually wither and die.

The pioneering work in education today seems to fall into three categories. First, there is the harnessing of modern technology to education. The tools and facilities of schooling are being transformed. Like so much of the current revolution in education, this industrialization of the schools seems inevitable in retrospect. A highly industrialized society, transformed from home to factory by such things as television, automation, and computers, simply cannot afford to drag behind it an inefficient edcational system still dependent on the blackboard and the slide projector.

Second, the conventional pattern of education—the way it trains, organizes, and uses teachers and students—is undergoing radical revision. The egg-crate school, composed of identical, self-enclosed classrooms, is giving way to a more flexible, functional arrangement. Teaching is frequently done in teams rather than solo, with each team member concentrating on his strongest technique or specialty. The system of grades has begun to disintegrate, with students permitted to progress at their individual rates in each subject. Our teachers are beginning to assume a new look, too, owing to programmes of training which stress broad liberal education, meaningful practice teaching, sophisticated professional courses, and training in the use of technology.

Third, the basic process of learning is slowly being altered by new ideas about how students acquire knowledge and understanding. We increasingly recognize the varieties of human ability unmeasured by IQ tests, and we are taking steps to motivate the student from within rather than by outside rewards and punishments.

This, then, is our map of the educational frontiers today. But what lies beyond the frontiers? What will the school of the future be like if we extrapolate the trends and possibilities which these pioneers describe?

The school of the future, recognizing that formal education is in large part a process of communication, will harness every kind of modern technology to its purpose. With complete control over various media—television, audio tapes, projectors of various kinds—teachers will design lessons for different groups of students, and even for individual students, drawing upon an extensive repertory of sight and sound materials. Teachers and school administrators will use technology as readily as businessmen or journalists use it. Nowadays if you walk through a factory with an industrial engineer you will see him wince every time he sees a worker performing some task which could be done far better and more cheaply by machine. In the school of tomorrow there will be the same aversion to having highly trained teachers deliver uniform lectures to different groups or run drill sessions—necessary tasks which can be done perfectly well by machines. As has happened in industry, the human being will be jacked up to truly skilled work by the use of machines for routine labours. "Any teacher who can be replaced by a machine," as B.F. Skinner has said, "should be."

The school of the future will be organized along lines which would today seem anarchic to most schoolmen. They are accustomed to the "necessity" for dividing students into groups which are homogeneous along some dimension or other: age, intelligence, ability. These groups then tend to remain fixed; one must, after all, know where the students *are*. The school of tomorrow will be so flexible that a student will proceed at his own rate in each subject, and, indeed, our idea of what constitutes a "subject" may change with the changing needs of each student. There will be so many ways of learning that students will think of themselves not as members of classes, but as colleagues of other students, working together to learn specific aspects of the various "subjects." And certainly the teachers will not generally gear their instruction to groups or classes, but to individual students.

Lloyd Trump, of the National Education Association, suggests that students in tomorrow's secondary school will spend 40 per cent of their time in independent study, 40 per cent in large groups, and the remaining 20 per cent in small group or tutorial sessions. Another educator, Jack Frymier, of Ohio State University, envisages a school in which students will see a master teacher for only one half-hour every two weeks, working the rest of the time under the tutelage of less trained instructors or on their own. The master teacher would function as a physician does, analyzing the students learning problems with the aid of full diagnostic reports and prescribing "treatment" to be administered by the lower-echelon teachers. We need accept neither of these images as the last word, but they are useful in stimulating our thinking about totally new ways of relating human beings to formal education. There is no self-evident reason for assuming that our current procedures, inherited from the one-room schoolhouse and the nineteenth-century urban school, are necessarily the best. In fact, it would be quite extraordinary, in the light of our new knowledge about the way human beings learn and the way they relate one to another, our new technology for instruction, and the new demands on the schools, if our traditional modes of education *were* the optimum ones for the second half of the twentieth century.

The school of the future will base its instructional strategy on new ideas about how children learn. Under the impact of findings in the social sciences we should come to view the school not as the place where students are taught a set body of knowledge, but as a place where every resource enhances their desire and competence to learn. Eventually we can probably leave much of the actual *learning* to the student himself, abetted by a wide range of materials and media which need not be provided by or at the school.

What will learning mean in the future? It will comprise many things, varying from student to student. In general, it will be characterized by an understanding of the ways of knowing proper to each of the standard fields of knowlege, a capacity to derive emotional as well as intellectual satisfaction out of knowing, and a fluency in using all the available personal resources of intelligence, creativity, and perseverance in the pursuit of knowledge.

Education's Industrial Revolution

America's schools were bypassed by the industrial revolution. While the world around them was being overrun by machines, our educational institutions remained virtually untouched by technology, and even today the machine seems out of place in the classroom. Recent developments in educational theory and practice, however, show that technology has finally invaded the schoolhouse.

First, education itself is coming to be thought of as our greatest industry, a vast enterprise employing more people than any other, engaging the full-time activity of at least a quarter of the nation, using a larger plant than the steel industry's and requiring a total budget dwarfed only by that for defense. The products of this massive industry are the "human resources" which we now recognize as the backbone of our technological society. The business of America has become, at least in part, education.

But the schoolmen are finding that they have a tiger by the tail. For the concept of education as an industry brings up a new question: is it efficient? To the extent that it is considered an industry, education is expected to match the efficiency of the nation's other productive enterprises. But *Fortune* magazine has reported that educational productivity has been declining since the turn of the century. Arguing that Americans are not getting a big enough return on their invested education dollar, *Fortune* calculated the efficiency of the schools by analyzing the number of pupils instructed and the time and personnel required to do the job. In their need to achieve efficiency in production, according to *Fortune*, the schools are no different from General Motors." Unless reforms are forthcoming, "the financial difficulties of the education industry will be compounded woefully."

Responding to such rebukes, the schools have recently undertaken some unprecedented innovations. The previous great wave of widespread experimentation in American education saw the establishment of progressive institutions in the early decades of this century. These schools and colleges questioned the basic goals of education. But the wave of experimentation which has swept American education during the 1960's has been concerned primarily with efficient techniques of instruction.

The national purpose newly assigned to education is the motive force behind much of this experimentation. There is an urgent need for scientific and technical "brainpower," and schools are assigned the task of filling that need. Many observers feel that the resulting scientific and technical preoccupation has tended to stifle humanistic education. But, for better or worse; the role assigned to education today has raised disturbing questions about the effectiveness of our schools in achieving the new national purpose, or indeed any true educational purpose.

In effect, the new wave of experimentation signalizes education's tardy recognition of the industrial revolution. The schools are admitting technology in its broadest definition, embracing processes and procedures as well as machines. The present revolution is of a wholly different order from the "scientific management" movement that obsessed school boards earlier in the century and that affected mainly such superficial aspects of school operation as cost accounting and book-keeping. Section II of this book samples the organizational changes whereby the schools are catching up with the idea of the division of labour and the benefits of liberating the skilled and the professional worker from routine tasks. In this opening section we shall see how the schools are overcoming their traditional antipathy to machines and are embracing all manner of mechanical and electronic aids to learning.

James D. Finn, professor of education at the University of Southern California, was the principal investigator for the

National Education Association's project on the educational implications of technology. In his essay on "Technology and the Instructional Process," he traces the history of technology in education, surveys the current scene, and offers some penetrating projections of the possible future. Finn sees us at a turning point in the "industrialization" of education.

After Finn's overview of the topic, we look at one of the most exciting of the new educational technologies: televised instruction. Television has revolutionized contemporary life, and its impact on education has been powerful, largely through support from the Ford Foundation and the federal government. Theodore R. Conant describes the extent of television teaching in American education today, analyzing its strengths and weaknesses. Conant, who is now with the National Film Board of Canada, served the Ford Foundation for several years as a programme specialist in instructional television.

The use of teaching machines caught the public imagination of Americans more than any other change in our schools in the fifties. The idea has spread faster, probably, than any other in the history of education. By 1962 an NEA survey revealed that school principals around the country thought that, of all the innovations currently being introduced, programmed learning would make the greatest gains in the next five years—their collective prediction was that its use would increase by 250 per cent.

The literature on teaching machines and programmed instruction has mushroomed in the last few years. An essential introduction is still the seminal essay by Professor B.F. Skinner, of Harvard University, the psychologist who gave this movement its initial stimulation in the fifties. (Sidney Pressey actually invented the prototype device in 1926, but it was designed more for testing than for teaching, and it never caught on.) Skinner explains why teaching machines were developed, exactly how they operate in the classroom, the experiments on which they are based, and the ways in which they could completely revolutionize education and learning theory. "The Science of Learning and the Art of Teaching" was published in 1954; it does not cover such subjects as the latest wrinkle in the arguments about "linear" versus "branching" programmes, the difficulties of good programming, or the final word on the dispute over machine versus programme. But it expounds the underlying psychological rationale which makes programmed learning so much more than educational gimmickry. Skinner also eloquently envisions what this movement could do for the schools.

The computer is probably the single device which to most people symbolizes the scientific culture which increasingly dominates our lives. But one rarely thinks of computers in education—a good example of the technological lag which James D. Finn excoriates in his essay. "Computers in Education," by Don D. Bushnell, president-elect of the Association for Educational Data Systems, explores the uses of computers in direct teaching, in making information accessible to the learner through information retrieval systems, in school administration, and in simulating educational situations for training and research. His piece makes it clear that we have at hand the otion—given sufficient imagination, dedication, and funds—to alter our educational system radically through the installation of computers at the very heart of teaching.

There seems little question that the rationalization and mechanization of the instructional process will proceed rapidly in American education during the coming decade. Education has been inordinately timid in harnessing technology to its purposes. It is a scandal that schools are not more efficient; this failure is one of the reasons teachers cannot be paid higher salaries. Any social etnerprise which goes to the public purse for support must be prepared to show that the money it gets is being used to the best effect.

But the "conventional wisdom" of education, formulated before the days of mass communication and teaching machines, recoils from the prospect of a school system which would be based as much on technology as on the hallowed personal contact between student and teacher. It is true that mechanization and rationalization can so transform an activity that it loses its unique character and value; farming is an example. "We have not yet learned to enjoy the blessings of automation without sacrificing human values in any area of activity," observes Harry Broudy, professor of education at the University of Illinois. "Is there reason to believe that we can do otherwise in automated instruction?"

Broudy wisely concludes that, despite the dangers, "we have no real choice but to try to outwit the machine age, to seek therein the potentialities for human values that it undeniably has." The schools have too long prided themselves on a kind of conspicuous inefficiency. The times demand a ruthless substitution of new pedagogical methods for old whenever the new techniques can provide more effective instruction, even if in the process we must eliminate some of the conventional amenities of school and college life. Educators must work out balanced judgements on the opportunities and hazards of the industrial revolution in education.

Moreover, there is no evidence that the use of technology in education *necessarily* undermines either humanistic or democratic values in the learning process. The use of such devices may well create new opportunities by making the best instruction available in every school. As suggested earlier, it is the purpose to which these neutral mechanisms are geared, not the mechanisms themselves, that is in question.

It is possible to use machines in education without turning schools and colleges into factories. Indeed, at a time when students come in tidal waves, technology's labour-saving teaching devices can free the time of the best teachers for more personal and specialized teaching. It may be the only way to *avoid* regimentation.

For example, small classes and personal contact with a teacher are clearly not basic educational values in themselves. If the teacher is incompoment, a small class merely gives him the opportunity to "communicate his mediocrity in an intimate environment," in the widely quoted words of the late President

Charles Johnson, of Fisk University. The value to be guarded is personal contact with an able, inspiring teacher when the student needs him most. At times, the student may not need this at all but could do much better if brought into electronic contact with a specialist via film or television, or with an expertly produced teaching-machine progamme. By insisting that quality education cannot take place unless the student is in the presence of a warm body, we have frequently sacrificed the genuine values of personal instruction to the formal requirements of a bureaucratic cliche.

In education, as everywhere else, technology increases alternatives, opens up new possibilities. It demands of those who would use it fully and well a firm grasp of their own basic purposes. Without such an understanding of fundamental concerns and priority goals, education's industrial revolution could bog down in a deluge of hardware. But guided by a clear understanding of educational purposes, it can make possible the most stimulating reorganization of the schools since the era of the progressives.

Broadly speaking the use of textbooks, audiovisual aids, programmed learning educational films, educational television and computers, for the realisation of educational objectives in the modern industrial culture is known as educational technology. All these factors have been discussed in this volume.

2

TECHNOLOGY AND THE INSTRUCTIONAL PROCESS

> *As an instrument of work engaging human energies in a manner far surpassing the lure of war, as a social dissolvent and readjuster, and as a philosophy of action, technology must be brought into the main stream of history, if the course of history is to be surveyed correctly and "the dark imminence of the unknown future" is to be in any way penetrated. . .*
>
> —Charles A. Beard (1932)

> *If we can grasp what John Stuart Mill called the "principia media" of a society, if we can grasp its major trends; in brief, if we can understand the structural transformation of our epoch, we might have "a basis for prediction." . . .*
>
> —C. Wright Mills (1959)

Recently, by way of the mass media, the American and, presumably, the Russian people were treated to a vigorous sporadic and, at times, heated debate between Vice President Nixon and Premier Khrushchev. The occassion, as is well known, was the opening, of the American exhibition in Moscow. The strange thing about this debate was its subject. Although the discussion ranged superficially over many cold war problems, the central subject of the debate was *technology*—both directly and by implication. Mr. Nixon and Mr. Khrushchev were debating the values of American *versus* Russian technology. Mr. Khrushchev's later visit to the United States merely continued the international colloquy.

Nothing could have emphasized the interests and commitments of the modern world more clearly than this clash between statesmen of the great opposing powers. They were singing, in effect, a gigantic and possibly terrifying version of the musical comedy favourite of some years ago—"Anything you can do, I can do better." And what is to be done involves the technology of washing machines, missiles, atomic power, mass production of housing, frozen orange juice, and lunar satellites, to mention only a few items. Technology, unlimited; technology, international; technology, totally competitive—in weapons, in commerce, even in the arts.

In addition, science, technology, and invention on a large scale have become such a handmaiden of industry in the United States that research and development are now regarded as the basic keys to progress in our economy. Research lengthens our lives and, until very recently, our automobiles; it filters our water and our tobacco smoke; it weaves miracles fabrics out of chemicals and television commercials out of our suppressed desires; it shoots missiles at Venus and attempts to construct a Venus out of every American woman with the aid of brassieres designed by engineers acquainted with the latest in stress technology.

Modern historians of technology emphasize the fact that American civilization is fundamentally a technological civilization. It is not surprising, then, to find that at a time of international crisis occuring simultaneously with the period in history remarkable for what is now generally called the "explosion" of knowledge, Americans would take the view that further development of science and technology is our number one national objective.

Technology, however, is more than invention—more than machines. It is a process and a way of thinking. And, as Mumford reminds us. "Every technical process tends, in its perfection, at eliminate the active worker from participation and to produce an effective substitute: the automation." And so in the midst of great national pressure to increase the number of scientists and engineers, to change the curricula of schools and colleges in the direction of more abundant and rigorous offerings in science and mathematics, to invent and apply new machines and systems in the armed forces, in government, in industry and commerce, it is also not surprising to see emerging powerful social pressures that are opposed to unrestrained technological development. The great strike of 1959 in the steel industry was, so the analysts tell us, at bottom an issue over automation, displaced jobs and the new role of the worker. The active worker has resisted, since the beginnings of the several industrial revolutions, his elimination by an automation—whether loom, sewing, machine, computer, television camera, or automatic steel puddler.

These two forces—the national (and private enterprise) drive for technological superiority and the resistance by special groups to the introduction of specific technologies into various segments of our society—are not new, but have certainly increased in degree until they are different in kind from similar actions in former times. In the long view, however, we do not see much visible effect upon the onward march of research, development, invention, and application.

The most powerful movement today is, without question, that associated with the *increase* of technology. Admiral Rickover, for example, is not an isolated phenomenon. While no scientist, he is a technical administrator and, to the public, he speaks with the voice of SCIENCE as he demands an increasingly technological education for all. Even 20 years ago the thought that an admiral in the U.S. Navy would become, almost in an official capacity, a spokesman for reform of the public school system of the United States would have been unthinkable. Today, many sectors of the general public expect that he should.

The result of all this pressure for increase is a sort of Parkinson's law of technology. One technician—be he pure scientist, applied scientist, or engineer—enters a new sector of development and four others automatically follow in his footsteps. And four more for each of the first four. Before long, a new territory has succumbed.

Technolology, in this sense, absolutely refuses to be confined. There are few areas of human interest that are saved from invasion. Religion, perhaps, but not love, nor poetry, nor the composition of symphonies, nor the teaching for the young. With this continual extension, there must be great temptation for the technologist, literally, to "take over." As an example of this phenomenon close to the hearts of educators, it might be well to examine the activities of the National Science Foundation and the National Academy of Sciences. It will be found, I suspect, that the two of them have already taken over some functions of the United States Office of Education, the NEA and its departments, and other possible "non-scientific" groups of educators, and are, in fact, busily spawning a "scientific" educational bureaucracy. Such a bureaucracy is but the beginning—and there are many others in other fields—of a movement I have dubbed "Neo-Technocracy." The Neo-Technocrats have, in fact, moved farther into positions of power and control in a few short years than Howard Scott ever imagined possible when he was promoting the original Technocracy in the days of the Depression.

Turning now to education, it becomes apparent under this national and international drive for technological superiority that: (1) those concerned professionally with education have not developed a well-conceived point of view and a position and/or positions concerning technology and education, (2) because of this lack of a point of view and because of certain cultural lag factors naturally associated with education, the acceleration of technological development has tended to bypass the entire educational enterprise until very recently, (3) professionals in education are not prepared now to deal with the tremendous impact that technology is beginning to have on the instructional process itself as, by the technological process of extension, technology begins to invade education in full force, and (4) the absence of understanding and a point of view among the profession creates a situation where the Neo-Technocrats not only can, but are beginning to move into the field of instruction.

STATEMENT OF RATIONALE

The statement of the rationale of this paper is best accomplished by presenting four propositions, as follows:

1. For purposes of analysis, the American educational system taken as a whole may be considered as a *society*.
2. The introduction, on a large scale, of technology into this (educational) society will be accompanied by the same types of stresses and strains, initiate the same types of problems, accomplish the same classes of objectives and force similar reorganizations as the introduction of large scale technology into any society, subject, of course, to modifications by the unique factors inherent in the specific (educational) society.
3. Because professional educators for the most part have not, up to this time, viewed current technological problems from this orientation, but rather, if at all, in specific contexts, (for example, problems associated with the sudden introduction of television into education) it will be necessary not only to review thoroughly current educational theories from this more general point of view, but to create new theories encompassing and anticipating the new technological directions.

4. This new orientation toward technology and education will require rigorous analysis of the nature and possible roles of specific technological developments, the relation of these to educational purposes, and the prediction of effects on the society.

The remainder of this paper will attampt to delineate some of the elements of this technological study, to relate and analyze current and predicted technological developments, and to suggest some educational implications that might bear examination by the profession.

DEFINITION OF TECHNOLOGY

In sophisticated quarters of the intellectual world, definition is usually left to popularizing speech makers, as definitions are often assumed—mistakenly, perhaps—in professional discourse. However, when considering technology in its relations with education, definition cannot be left to chance. Many curriculum specialists, philosophers, administrators, and subject-matter experts are inclined to think of technology exclusively as *machines*. Nothing could be further from the truth. Machines are, of course, an indispensable part of technology. Even the dictionary definition, however, goes beyond machinery. The *Funk and Wagnalls College Dictionary* (the one I have closest at hand) defines technology as: (1) "Theoretical knowledge of industry and the industrial arts," and (2) "The application of science to the arts."

A much more useful concept for our purposes is contained in a little-known discussion of technology by Charles A. Beard. Beard says, in part:

> What then is this technology which constitutes the supreme instrument of modern progress? Although the term is freely employed in current writings, its meaning as actuality and potentiality has never been explored and defined. Indeed, so wide-reaching are its ramifications that the task is difficult and hazardous. Narrowly viewed, technology consists of the

totality of existing laboratories, machines, and processes already developed, mastered, and in operation. But it is far more than mere objective realities.

Intimately linked in its origin and operation with pure science, even its most remote mathematical speculations, technology has a philosophy of nature and a method—an attitude toward materials and work—and hence is a subjective force of high tension. It embraces within its scope great constellations of ideas, some explored to apparent limits and others in the form of posed problems and emergent issues dimly understood.

The educationist, in considering the effect of technology on the instructional process, must remember that, in addition to machinery, technology includes processes, systems, management and control mechanisms both human and non-human, and above all, the attitude discussed by Beard—a way of looking at problems as to their interest and difficulty, the feasibility of technical solutions, and the economic values—broadly considered—of those solutions. This is the context in which the educator must study technology.

THE POSSIBLE RELATIONS OF TECHNOLOGY WITH EDUCATION

Technology relates to education in at least three major ways. First in a society in which science and technology are primary, such as America, the society requires that the educational system insure an adequate supply of scientists and associated technicians. This requirement sets a curriculum problem, an organization problem, and many other problems associated with the screening, selection, and education of young people as potential additions to the nation's technical manpower.

Second, as a society becomes more and more technologically oriented and controlled, the question of the general education of all citizens is raised. The survival and management of the whole society theoretically requires more general education in the sciences and technology for all. Pressures arise for more mathematics and science to be taught to the entire population. Again, curriculum problems, organization problems, and a host of nagging, persistent general education problems arise.

Third, because of the tendency for technology to have no limits and constantly to extend into new areas, it is inevitable that, in an advanced technical society, technology should begin to extend into the instructional process itself. As will be shown, this is particularly true when education has been, for a century or more, one of the areas of American society which has walled itself off from technological advances and, consequently, has created a technological vacuum. That vacuum is now rapidly being filled.

It is with this third relationship – the application of technology to the educational, or to be more precise, to the instructional process—that the balance of this paper is concerned. The three relationships just discussed—development of technicians, general education in technology, and the application of technology to the instructional process—cannot eventually be completely separated. However, the third relationship is sufficiently different to merit thorough analysis.

Again, for purposes of this paper, a finer distinction will now be drawn. Within the educational process itself, there are three general areas in which technology can or is being applied. These are: (1) general administration, (2) testing, and (3) instruction. The uses of technical management systems, modern equipment, etc., represent the fairly obvious applications to the field of general administration. While it probably can easily be shown that this area of management is, taken as a whole, two or three decades behind its counterpart in industry, the problems associated with technology and school management are not as difficult as some of the others and will not, at this time, be considered. This is not to say that administration is not highly interrelated with the other two areas of testing and instruction, but the position can be taken that the problems arising from the latter two should guide the technical solutions in administration, not the other way around.

The second category, testing, is in many respects the most highly developed technology at present existing in American education. This is true both from a machine and from a systems standpoint. Further, the close relationships between psychological, achievement, and other types of testing and the instructional process are so well defined as to need no comment. However, with some exceptions, the technology of the instructional process can, for purposes of analysis, be isolated from testing. This arbitrary decision is made here in order to further the remainder of the discussion. We are left, then, with the instructional process by itself and can now turn to the impact of technology upon that process.

THE DEVELOPMENT OF INSTRUCTIONAL TECHNOLOGY

The development of a technology of the instructional process is relatively new. For guidance as to this development, the reader may refer to Chart I, which roughly compares the development of industrial technology with instructional technology. In the preindustrial phases of both education and industry while industry was principally at the handwork, artisan level, the instructional process relied upon such devices as the slate, the hornbook, the blackboard, chalk, and limited single textbooks with few illustrations. Although attention will be confined principally to some of the symbols of technology—equipment and machines—it should be emphasized that other factors—organization, etc.—were in the same state. As is well known, for example, the graded school is a late development.

At the beginning of the nineteenth century we note the famous changes in industry—the invention of a group of related machines for power, spinning, weaving, etc.—which made possible the factory system. Based on the work of Toynbee the elder, the term "Industrial Revolution" is applied to this period. However, in education the same revolution did *not* occur and instructional technology (with some exceptions here and there) remained at the pre-industrial level. During the last quarter of the century, there was some indication of a change. Oliver notes that an exhibit from an American school "with maps, charts, textbooks, and other equipment" won admiration at the International Exposition in Vienna in 1873. He adds that the American school display at Paris in 1878 was even more outstanding. Significantly, Oliver's last mention of international attention to American instructional technology was at Melbourne in 1880.

By 1900, on the other hand, industry had established factories and was moving into assembly line operations; had begun to apply, in a crude way, research and development concepts; had introduced the beginnings of modern management; and had developed a sophisticated financial system. Developments had reached such a state that the perceptive Henry Adams, the true prophet and seer of technology, foretold the coming of the Age of the Atom and the problems it would bring. In the years to 1950, aided by the acceleration of two wars, technology burgeoned and developed, piled machine upon machine, system upon system, added fantastically to power, and invented the method of invention. Technology transformed American society, philosophy, and art.

Technology, however, during the period from 1900 to 1950 only washed lightly upon the shores of instruction. During this same time span, when high speed printing techniques, radio, sound motion pictures, television, and other pieces of communication technology were invented, developed, and exploited, American education failed to apply these devices in quantity to the instructional process and failed to develop the appropriate technological systems necessary for this application. There were always rumblings, to be sure, as evidenced by the statement attributed to Edison in 1916 that the motion picture would replace the teacher. However, looked at from the vantage point of 1960, laboratories, project methods, libraries, and minute arrangements for audiovisual materials—the provisions to 1950—constituted what was still a pre-industrial technology for instruction.

By 1950, industry had entered what may be called the pre-automation period, which heralded the beginning of a

CHART I

Industrial vs. Instructional Technology

(all dates rough approximations)

Industry	*Instruction*
Pre-industrial Production Technology . . artisans, handwork, etc. . . invention of specific machines, and technics. *to 1800*	*Pre-industrial Instructional Technology* . . hornbook, slate, blackboard and chalk, limited single textbooks, few illustrative and graphic materials.
Mass Production Technology . . establishment of factories; gradual development of machines . . assembly lines . . modern capitalism . . management concepts . . new power sources, etc.	. . some signs of American leadership . . maps, globes, blackboards, etc. (1875) *to 1900* . . addition of laboratories, project methods, libraries, very small amounts of audiovisual materials . . *Still Pre-industrial in Concept and Execution*
to 1950	
Pre-Automation Period . . "Detroit automation," working computers . . development of systems and operational concepts. *to 1955*	*Potential Mass Production Technology (Unrealized)* . . Legacy of WWII for AV Materials . . ETV possible . . "saturation concept" . . all not applied significantly.
Automation Period Dawns . . the automatic factory . . the space age. *to 1960*	*Eurich-Stoddard Mass Production Period Dawns* . . the pressure for ETV and mass instruction with master teachers . .
	Potential for Educational Automation Appears . . the era of teaching machines . . stratovision . . the automatic classroom.

By 1959, in actuality, instructional technology had by no means reached the mass production stage on any scale.

movement toward true automation. At this time, much of the basic work on computers and other control mechanisms had been done. At this time also, mechanical systems of transporting work goods between machines had integrated some production lines into a system of mechanical or "Detroit automation." The period of automation was dawning, and I have arbitrarily set 1955 as the date at which this electronic-mechanical-systems analysis procedure began to be significantly applied. It is no accident that man began to push toward space at about the same time.

By 1950, American education had the potentiality, to carry on with the analogy, of a mass production technology. The hardware—projectors, recorders, television—and the materials were present. The systems concepts—saturation with audio-visual materials at the point of an instructional problem, for example, a concept derived from the military experience of World War II—were developed and known in a few audio-visual circles. A certain amount of incentive and public acceptance, also derived from World War II experience, could be drawn upon. The cake of custom, however, proved to be too tough and the mass production stage, at least 100 years behind industry, was not entered except here and there on isolated little islands.

At this point, approximately 1955, the god came out of the machine in the form of the Ford Foundation and Dr. Alvin C. Eurich (and a little later, his associate, Dr. Alexander J. Stoddard) to give the instructional processes of American education a sharp push into a mass production technology. The time was ripe. There was a shortage of teachers; education and educationists were under fire from all sides; Neo-Technocracy was turning its attention to education; the race with Russia was underway; the natives were restless indeed.

There was several interesting facets to this shove into mass instructional technology. First, television, both closed-circuit and broadcast, was chosen as the prime hardware. This was due, I think, to the unconsciously assumed basic concept of *mass production*, usually stated in terms of a shortage of teachers, large classes, and quality instruction. Second, the Ford impetus made provision, for the first time, for a technology of systems to go along with the hardware. Stoddard's own work in designing the school of tomorrow and the work of Trump and his associates in drawing the instructional images of the future for the American secondary school are, essentially, proposed systems.

Third, the Ford group made use of technology in creating the impetus in the first place. The technology of social psychology and public relations was drawn upon; educational decision-makers were the prime targets, and the means used, including high-priced public relations counsel, were the best available. This accounts for the fact that the teaching profession in general and audiovisual specialists in particular—really the only technologists of the profession—were for the most part left out of this move into technology.

Instead, the Foundation went to administrators and borad members and influential opinion makers of all types. New organizations were approached—the National Educational Television and Radio Center (now, I believe, related to something called the Learning Resources Institute), the revitalized National Association of Educational Broadcasters, and the Educational Facilities Laboratories, Inc. Others were created. As a sign of this policy to short-circuit the profession, it is significant that, except for a small grant to promote a seminar or two, the Department of Audio-visual Instruction of the NEA was left out of the largesse.

The Ford people assumed, I think, that if the cake of custom was to be broken the priesthood was not the agency to break it. This may mean, in part and as far as audiovisual and curriculum people are concerned, that to an outsider their technological orientation is at the level of the water wheel and the hand-loom, not the computer and the rocket. It is something to think about. On the other hand, it may also mean in part that the Ford Foundation is merely another instrument of

Neo-Technocracy and that these actions forecast even more loss of control of education by the existing pre-technological profession.

THE IMPACT OF PRESENT TRENDS

With this background of development, we can now come to grips with the impact of the present technology. Here, our first principle should be recalled. If we consider education as a societal universe, what happens when we introduce energy into that universe suddenly and on a large scale? That is apparently what is happening. Two general effects, based on two analogous concepts can be predicted. If the concept of entropy holds good in this connection, the educational system will become more highly organized and less random in nature (negative entropy will increase); if the observed historical-anthropological law of the introduction of a system of technology into a culture holds good, the distortions, stresses, and non-predictable effects will increase until the culture becomes unrecognizable. Two historical events serve as examples—one taken from Mumford, the introduction of the clock to regulate the habits of monks, and one from Muher, the invention of writing in Egypt for the purpose of keeping accounts. Both changed the world several times over and the effects of neither were, of course, predictable.

What then, are the present trends? If you don't count the continuous, grinding, sweating struggle carried on by audio-visual specialists, dealers, manufacturers, and producers to introduce, one item at a time, film libraries, projectors, recorders, etc., into the educational system in the slow process of conversion from a pre-industrial technology, two major trends can be identified. These two trends, at the moment, lead in opposite directions.

The first is the trend toward a mass instructional technology and is governed by machines and systems suitable for that purpose. Foremost, of course, is television, of which there are four instructional types: (1) broadcast on an educational channel, (2) broadcast on a commercial channel, (3) closed-circuit of the Hagerstown-Penn State type in which live instructors are used either to supplement instruction or to provide direct instruction exclusive of classroom teachers, and (4) the Compton type in which filmed lectures are distributed via the closed-circuit medium is replacement for classroom teachers. In all cases, the desire is to reach more students with fewer teachers or to obtain "quality" instruction.

Mass instruction technology in another form includes, of course, the massed film systems. The prime example is the EBF series in physics and chemistry, amounting to over 300 half-hour motion pictures intended to be used where there are no science teachers, where there are teachers not considered qualified, as audiovisual aids to more qualified teachers, and with very large groups of students. These films, of course, may theoretically be used over television. The exploitation of the overhead transparency projector is another example of mass instructional technology as shown in the Newton (Massachusetts) experiment in English grammar and composition.

In opposition to this trend of mass instruction is a growing technology for individual instruction. This trend is the audiovisual wave of the future (for the moment). The most dramatic development here is that class of systems and instruments known as teaching machines. Actually, I would class all teaching equipment designed for individual or near-individual operation as being in the category of teaching machines. At present, then, there are approximately five types, listed here on an ascending scale of sophistication: (1) individual reading pacers and similar devices, (2) individual viewing and listening equipment for existing slides, filmstrips, motion pictures, and recordings, (3) language laboratories of all types, (4) specifically programmed printed materials such as serambled textbooks, the proposed Lumsdame notebook, etc., and (5) true teaching machines of the Skinner or Pressey type containing carefully worked out verbal or pictorial programmes with various ingenious mechanical or electronic arrangements to test student reaction, inform him of his progress, errors, etc.

EXTRAPOLATION I

These two major trends toward technologies of mass and of individual instruction are not science fiction; they are with us now. Assessment of this impact is our most pressing and difficult problem. It does not take much of a crystal ball to see that a combination of these two technologies is the next immediate step. For example, let us take Maurice Mitchell's new series for his chemistry course on 150 plus films. Let us further assume that Mr. Mitchell makes a deal with the Rheem Califone Corporation to programme their multiple-choice Didak teaching machine with material to go along with the chemistry films (Mr. Eurich might have to put up the money for the initial effort). Let us continue by saying we will project the films hourly on the Compton College closed-circuit television film distribution system and place the machines in proper cubbyholes for Compton College students to work at specified times. We could get, almost immediately, to what can be called total educational automation.

Or, in another context, let us suppose that the new Ford creation, the Learning Resources Institute, initiates another Continental Classroom in mathematics over national broadcast television; and that the new audiovisual teaching machines now being developed by Hughes Aircraft are programmed to relate to this new series; and that these machines are placed by the Foundation in every public library in America; and that, at the conclusion of the instructional period, students report to designated centers where the Educational Testing Service examines them and certifies them to the colleges of their choice. Think, for a moment, about that one. It is now possible, not only to eliminate the teacher, but the school system.

These may be considered extreme applications, but such applications, at least experimentally, are inevitable. In fact, one such study, testing the combination of these two technologies, is now underway. The point is that both the mass instruction systems and the technology of individual instruction—teaching machines—are getting terrific momentum. These technologies are going to hit education with a million-pound thrust. What will be the effect upon our educational society? What is the role of the teacher, the audiovisual specialist, the curriculum director? *Quo vadis* the curriculum itself? This last question is particularly pertinent if the medium or image governs the message, as McLuhan maintains.

EXTRAPOLATION II

Technology never sits still. The extrapolations given in the last section are immediate. What of those that can be made for a time slightly farther into the future? I see several developments. First, it is reasonable to expect that programming for teaching machines will move from the verbal-Socratic-Skinner type to the audiovisual-branching type. That is, the machines will present, based upon student pre-tests, conceptual content using films, slides, filmstrips, tapes, and/or video tape as the medium. The presentation sequences will be longer and the student will be given an opportunity to select additional sequences for further explanation if the machine, through testing, informs him that he needs it. Records, of course, will be maintained instantaneously by miniaturized computers.

Secondly, the work in England of Ashby, Pask, and others with teaching machines based on the design concepts of biological computers will affect the technology of the present teaching machine much as transactional psychology affects stimulus-response psychology. Pask has already produced a machine which, in training key punch operators, actually senses the characteristics of the student as he works and automatically adjusts the programme of the machine to the student's individual needs. This is a pure transaction, and Pask maintains he can develop such a machine to teach decision-making with present hardware and know-how.

A second development of the future begins next year with the stratovision experiment of the Ford Foundation over a city in Indiana....One or more airplanes carrying multiple television transmitters circling overhead can receive multiple signals from the ground and broadcast them over much greater distances than conventional tower transmission. The programmes will go into several states and, because of the location, into both urban and rural areas and into innumerable heretofore independent school districts...Nothing technical would prevent, by the way, a national network of such aircraft as an addition to our other national means of transmission.

A third predicted development is based on information that it is technically possible, although not yet economically feasible, to produce a motion picture film with characteristics similar to the Polaroid film that is instantaneously developable. What this would do to video tape, to production techniques, and to the possibilities of local production of materials is of great interest to the audiovisual field.

The fourth development that can be anticipated is the most spectacular. Essentially, it is based on a systems concept. It is theoretically possible now to design an automatic classroom under the control of the teacher. Most of the elements are present or can be designed. Such a classroom would have total light and air control, automatic projection and television systems, technical provision for the best possible discussion environments, display situations, etc., which could be changed at will. By planned programming the classroom could be made to function for major presentations, small group discussions, individual work at teaching machines, creative periods, etc. All of this *could be* under the control of the teacher. The classroom then would become the teaching machine. Adrian TerLouw at Eastman Kodak has done some work in this area and it is, of course, implied in the provocative article by Simon Ramo which is so often cited in discussions of teaching machines. An acquaintance of mine refers to this concept as the "mad scientist" classroom.

If we look at this series of possibilities, we can sense a change in trend. Of the four cited, only one—the stratovision experiment—is clearly on the side of mass production. The other three lean toward the technology of individual instruction. The automatic classroom is a combination of both, but one in which the human element still plays the central part with the machines being the slave of man, not the other way around.

IMPLICATIONS

To assess the implications of this current and predicted impact of technology on the instructional process is not easy. At with any such speculation, it is also hazardous. It is, however, a job we must attempt.

We have to start, I think, with the proposition that, based upon the historical development of instructional technology, our educational society is in the position of a backward or underdeveloped culture suddenly assailed by the twentieth-century engineer. In addition, reactions in some professional circles to the advent of television are similar to those factory workers of the nineteenth century who attempted to destroy the machines that were replacing their jobs. In the long run, the machines remained; instructional technology is, no doubt, here to stay. Our problem becomes one, not so much of how to live with it on some kind of feather-bedding basis, but how to control it so that the proper objectives of education may be served and the human being remain central in the process.

Certain things are obvious. I think the concept of negative entropy will hold. The thrust and energy of technology will force a greater organization upon us *at every point at which it is applied to instruction.* Such an arrangement as the stratovision experiment will require a tighter and different organization in those five or six states and in those many school districts of the Midwest. The closed-circuit experiment just beginning in Anaheim, California, is already, it seems to me, making requirements for organization—of scope and sequence in the curriculum, of the district itself, and of the nature of the television presentations—the rigor of which has never been felt before in Anaheim.

Programming, in its machine, computer, and automation sense, is a matter of extreme organization—the piling up of energy. Most of the devices and systems of the new technology require, one way or another, this type of programming—television, teaching machines, mass films, language laboratories. This means that programmers are needed. Who is to do this? This is essentially, in the old sense, both a curriculum and an audiovisual problem. It is also a social problem. The heartland is programming. He who controls the programming heartland controls the educational system. Will it be a foundation, a committee of scientists, textbook publishers and film producers, the NEA, the school superintendent, the board of education, the students, or the general public?

Too, how many of us will go overboard and sink with the old concepts that will be absorbed or outmoded and tossed to the sharks by the new technology? Take the concept of instructional materials which some curriculum specialists love so well and which caused quite a controversy in DAVI circles a few years ago. The fight was futile, as is the love. The concept of programming and the systems and systems analysis it implies completely absorbs the idea of materials. Instructional materials becomes an outmoded atomistic, pre-technological concept useful mainly to the historians of education.

The concept of audiovisual education may accompany instructional materials down to drain, or it may not, depending on whether or not it can be redefined acceptably. The Skinner and Pressey type teaching machines and their descendants are, for example, primarily verbal devices, and yet their management, programming, etc., as technical electronic devices belongs somewhere. At a practical level, within a school situation, someone is going to have to worry about them. It is my position that the audiovisual field is in the easiest position to help integrate these mechanisms properly into the instructional process. They are not primarily audiovisual; they are primarily technological. The AV field, I think, must now suddenly grow up. We, the audiovisual specialists, are, of all educational personnel, the closest to tecnnology now; we have, I think, to become specialists in *learning technology*—and that's how . would redefine audiovisual education.

What of the curriculum people? Their work is just begin-ni g. It can become infinitely more rigorous and, at the same time, more satisfying. I suspect some of the emotional Rousseauians will have to get out of the curriculum business. The rest can step in and face this problem of programming a learning technology in human terms and find great excitement and reward.

Finally, we must remember the stresses and strains of introducing technology into our pre-industrial culture and the unpredictable consequences of any technological advance. If the profession continues to react like the California Teachers Association did toward television, we'll end up with a new profession. Not that I approve of the so-called Compton concept which shocked the CTA, because emphatically I do not. The great mistake of the CTA statement was that, at a point where precision was an absolute necessity, the CTA chose to lump all educational television—broadcast and closed-circuit, general and in-school—into one pile and then indicate that the CTA was against sin in favour of home and mother. The statement was unrealistic, imprecise, and failed to deal with the issues. We have a right to expect better from a large professional association of teachers. The profession as a whole must be made to sense this powerful movement to instructional technology and be made ready to seize the great opportunity it offers to make *all* teachers highly professional.

THE PHILOSOPHY OF ADVENTURE

In closing, I should like to return to the position I took in my Los Angeles address to the DAVI National Convention in 1955. Whitehead has said that it is the business of the future to be dangerous. Technology certainly has made this aphorism into the outstanding fact of our time. Technology is now making the future of instruction capricious and hazardous. But in doing so it has presented us with more opportunity and more choices than ever before. If the future is an adventure, it is an adventure *because* of technology. The cost of civilization is the fact that we can make wrong choices because of the alternatives technology presents. The reward of civilization is the freedom provided by technology and the opportunity to make the right choices. This cost and this reward we now face with the technology of the instructional process. We *must* look forward to the adventure and not present what Herbert Muller noted as "the curious spectacle of civilized man forever marching with his face turned backward—as no doubt the cave man looked back to the good old days when men were free to roam instead of being stuck in a damn hole in the ground." The "good old days" are gone; approached with intelligence and zest, the days of the future will be better.

Future Role of Technology

I will discuss some of the general kinds of changes in edcational capabilities that should result from the effective utilization of appropriate technologies, and will suggest their implications, especially for future planning.

FORECASTING AND FORECASTS

If there is value in the proposed approach (and I am increasingly convinced that there is) it arises from the uncertainty which surrounds specific technological developments. These are in part determined by the present state of the art, which can be assessed. They are also affected by a variety of other factors which are difficult to identify with any reliability, except to know that they are always potentially important. Economic conditions, congressional fads, rediscovering the poor, changes in the Department of Defense structure and concerns, modifications in corporate goals and teacher-student revolutions are illustrations of such variables. They can have surprising and unpredictable effects on advances in education. World War II, in every sense, probably did as much indirectly to refine education as any other single phenomenon. The training demands of the massive military mobilization overwhelmed educational capabilities. The need for greater capabilities was extremely critical, and new capabilities were created almost overnight. But we cannot conclude that critical periods of national defense necessarily encourage the development of new educational capabilities. Conditions change. In the last few years, funds for incrasing educational capabilities have been made available—this time, to the educational community itself. However, the continuing war has been a direct cause of reducing this support.

There are other illustrations of the problems involved in forecasting specific developments and capabilities. It appeared obvious to many in 1960, for example, that programmed instruction was well on its way to becoming commonplace in classrooms throughout the country. Dozens of firms began marketing—or at least advertising—hardware and software; professional associations and publications devoted to programmed instruction were formed; and a few colleges began to offer course work in programming procedures. What happened? Several explanations have been offered, but my point is that what appeared to be an obviously valid forecast did not materialize. Will the same be true, for example, of computer-assisted-instruction? We hear much talk and promise about the impact of CAI in the near future. But many of my school district friends are asking: Where is the necessary software? Will it be developed, and when, and by whom?

One of the more important problems in attempting forecasts about technological developments in education, it seems to me, is that as a result of our excitement about hoped-for improvements, we have tended to be premature, and often have been careless in judging the readiness of a given technological development for use in schools. Many of us, in our enthusiasm. describe an idea to the practicing educator but fail to note the state of the concept in the research and development process. We tend to get our tenses mixed. We often say *is* when we mean *will*, or even worse, *could*, or the most unpardonable *might*. The problem is that in all phases of the research and development process we have learned more not only about the technology, but also about what we should be seeking to do in education. The communication process being what it is, many of us operate in blissful ignorance of more recent findings and, more important, about revised decisions and plans.

The resolution of this problem can be expensive. For example, a pilot friend who is responsible for navigation training for a major air line was directed to mount a "crash" programme for training flying officers in the use of a revolutionary new navigation system which was in its final test stage. The system manufacturer gave assurances that it was reliable, extremely accurate, and permitted a San Francisco to Honolulu runway-to-runway trip without the necessity for any human calculations except perhaps for some minor adjustments in the course plotted by the system. By turning dials and flicking switches, the captain and crew could obtain displays of all pertinent navigation information. In addition, the computer was prepared to effect, automatically, changes in aircraft performance indicated by the data. In effect, the system eliminated the second officer navigation function. It was "fail safe"—the probabilities of the dual system malfunctioning were equal to those of the captain and the first officer dying of heart attacks on the same trip. Midway into a tremendously expensive training programme designed to teach all cockpit personnel to use the system, the impossible happened. Both the captain's and the first officer's systems failed on a training flight over the Pacific. All went well due to a trusty compass and dead reckoning. The educational implications, however, were serious. The air line had counted on the system and had *planned* on using it. Based on an assumed validity of the technological development, the company mounted a significant, far reaching, and expensive training programme which had to be abandoned. In this situation considerable savings could have been effected had the forecasting been more accurate.

This little drama, admittedly, has implications only for a relatively short range forecast regarding educational plans based on technological developments. While planning for a ten to twenty-year time span can be much more general, and thus more flexible and amenable to changes because of revised technological forecasts, there is still a point at which educational leaders must make a commitment. We cannot wait until the technology has proven itself before deciding to go along with it—that is, to gear up our institutions to accept a capability. To do so would be to engage in a never ending waiting game involving those who are primarily concerned with developing technology, and those who are mainly interested in using it.

It is appropriate to complete this perspective for forecasting changes in educational capabilities resulting from technology with the addition of one more concept: The nature of technology being what it is, we should not rule out anything! Timing of course is important and affects the relevancy of what to consider and for what to plan. As suggested above, if the task is to decide, plan, and implement, then a relatively conservative forecast is appropriate. But when the task is to begin developing strategy for the next two decades, I would argue that we should not rule out any kind of potential educational capability.

With all of these challenges and cautions in mind, I want to suggest several kinds of educational capabilities that will be changed as a result of using emerging technology, and which we should explore carefully within the immediate future. Such an exploration, I believe, will lead to more specific and valid forecasts.

What follows should be qualified by "it could be possible." What takes place—that is, the capabilities that actually evolve —will depend in part upon what we and many others like us do about existing technology.

I have the vague feeling that we are really only in the mechanical phase of the technological revolution in education. Nearly all of the man-machine systems in education which are now being operated are, in a relative sense, clumsy. Admittedly, they are exciting, but so was the Model T as compared with what it replaced—that is, brute force. Computer applications in education to date are actually quite cumbersome. They seldom work as well as predicted; they cause many inconveniences; and they usually require a fairly constant application of technological bailing wire. As a number of users have commented, for example, the only trouble with flexible scheduling is that it is highly inflexible. If its goal is to make possible individualized instruction, then flexible scheduling will have succeeded on the day that we no longer need to schedule students.

COMPUTER BASED DATA SYSTEMS

Perhaps the most obvious increased capability is that of storing, retrieving and manipulating large amounts of data about students. Computer technology should result in the development of large and flexible learning data systems. These will have two main functions: (1) instructional management, and (2) educational research. The first is absolutely essential for individualized instruction which requires constant monitoring and analysis of student learning behaviour. The second offers one of the greatest opportunities for making substantial improvement in the teaching-learning process. It should be helpful to describe in some detail at least, the components of such a system. Several are under development, including one at the American Institutes for Research and another by the Portland, Oregon, schools. The one with which I am most familiar is called System for Individualized Instruction Management (SIIM).

This system includes two basic computer files: a curriculum file and a student file. The system can have one or several input/output modes. Fig. 2.1 shows the kind of reports that can be generated, as well as the research and evaluation activities that can be undertaken by using the system. Probable types of output from an initial version include:

Student appraisal reports;

Student status reports:

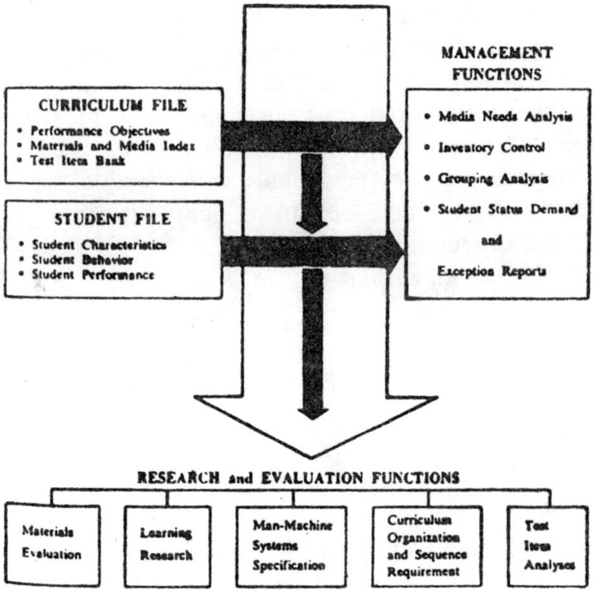

Fig. 2.1: System for Individualized Instruction Management

Warning messages for students not meeting expectations;

Suggestions for instructor-directed presentation groupings;

Individualized instructional materials list;

Instructional materials inventory lists; and

Indications of special interest groups.

Research generated by the system would include:

Evaluation of specific materials to various kinds of pupils;
Studies of objective sequence patterns;

Studies of teacher and student use in reactions to various input/output formats and modes;

Studies of information volume and space limitations and instruction; and

Studies of comparative instructional systems and procedures.

There is a master curriculum file (map) for each course unit as well as an individual curriculum map for each student. The master file contains performance objectives, an instructional materials index, a test item bank, sequence dependencies, and classifications of intellectual activity. All test items and instructional materials are indexed to the performance objectives. The curriculum file serves as a unique driver for the system that permits the development of generalized programme design, applicable in different subject-matter areas and different environments.

The student file contains the individual curriculum map; characteristics such as age, aptitude, and interest; behaviour records (materials and activities involved in the student's work); and his performance record (test scores).

Given the initial curriculum map and student file, daily or weekly recommended changes for the map are based on updated performance objectives. An analysis is made of the student's subject matter strengths and weaknesses, as well as of his intellectual activity. Recommendations might include: a change in the sequence of performance objectives; substitution for an objective where unexpected strength has been revealed; or the addition or repetition of an objective to overcome an indicated weakness. (A print-out of this record would be provided at regular intervals as requested, or when changes are to be recommended.)

An analysis also is made of the instructional materials used; this is based on recorded data and student performance. The analysis indicates materials best suited for a particular individual, as well as a broader evaluation of the effectiveness of the materials in instruction.

The test item bank assembles tests, and incorporates review items based on objectives already attained. Students concurrently working on the same objective could receive different test items, depending on analysis results. Extensive item analysis procedures would be completed, including the determination of difficulty and discrimination indexes for test items. An instructor might begin the day by studying a report summarizing student status. He would note those who need special attention organize instructor-directed presentations, determine special instruction materials requirements for the day, and determine the points of emphasis of the group's study. Instructor-aide assignments would be made, and anticipated tests ordered and printed. He would make inputs on student behaviour and performance during the day. If appropriate, he might receive warning messages regarding students having difficulty with their contracted objectives. Toward the close of the day, the instructor would input requests for data and materials needed for the next day. The administrator, counselor, and other support personnel would monitor the instructional programme daily as a basis for guiding their own efforts. The system should be available to both students and staff, on demand, as well as on an exception report basis.

Consider the research function of such a system. Imagine that we have 50,000 pupils in several districts, all served by the system. Each pupil has a file in the system. The file contains data about personal and social characteristics, specific research of past achievement, and measures of interest and personality. As each pupil pursues an educationl objective (defined in operational terms) the following are input to the system: (1) descriptions of the material and procedures he uses; (2) his reactions to these; (3) teacher observations; and (4) the student's actual terminal behaviour. We also have definitive descriptions of the materials and procedures.

An important capability would be that of providing answers to research questions of several levels and kinds. Relatively simple analyses of alternate materials designed or proclaimed to teach similar objectives could be made. For example, a sample of students could be drawn, each of whom had been pursuing similar objectives, but with different instructional materials—for example, using three different texts. One could easily compare the learning achievement of each of the groups. A more sophisticated analysis would be a comparison of different sequence patterns. My guess is that instead of a single sequence, we would discover a number of ways of sequencing instructional material, and that these would vary in effectiveness with students who manifest different characteristics. Most of us, I assume, have reacted—after reading a book, listening to a lecture, or viewing a film—with a comment such as "If he had said that earlier I would not have been confused all this time," and at the same time, being aware that the fellow in the next seat—no more or no less bright—*had* understood—that is, the sequence of instruction was totally adequate for him.

The capability of a research based instructional system could, if we would use it, revolutionize education as it now exists. The capability obviously would not be limited to instruction per se, but should be applied to staffing and any other aspect of education.

SATELLITE SUPPORTED INSTRUCTION

One of the more exciting capabilities will be that of providing what might be termed *real time instruction* rather than historical instruction, by increased use of television, and especially by the use of worldwide satellite systems. Given increased technological facilities and personnel, students at all age levels—even in the smallest and most remote schools—should be able to observe and view events as they occur throughout the world. Whether it is a riot in Chicago, a debate in the British Parliament, or a ten-week series of half hour programmes on experimental farming in Arabia, the capability will exist for pupils to observe what is taking place *at the time it takes place*. This worldwide communication facility has many obvious advantages for education. Not the least among them is the elimination of much of the provincialism characteristic of elementary education. I am not suggesting that there is no value in acquainting students with a local and regional history. I am convinced that there is. Perhaps such study is becoming even more important as a way of assisting young people to gain an appreciation for and learn the benefits that can be derived from understanding the cultural micro-environment in which they live, and which, at least on a day to day basis, is the arena in which they work, play, love, and exert a personal influence on their fellow men.

At the same time, it is clear that we must become more cognizant of a world society. Traditional schools have attempted something like this through the study of either ancient civilization or of a regional history. In the case of my own region, for example, elementary children spend what seems to me an unreasonable amount of time examining the living habits of Northwest Indians, in part—according to curriculum guides—as a means of studying primitive and developing countries such as those in Africa. Meanwhile, the new nations of Africa queue up until grade nine when they finally receive some systematic study. One reason that this is done, of course, is that materials exist on the Northwest Indians, while they are much more difficult to find on the emerging African nations. The problem has been—and to some extent still is—one of educational capability. Movies are expensive and, in the area of social studies, they are frequently out of date before they are available for classroom use. Video tapes are relatively inexpensive, and the lag between recording and use is practically insignificant.

Grant then, if you will, the future existence of a rather tremendous worldwide satellite assisted audio-video network capability for education. It is clear. I believe, that some such system will develop, even though the specific characteristics will be unpredictable at this time. Educators should therefore begin thinking about how they can make the best use of the capabilities. There are a number of serious problems and difficult tasks which lay between the existence of the capability and its effective use in education. One problem is especially critical. It involves the level of inference of presentations and displays of the subject matter, whether it is by lecture, book, film, tour or some other medium.

A certain amount of abstracting or selecting takes place in the preparation of content for presentation. Usually this is done with some degree of purpose by the teacher or preparer of materials which, of course, implies that contol of time is important. While there may be considerable and significant disagreement among us regarding the substance of the editing and abstracting process, there is undoubtedly agreement that this function is important. The learner's time is too valuable to waste on irrelevant and needlessly repetitious materials.

Given the real time nature of an audio-visual worldwide communications capability, we must deal with two kinds of questions: How can we be selective, given the short time frame? What shall we select, or more to the point, what shall we use as selective criteria? The first problem apparently can be solved reasonably satisfactorily. In general, representatives from television suggest buffer systems in which "raw" information is temporarily stored, analyzed, edited, rearranged, merged, or whatever is appropriate, and then displayed to the learner. They are quick to point out that the real problem relates to what is selected. It is not so much a technological capability problem—that is, a machine problem—but rather is a criterion problem—the human problem—which is basic. This is the problem which has been part of the whole technological revolution in education. The machines exist in some usable form, but before they can be useful, one has to know the purposes or objectives of the educator. The issue itself, particularly in a world oriented educational enterprise, can be deceptively complex. It is even more complex when the educational vehicle has the real time characteristic noted above.

A good part of the deception results from the problem of omission because of unawareness. The current concern over whether or not history texts give adequate attention to Negro history and its contribution to the development of America is illustrative. It is apparent that the critics are correct. And while it could be that the omission was willful in the case of some small number of authors and publishers, the important reason for the omission of research in writing is really insensitivity, or middle class cultural blindness. The Negro was not maliciously left out of history books (he was, however, maliciously left out of history); he was simply seldom seen. Apparently in the eyes of many writers he did not exist in spite of the long time frame available to them for study. How can we avoid the same kind of error in using an audio-visual technology capability?

The immediate interpretation of an event may be revised significantly with the perspective of time. When the publication lag no longer exists and serves as a tempering mechanism, how can we guard against teaching concepts which may soon need to be "untaught"?

PUBLISHING CAPABILITIES

Another capability resulting from computer technology and increased audio-visual reproduction devices will have great impact on the primary medium of instruction, namely books. This capability can destroy the basic one book-one course educational model. It will be possible to go from author manuscript to indexing to magnetic storage, to generating hard copies of such things as CBI (Computer Based Instruction) programmes in response to specifications provided by teachers. Authors will not be contracted to write or revise texts, as is now the case, but rather to update data banks and materials. Ideally, a teacher—or "instructional team leader" will indicate the learning objectives for one or more students, and the computer will search its files and produce a combination of materials best suited to the objectives. The chief problem, as always, will involve the issue of stating objectives. Whether we call them performance criteria or behavioural objectives, *this kind of capability will make a significant contribution only after learning objectives are stated in precise terms*. Our experience to date has taught us that this is an extremely difficult task. Until we achieve it, however, what is done, essentially, is to index the subsections of books, and treat these as entities. This, in itself, offers at least certain economic advantages and somewhat greater flexibility, but falls short of individualized or prescribed instruction which is truly responsible to the needs of pupils.

INSTRUCTION THAT IS INDEPENDENT OF TEACHERS

The technology . . . can be viewed from another perspective: that is, the changed role and function of the teacher and student in the educational process. Much has been written about the impact of technology on the role of teachers, but I would suggest that *more attention should be given to the changed role and responsibilities of the student.* We really cannot appreciate the importance of technology for the teacher's role without considering what will happen to students.

It appears obvious to many that the application of sophisticated technology in education will reduce the need for the teacher "interface" function between instructional materials (content or substance) and the learner. In other words, *the capability for teacher-independent instruction will be increased.*

The teacher's function as a presenter of information could easily be eliminated entirely. He will continue to interpret, synthesize, and clarify information displayed in another mode. The question as to whether the predicted amount of time which the teacher and student will spend together will be decreased has caused concern among some educators. They ask if this will dehumanize education. It could lead in this direction, but I doubt that it will, due to the quality of much of the student-teacher interaction. The term "interaction" is probably an inaccurate designation of what actully takes place in the lecture hall. *A reduction in the traaitional kind of student-teacher relationship, and a concomitant increase in task or problem oriented student-teacher interaction may in fact increase the humaneness of instruction.*

A more important outcome of the teacher independent instructional capability for students is, by definition, the increase in responsibility which students must assume for their own learning behaviour. I am not sure what this means, but it is such a radical change from the tight control teachers have maintained over students in the past that the role of the student will certainly change. The freedom to explore and to set his own pace, plus a comprehensive in-depth instructional capability to support independent learning behaviour, should lead to the development of a new breed of students. Their perceptions of "school" will be very different from that of counterparts of today, and they will in turn be perceived differently by teachers. The burden, it can be added, will be on educators, for the "newness" will be limited to their experiences. Students, having nothing for contrast, will accept the new as if it were always so.

TECHNOLOGY AND THE ROLE OF TEACHERS

Increased technological capabilities will obviously have an impact on the role of teachers. Technology will both provide new educational tools directly, and thus cause changes in what teachers do in the teaching process, and in a less direct manner. cause teachers to become involved in new kinds of educational functions. Most of what has been said so far has been about the first kind of educational capability. A few comments regarding the second kind of capability—namely changes in educational personnel capabilities—are appropriate at this point.

The Teacher

Traditionally, a teacher has had to build his own teaching methods and materials (for example, charts, pictures, audio-visual presentations, and so on). The economics of time provides strong support for the concept of staying with a few tested teaching procedures, with tested instructional materials, and perhaps to an extent greater than commonly recognized, with the same subject matter. However, *when the teacher's role and responsibilities change* from those of the generalist who must be responsible for the total teaching process (including the development of many instructional materials) *to those of the professional specialist responsible for designing instructional programmes for individual pupils, the emphasis shifts to decision*

making and planning. While still involved in implementing the plan, the teacher focuses more than before on defining the needs of individual pupils, synthesizing these, and communicating them to others who then make the appropriate resources available to the pupil in the most appropriate teaching mode.

The Non-Teaching Specialist's Team

One hesitates at this point to apply labels to the new kinds of personnel in education, because it is far from clear what particular combinations of competencies will be most desirable. If we keep in mind that the labels are merely suggestive, *it is reasonable to assume that at least four areas of non-teaching specialists will emerge in regard to man-machine systems in education.* They are: (1) content research specialist, (2) media specialists, (3) educational systems specialists, and (4) educational engineers. People in these four areas of specialty will serve as a kind of support team to teachers.

It should be helpful to speculate briefly on a competencies in the four areas of specialization suggested, since they will constitute increased educational capabilities. *The team concept is critical and the maximum contribution by each area cannot be made independently of the others.* Perhaps the most effective way to describe the function of each is to illustrate how they might operate in a school employing new capabilities.

The teacher's first responsibility would be to determine the learning objectives for pupils and to communicate these to the supporting team of specialists. Before members of the team can function, they must know what the teacher-leader wants to achieve. Precisely what behaviours of his students does he think should be modified, promoted, or eliminated? This is not an easy task, but given a statement of objectives and information about the pupils to be taught, the content researcher, media specialist, and systems specialist could assist the teacher to develop appropriate instructional systems.

Content Research Specialists. The content researcher would have the responsibility of identifying and synthesizing subject matter relevant to the particular objectives. In part a librarian, he would have at his disposal an information-retrieval system much more sophisticated and sensitive than traditional manual classification systems. The task would be to identify the most appropriate materials for the instructional objectives stated—those which are maximally sensitive to the characteristics of the learners. In order to accomplish this, of course, he must have the capability to analyze great amounts of materials in terms of both content and learning criteria.

Media Specialists. Given the learning goals, learners' characteristics, and a pool of material from which to work, the media specialist will have to determine the most effective modes of presentation and then assemble and construct instructional materials. While libraries of materials and collections of equipment should certainly continue to be available, an equally important resource would be a media laboratory and production shop. Media specialists will include artists, audio-visual production specialists, material programmers, and so on.

Educational Systems Specialists. In regard to new personnel, the educational systems specialist represents the greatest innovation entailed in man-machine systems in education. While the extent of assistance from resource materials and media entailed in man-machine systems in education represents a radical change, the concept of providing this kind of support for teachers is certainly not new. In the past, however, it has been the instructor's responsibility to integrate these resources into his own classroom procedures. Man-machine systems in education entail a level of complexity and coordination and a knowledge of machines which the teacher, as defined above, cannot reasonably be expected to master. The systems specialist has responsibility for putting the various resources together and designing a control procedure which will enable the teacher to exercise and maintain maximum surveillance and control over the teaching and learning processes. The basic goal of man-machine systems in education is to achieve the ultimate in individualized instruction, and the closer one comes toward achieving this goal, the more complex the systems will become.

The potential for chaos—the failure to instruct anybody in much of anything—also increases. All of the "what happens if" and "what should be done when this takes place" questions must be anticipated and thought through, with solutions provided and built into the system. This is the task of the systems specialist, to assemble piece by piece the components of instruction constructed by the resoure and material specialists according to the specifications determined by the teacher. In a more sophisticated systems, the educational systems are undoubtedly will require the skills of computer programmers.

Educational Engineers. In larger schools and colleges the efficient use, maintenance, and modification of complex man-machine educational systems will require a staff of engineers familiar with the school or college and with education in general.

BIO-ELECTRONIC LEARNING

Only a few of the many kinds of possible new educational capabilities have been discussed here. However, I would not want to leave this brief exercise in forecasting, without at least mentioning a kind of future capability which represents a new dimension, rather than an extension, of education. The capabilities discussed to this point are in a sense, refinements of educational psychology—centered especially on perceptual problems and issues. In a word, they are all "outside" of the individual—that is, they stop short of making direct changes in the organism. Rather, they attempt to make it easier for the organism to change itself.

We will soon see, I believe, the clear emergence of capabilities for making direct changes in the organism for learning purposes. Such things as laser beam technology, advances in endocrinology, bio-chemical control of genetics, and preconscious cognition techniques will provide both an exciting and somewhat frightening educational capability. They will be exciting because of the tremendous potential for enhancing learning—and frightening because they entail moral, ethical, and philosophical problems with which we have not had to deal. Admittedly, while not as immediate as other kinds of emerging technology, educational planning which does not give them at least some serious consideration, is short sighted.

IN SUMMARY

The main obstacle to the development and use of sophisticated data banks and information systems, I suspect, is not the technology itself, but the threat posed to the educational establishment. American education operates on a set of myths which have evolved from the time that only a few had access to stored knowledge (print on pages) and thereby had the power to influence tremendously who should learn what. The educational elite—that is, "the establishment"—guarded its capability closely, and carefully handed it down to each new generation. More recently the professors of administration largely decided what the practicing administrator should know. The administrator in turn decided what teachers could know and do, and the teachers (which is only fair, of course) decided what materials the pupils should learn. Somewhere in the shuffle professors of teacher education tended to get bumped aside. But the bastion around educational capabilities is crumbling, and capabilities are cropping up in other places. The old restrictions on classroom content are made ineffective by information available through such sources as movies, television, and greater freedom in the printing and distribution of materials.

The point is simply that new and powerful educational capabilities exist outside the school, and out of control of the educational establishment. This emerging trend will continue, and educators will either "get with it" or find learners increasingly dissatisfied with their offering and teachers who are unable to hold their attention. This is happening now on college campuses in the form of student initiated courses. The most significant aspect of the student revolt is not their questioning of the appropriateness of subject matter or content. It is, instead, their increasing rejection of traditional educational procedures. They are asking—perhaps demanding—"When are you going to use your new educational capabilities?", and when they hear no satisfactory response, they set out to try to use them independently.

THE SCIENCE OF LEARNING AND THE ART OF TEACHING

Some promising advances have recently been made in the field of learning. Special techniques have been designed to arrange what are called "contingencies of reinforcement"—the relations which prevail between behaviour on the one hand and the consequences of that behaviour on the other—with the result that a much more effective control of behaviour has been achieved. It has long been argued that an organism learns mainly by producing changes in its environment, but it is only recently that these changes have been carefully manipulated. In traditional devices for the study of learning—in the serial maze, for example, or in the T-maze, the problem box, or the familiar discrimination apparatus—the effects produced by the organism's behaviour are left to many fluctuating circumstances. There is many a slip between the turn-to-the-right and the food-cup at the end of the alley. It is not surprising that techniques of this sort have yielded only very rough data from which the uniformities demanded by an experimental science can be extracted only by averaging many cases. In none of this work has the behaviour of the individual organism been predicted in more than a statistical sense. The learning processes which are the presumed object of such research are reached only through a series of inferences. Current preoccupation with deductive systems reflects this state of the science.

Recent improvements in the conditions which control behaviour in the field of learning are of two principal sorts. The "law of effect" has been taken seriously; we have made sure that effects *do* occur and that they occur under conditions which are optimal for producing the changes called learning. Once we have arranged the particular type of consequence called a reinforcement, our techniques permit us to shape the behaviour of an organism almost at will. It has become a routine exercise to demonstrate this in classes in elementary psychology by conditioning such an organism as a pigeon. Simply by presenting food to a hungry pigeon at the right time, it is possible to shape up three or four well-defined responses in a single demonstration period—such responses as turning around, pacing the floor in the pattern of a standing still in a corner of the demonstration apparatus, stretching the neck, or stamping the foot. Extremely complex performances may be reached through successive stages in the shaping process, the contingencies of reinforcement being chánged progressively in the direction of the required behaviour. The results are often quite dramatic. In such a demonstration one can *see* learning take place. A significant change in behaviour is often obvious as the result of a single reinforcement.

A second important advance in technique permits us to maintain behaviour in given states of strength for long periods of time. Reinforcements continue to be important, of course, long after an organism has learned *how* to do something, long after it has acquired behaviour. They are necessary to maintain the behaviour in strength. Of special interest is the effect of various schedules of intermittent reinforcement. Charles B. Ferster and the author are currently preparing an extensive report of a five-year research programme, sponsored by the Office of Naval Research, in which most of the important types of schedules have been investigated and in which the effects of schedules in general have been reduced to a few principles. On the theoretical side we now have a fairly good idea of why a given schedule produces its appropriate performance. On the practical side we have learned how to maintain any given level of activity for daily periods limited only by the psysical exhaustion of the organism and from day to day without substantial change throughout its life. Many of these effects would be traditional assigned to the field of motivation, although the principal operation is simply the arrangement of contingencies of reinforcement.

These new methods of shaping behaviour and of maintaining it in strength are a great improvement over the traditional practices of professional animal trainers, and it is not surprising that our laboratory results are already being applied to the production of performing animals for commercial purposes. In a more academic environment they have been used for demonstration purposes which extend far beyond an interest in learning as such. For example, it is not too difficult to arrange the complex contingencies which produce many types of social behaviour. Competition is exemplified by two pigeons playing a modified game of ping-pong. The pigeons drive the ball back and forth across a small table by pecking at it. When the ball gets by one pigeon, the other is reinforced. The task of constructing such a "social relation" is probably completely out of reach of the traditional animal trainer. It requires a carefully designed programme of gradually changing contingencies and the skillful use of schedules to maintain the behaviour in strength. Each pigeon is separately prepared for its part in the total performance, and the "social relation" is then arbitrarily constructed. The sequence of events leading up to this stable state are excellent material for the study of the factors important in non-synthetic social behaviour. It is instructive to consider how a similar series of contingencies could arise in the case of the human organism through the evolution of cultural patterns.

Cooperation can also be set up, perhaps more easily than competition. We have trained two pigeons to coordinate their behaviour in a cooperative endeavour with a precision which equals that of the most skillful human dancers. In a more serious vein these techniques have permitted us to explore the complexities of the individual organism and to analyze some of the serial or coordinate behaviours involved in attention, problem solving various types of self-control, and the subsidiary systems of responses within a single organism called "personalities." Some of these are exemplified in what we call multiple schedules of reinforcement. In general, a given schedule has an effect upon the rate at which a response is emitted. Changes in the rate from moment to moment show a pattern typical of the schedule. The pattern may be as simple as a constant rate of responding at a given value, it may be a gradually accelerating rate between certain extremes, it may be an abrupt change from not responding at all to a given stable high rate, and so on. It has been shown that the performance characteristic of a given schedule can be brought under the control of a particular stimulus and that different performances can be brought under the control of different stimuli in the same organism. At a recent meeting of the American Psychological Association, Dr. Ferster and the author demonstrated a pigeon whose behaviour showed the pattern typical of "fixed-interval" reinforcement in the presence of one stimulus and, alternately, the pattern typical of the very different schedule called "fixed ratio" in the presence of a second stimulus. In the laboratory we have been able to obtain performances appropriate to *nine* different schedules in the presence of appropriate stimuli in random alternation. When Stimulus 1 is present, the pigeon executes the performance appropriate to Schedule 1. When Stimulus 2 is present, the pigeon executes the performance appropriate to Schedule 2. And so on. This result is important because it makes the extrapolation of our laboratory results to daily life much more plausible. We are all constantly shifting from schedule to schedule as our immediate environment changes, but the dynamics of the control exercised by reinforcement remain essentially unchanged.

It is also possible to construct very complex *sequences* of schedules. It is not easy to describe these in a few words, but two or three examples may be mentioned. In one experiment the pigeon generates a performance appropriate to Schedule A where the reinforcement is simply the production of the stimulus characteristic of Schedule B, to which the pigeon then responds appropriately. Under a third stimulus the bird yields a performance appropriate to Schedule C where the reinforcement in this case is simply the production of the stimulus characteristic of Schedule D, to which the bird then responds appropriately. In a special case, first investigated by L. B. Wyckoff, Jr., the organism responds to one stimulus where the reinforcement consists of the *clarification* of the stimulus controlling another response. The first response becomes, so to speak, an objective form of "paying attention" to the second stimulus. In one important version of this experiment, as yet unpublished, we could say that the pigeon is telling us whether it is "paying attention" to the *shape* of a spot of light or to its *colour.*

One of the most dramatic applications of these techniques has recantly been made in the Harvard Psychological Laboratories by Floyd Ratliff and Donald S. Blough, who have skillfully used multiple and serial schedules of reinforcement to study complex perceptual processes in the infrahuman organism. They have achieved a sort of psycho-physics without verbal instruction. In a recent experiment by Blough, for example, a pigeon draws a detailed dark-adaptation curve showing the characteristic breaks of rod and cone vision. The curve is recorded continuously in a single experimental period and is quite comparable with the curves of human subjects. The pigeon behaves in a way which, in the human case, we would not hesitate to describe by saying that it adjusts a very faint patch of light until it can just be seen.

In all this work, the species of the organism has made surprisingly little difference. It is true that the organism studied have all been vertebrates, but they still cover a wide range. Comparable results have been obtained with pigeons, rats, dogs, monkeys, human children, and most recently—by the author in collaboration with Ogden R. Lindsley—with human psychotic subjects. In spite of great phylogenetic differences, all these organisms show amazingly similar properties of the learning process. It should be emphasized that this has been achieved by analyzing the effects of reinforcement and by designing techniques which manipulate reinforcement with considerable precision. Only in this way can the behaviour of the individual organism be brought under such precise control. It is also important to note that through a gradual advance to complex interrelations among responses, the same degree of rigor is being extended to behaviour which would usually be assigned to such fields as perception, thinking, and personality dynamics.

From this exciting prospect of an advancing science of learning, it is a great shock to turn to that branch of technology which is most directly concerned with the learning process—education. Let us consider, for example, the teaching of arithmetic in the lower grades. The school is concerned with imparting to the child a large number of responses of a special sort. The responses are all verbal. They consist of speaking and writing certain words, figures, and signs which, to put it roughly, refer to numbers and to arithmetic operations. The first task is to shape up these responses—to get the child to pronounce and to write responses correctly, but the principal task is to bring this behaviour under many sorts of stimulus control. This is what happens when the child learns to count, to recite tables, to count while ticking off the items in an assemblage of objects, to respond to spoken or written numbers by saying "odd," "even," "prime," and so on. Over and above this elaborate repertoire of numerical behaviour, most of which is often dismissed as the product of rote learning, the teaching of arithmetic looks forward to those complex serial arrangements of responses involved in original mathematical thinking. The child must acquire responses of transposing, clearing fractions, and so on, which modify the order or pattern of the original material so that the response called a solution is eventually made possible.

Now, how is this extremely complicated verbal repertoire set up? In the first place, what reinforcements are used? Fifty years ago the answer would have been clear. At that time educational control was still frankly aversive. The child read numbers, copied numbers, memorized tables, and performed operations upon numbers to escape the threat of the birch rod or cane. Some positive reinforcements were perhaps eventually derived from the increased efficiency of the child in the field of arithmetic, and in rare cases some automatic reinforcement may have resulted from the sheer manipulation of the medium-from the solution of problems or the discovery of the intricacies of the number system. But for the immediate purposes of education the child acted to avoid or escape punishment. It was part of the reform movement known as progressive education to make the positive consequences more immediately effective, but anyone who visits the lower grades of the average school today will observe that a change has been made, not from aversive to positive control, but from one form of aversive stimulation to another. The child at his desk, filling in his workbook, is behaving primarily to escape from the threat of a series of minor aversive events—the teacher's displeasure, the criticism or ridicule of his classmates, an ignominious showing in a competition, low marks, a trip to the office "to be talked to" by the principal, or a word to the parent who may still resort to the birch rod. In this welter of aversive consequences, getting the right answer is in itself an insignificant event, any effect of which is lost amid the anxieties, the boredom, and the aggressions which are the inevitable by-products of aversive control.

Secondly, we have to ask how the contingencies of reinforcement are arranged. When is a numerical operation reinforced as "right"? Eventually, of course, the pupil may be able to check his own answers and achieve some sort of automatic reinforcement, but in the early stages the reinforcement of being right is usually accorded by the teacher. The contingencies she provides are far from optimal. It can easily be demonstrated that, unless explicit mediating behaviour has been set up, the lapse of only a few seconds between response and reinforcement destroys most of the effect. In a typical classroom, nevertheless, long periods of time customarily elapse. The teacher may walk up and down the aisle, for example, while the class is working on a sheet of problems, pausing here and there to say right or wrong. Many seconds or minutes intervene between the child's reponse and the teacher's reinforcement. In many cases—for example, when papers are taken home to be corrected—as much as 24 hours may intervene. It is surprising that this system has any effect whatsoever.

A third notable shortcoming is the lack of a skillful programme which moves forward through a series of progressive approximations to the final complex behaviour desired. A long series on contingencies is necessary to bring the organism into the possession of mathematical behaviour most efficiently. But the teacher is seldom able to reinforce at each step in such a series because she cannot deal with the pupil's responses one at a time. It is usually necessary to reinforce the behaviour in blocks of responses—as in correcting a work sheet or page from a workbook. The responses within such a block must not be interrelated. The answer to one problem must not depend upon the answer to another. The number of stages through which one may progressively approach a complex pattern of behaviour is therefore small and the task so much the more difficult. Even the most modern workbook in beginning arithmatic is far from exemplifying an efficient programme for shaping up mathematical behaviour.

Perhaps the most serious criticism of the current classroom is the relative infrequency of reinforcement. Since the pupil is usually dependent upon the teacher for being right and since many pupils are usually dependent upon the same teacher, the total number of contingencies which may be arranged during, say, the first four years is of the order of only a few thousand. But a very rough estimate suggests that efficient mathematical behaviour at this level requires something of the order of 25,000 contingencies. We may suppose that even in the brighter student a given contingency must be arranged several times to place the behaviour well in hand. The responses to be set up are not simply the various items in tables of addition, subtraction, multiplication, and division; we have also to consider the alternative forms in which each item may be stated. To the learning of such material we should add hundreds of responses concerned with factoring, identifying primes, memorizing series, using short-cut teachniques of calculation, constructing and using geometric representations or number forms, and so on. Over and above all this, the whole mathematical repertoire must be brought under the control of concrete problems of considerable variety. Perhaps 50,000 contingencies is a more conservative estimate. In this frame of reference the daily assignment in arithmetic seems pitifully meagre.

The result of all this is, of course, well known. Even our best schools are under criticism for their inefficiency in the teaching of drill subjects such as arithmetic. The condition in the average school is a matter of widespread national concern. Modern children simply do not lean arithmetic quickly or well. Nor is the result simply incompetence. The very subjects in which modern techniques are weakest are those in which failure is most conspicuous, and the wake of an ever-growing incompetence come the anxieties, uncertainties, and aggressions which, in their turn, present other problems to the school. Most pupils soon claim the asylum of not being "ready" for arithmetic at a given level or, eventually, of not having a mathematical mind. Such explanations are readily seized upon by defensive teachers and parents. Few pupils ever reach the stage at which automatic reinforcements follow as the natural consequences of mathematical behaviour. On the contrary, the figures and symbols of mathematics have become standard emotional stimuli. The glimpse of a column of figures, not to say an algebraic symbol or an integral sign, is likely to set off—not mathematical behaviour—but a reaction of anxiety, guilt, or fear.

The teacher is usually no happier about this than the pupil. Denied the opportunity to control via the birch rod quite at sea as to the mode of operation of the few techniques at her disposal, she spends as little time as possible on drill subjects and eagerly subscribes to philosophies of education which emphasize material of greater inherent interest. A confession of weakness is her extraordinary concern lest the child be taught something unnecessary. The repertoire to be imparted is carefully reduced to an essential minimum. In the field of spelling, for example, a great deal of time and energy has gone into discovering just those words which the young child is going to use, as if it were a crime to waste one's educational power in teaching an unnecessary word. Eventually, weakness of technique emerges in the disguise of a reformulation of the aims of education. Skills are minimized in favour of vague achievements —educating for democracy, educating the whole child, educating for life, and so on. And there the matter ends, for unfortunately, these philosophies do not in turn suggest improvements in techniques. They offer little or no help in the design of better classroom practices.

There would be no point in urging these objections if improvement were impossible. But the advances which have recently been made in our control of the learning process suggest a thorough revision of classroom practices, and, fortunately, they tell us how the revision can be brought about. This is not, of course, the first time that the results of an experimental science have been brought to bear upon the practical problems of education. The modern classroom does not, however, offer much evidence that research in the field of learning has been respected or used. This condition is no doubt partly due to the limitations of earlier research. But it has been encouraged by a too hasty conclusion that the laboratory study of learning is inherently limited becacuse it cannot take into account the realities of the classroom. In the light of our increasing knowledge of the learning process we should, instead, insist upon dealing with those realities and forcing a substantial change in them. Education is perhaps the most important branch of scientific technology. It deeply affects the lives of all of us. We can no longer allow the exigencies of a practical situation to suppress the tremendous improvements which are within reach. The practical situation must be changed.

There are certain questions which have to be answered in turning to the study of any new organism. What behaviour is to be set up? What reinforcers are at hand? What responses are available in embarking upon a programme of progressive approximation which will lead to the final form of the behaviour? How can reinforcements be most efficiently scheduled to maintain the behaviour in strength? These questions are all relevant in considering the problem of the child in the lower grades.

In the first place, what reinforcements are available? What does the school have in its possession which will reinforce a child? We may look first to the material to be learned, for it is possible that this will provide considerable automatic reinforcement. Children play for hours with mechanical toys, paints, scissors, and paper, noise-makers, puzzles—in short, with almost anything which feeds back significant changes in the environment and is reasonably free of aversive properties. The sheer control of nature is itself reinforcing. This effect is not evident in the modern school because it is masked by the emotional responses generated by aversive control. It is true that automatic reinforcement from the manipulation of the environment is probably only a mild reinforcer and may need to be carefully husbanded, but one of the most striking principles to emerge from recent research is that the *net* amount of reinforcement is of little significance. A very slight reinforcement may be tremendously effective in controlling behaviour if it is wisely used.

If the natural reinforcement inherent in the subject matter is not enough, other reinforcers must be employed. Even in school the child is occasionally permitted to do "what he wants to do," and access to reinforcements of many sorts may be made contingents upon the more immediate consequences of the behaviour to be established. Those who advocate competition as a useful social motive may wish to use the reinforcements which follow from excelling others, although there is the difficulty that in this case the reinforcement of one child is necessarily aversive to another. Next in order we might place the good will and affection of the teacher, and only when that has failed need we turn to the use of aversive stimulation.

In the second place, how are these reinforcements to be made contingent upon the desired behaviour? There are two considerations here—the gradual elaboration of extremely complex patterns of behaviour and the maintenance of the behaviour in strength at each stage. The whole process of becoming competent in any field must be divided into a very large number of very small steps, and reinforcement must be contingent upon the accomplishment of each step. This solution to the problem of creating a complex repertoire of behaviour also solves the problem of maintaining the behaviour in strength. We could, of course, resort to the techniques of scheduling already developed in the study of other organisms but, in the present state of our knowledge of educational practices, scheduling appears to be most effectively arranged through the design of the material to be learned. By making each successive step as small as possible, the frequency of reinforcement can be raised to a maximum, while the possibly aversive consequences of being wrong are reduced to a minimum. Other ways of designing material would yield other programmes of reinforcement. Any supplementary reinforcement would probable have to be scheduled in the more traditional way.

These requirements are not excessive, but they are probably incompatible with the current realities of the classroom. In the experimental study of learning it has been found that the contingencies of reinforcement which are most efficient in controlling the organism cannot be arranged through the personal mediation of the experimenter. An organism is affected by subtle details of contingenices which are beyond the capacity of the human organism to arrange. Mechnical and electrical devices must be used. Mechanical help is also demanded by the sheer number of contingencies which may be used efficeintly in a single experimental session. We have recorded many millions of responses from a single organism during thousands of experimental hours. Personal arrangement of the contingencies and personal observation of the results are quite unthinkable. Now, the human organism is, if anything, more sensitive to precise contingencies than the other organisms we have studied. We have every reason to expect, therefore, that the most effective control of human learning will require instrumental aid. The simple fact is that, as a mere reinforcing mechanism, the teacher is out of date. This would be true even if a single teacher devoted all her time to a single child, but her inadequacy is multiplied many-fold when she must serve as a reinforcing device to many children at once. If the teacher is to take advantage of recent advances in the study of learning, she must have the help of mechanical devices.

The technical problem of providing the necessary instrumental aid is not particularly difficult. There are many ways in which the necessary contingencies may be arranged, either mechanically or electrically. An inexpensive device which solves most of the principal problems has already been constructed. It is still in the experimental stage, but a description will suggest the kind of instrument which seems to be required. The device consists of a small box about the size of a small record player. On the top surface is a window through which a question or problem printed on a paper tape may be seen. The child answers the question by moving one or more sliders upon which the digits 0 through 9 are printed. The answer appears in square holes punched in the paper upon which the question is printed. When the answer has been set, the child turns a knob. The operation is as simple as adjusting a television set. If the answer is right, the knob turns freely and can be made to ring a bell or provide some other conditioned reinforcement. If the answer is wrong, the knob will not turn. A counter may be added to tally wrong answers. The knob must then be reversed slightly and a second attempt at a right answer made. (Unlike the flashcard, the device reports a wrong answer without given the right answer). When the answer is right, a further turn of the knob engages a clutch which moves the next problem into place in the window. This movement cannot be completed, however, until the sliders have been returned to zero.

The important features of the device are these: Reinforcement for the right answer is immediate. The mere manipulation of the device will probably be reinforcing enough to keep the average pupil at work for a suitable period each day, provided traces of earlier aversive control can be wiped out. A teacher may supervise an entire class at work on such devices at the same time, yet each child may progress at his own rate, completing as many problems as possible within the class period. If forced to be away from school, he may return to pick up where he left off. The gifted child will advance rapidly but can be kept from getting too far ahead either by being excused from arithmetic for a time or by being given special sets of problems which take him into some of the interesting bypaths of mathematics.

The device makes it possible to present carefully designed material in which one problem can depend upon the answer to the preceding and where, therefore, the most efficient progress to an eventually complex repertoire can be made. Provision has been made for recording the commonest mistakes so that the tapes can be modified as experience dictates. Additional steps can be inserted where pupils tend to have trouble, and ultimately the material will reach a point at which the answers of the average child will almost always be right.

If the material itself proves not to be sufficiently reinforcing, other reinforcers in the possession of the teacher or school may be made contigent upon the operation of the device or upon progress through a series of problems. Supplemental reinforcement would not sacrifice the advantages gained from immediate reinforcement and from the possibility of constructing an optimal series of steps which approach the complex repertoire of mathematical behavour most efficiently.

A similar device in which the sliders carry the latters of the alphabet has been designed to teach spelling. In addition to the advantages which can be gained from precise reinforcement and careful programming, the device will teach reading at the same time. It can also be used to establish the large and important repertoire of verbal relationships encountered in logic and science. In short, it can teach verbal thinking. As to content instruction, the device can be operated as a multiple-choice self-rater.

Some objections to the use of such devices in the classroom can easily be foreseen. The cry will be raised that the child is being treated as a mere animal and that an essentially human intellectual achievement is being analyzed in unduly mechanistic terms. Mathematical behaviour is usually regarded not as a repertoire of responses involving numbers and numerical operations, but as evidences of mathematical ability or the exercise of the power of reason. It is true that the techniques which are emerging from the experimental study of learning are not designed to "develop the mind" or to further some vague "understanding" of mathematical relationships. They are designed, on the contrary, to establish the very behaviours which are taken to be the evidences of such mental states or processes. This is only a special case of the general change which is under way in the interpretation of human affairs. An advancing science continues to offer more and more convincing alteranatives to traditional formulations. The behaviour in terms of which human thinking must eventaully be defined is worth treating in its own right as the substantial goal of education.

Of course, the teacher has a more important function than to say "right" or "wrong". The changes proposed would free her for the effective exercise of that function. Marking a set of papers in arithmetic—"Yes, 9 and 6 *are* 15; no, 9 and 7 *are not* 18"—is beneath the dignity of any intelligent individual. There is more important work to be done—in which the teacher's relations to the pupil cannot be duplicated by a mechanical device. Instrumental help would merely improve these relations. One might say that the main trouble with education in the lower grades today is that the child is obviously not competent and *knows it* and that the teacher is unable to do anything about it and *knows that too.* If the advances which have recently been made in our control of behaviour can give the child a genuine competence in reading, writing, spelling, and arithmetic, then the teacher may begin to function, not in lieu of a cheap machine, but through intellectual, cultural, and emotional contracts of that distinctive sort which testify to her status as a human being.

Another possible objection is that mechanized intruction will mean technological unemployment. We need not worry about this until there are enough teachers to go arround and until the hours and energy demanded of the teacher are comparable to those in other fields of employment. Mechnical devices will eliminate the more tiresome labours of the teacher, but they will not necessarily shorten the time during which she remains in contact with the pupil.

A more parctical objection. Can we afford to mechanize our schools? The answer is clearly "Yes." The device I have just described could be produced as cheaply as a small radio or phonograph. There would need to be far fewer devices than pupils, for they could be used in rotation. But even if we suppose that the instrument eventually found to be most effective would cost several hundred dollars and that large numbers of them would be requird, our economy should be able to stand the strain. Once we have accepted the possibility and the necessity of mechanical help in the classroom, the economic problem can easily be sur-mounted. There is no reason why the schoolroom should be any less mechanized than, for example, the kitchen. A country which annually produces millions of refrigerators, dishwashers, automatic washing machines, automatic clothes driers, and automatic garbage disposers can certainly afford the equipment necessary to educate its citizens to high standards of competence in the most effective way.

There is a simple job to be done. The task can be stated in concrete terms. The necessary techniques are known. The equipment needed can easily be provided. Nothing stands in the way but cultural inertia. But what is more characteristic of America than an unwillingness to accept the traditional is inevitable? We are on the threshold of an exciting and revolutionary period, in which the scientific study of man will be put to work in man's best interests. Education must play its part. It must accept the fact that a sweeping revision of educational practices is possible and ivevitable. When it has done this, we may look forward with confidence to a school system which is aware of the nature of its tasks secure in its methods, and generously supported by the informed and effective citizens whom education itself will create.

3

TEXT BOOKS

An analysis of the school textbooks used in the past reveals a truer history of what was taught in the earliest schools than does a study of past educational theories alone. This is particularly true for the early American schools. The teachers in the early days of our country were so meagrely trained and educated that they depended strongly on the textbooks for what to teach and how to teach. Most authorities agree that in the United States the old textbooks in use in any particular school largely constituted the school's course of study. And so an analysis of old American school textbooks reflects the evolution of the American school curriculum and the teaching and learning methods.

My study attempts to show only the development of the socalled "Common School" subjects. The Common School was the term applied to the schools first established at various dates in the different states of the Union for all children—the schools now known as the Elementary Schools. A full chapter is devoted to each of the following: spelling, reading, grammar, arithmatic, and geography. The author hopes that his second book will present the evolution of the important secondary school textbooks.

I have made a serious attempt to present as true a picture as reasonably possible of the changing nature of American

"Common School" textbooks published before 1900. Two reasons may be given for selecting the terminal date: (1) Most persons reading this book will be more or less versant with the more recent textbooks; and (2) the scientific influence on American education began about 1900, causing the textbooks to change markedly after that date.

CHANGING CHARACTERISTICS

Size. In most subject fields, the older the textbooks the smaller they were, particularly those used in the elementary level. This is objectively shown for the texts in several fields in Table 3.1.

TABLE 3.1

A Comparison in the Size of Old and Recent Textbooks in Several Fields

Field	*Period*	*Books*	*Average Pages*
Geography:			
Old	1784-1895	134	211
Recent:			
Ele.	Since 1895	24	253
Jr. H.S.	Since 1895	54	309
American History:			
Old	1795-1885	54	295
Recent	Since 1885	28	639
Civics:			
Old	1789-1889	70	210
Recent	Since 1889	33	566
Physiology:			
Old	19th Century	62	242
Recent	1900-1940	19	286

The older books not only contained fewer pages, but commonly the pages were much smaller. For example, the pages of many of the earliest editions of the *New England Primer* were 3¼ by 4½ inches in size. The pages of the *Elements of Geography* (1796) by Jedidiah Morse were 3 by 4¾ inches. Nearly all very early geography textbooks were small and contained only a few folded maps, if any at all. However, by the 1880's geographies became very large, even larger than they are at present and contained large maps.

Bindings and Paper. In general, the bindings of the books intended for elementary children were very different from those for secondary school youth. For example, most editions of the *New England Primer* were bound either in rather limp paper covers or with very thin wooden boards covered with paper. On the other hand, most Latin and Greek grammars were bound in leather. A few were bound with homespun linen over stiff board covers. In many the leather covered very thin wooden boards.

Most of the earliest spellers were bound either in stiff paper cardboard with leather spines or in full leather. The later spellers were commonly bound in stiff paper cardboard covers and cloth spines. Leather bound books on the elementary level were rare after 1800. However, the texts for the upper grades and secondary schools often continued to appear bound in leather until about 1850.

Nearly all old textbooks were printed on rag paper. Thus the paper in texts over 400 years old is commonly still in rather good condition. More recent texts commonly are printed on less durable pulp paper which ultimately disintegrates. Thus further textbooks collectors may find textbooks difficult to preserve.

Print and Pictures. In general, old textbooks were printed in much smaller type than the later ones. Two of the oldest readers written in America were by Noah Webster and Caleb

Bingham. Webster's book was printed with 9 point type and Bingham's with 8 point. McGuffey's *Primer* (1849), as well as most other primers of that period, was printed with 12 point type. Commonly, recent primers are printed with 18 or 24 point type. Incidentally, the first edition of Webster's *Compendious Dictionary* (1806) was printed with 3 point type. It is evident that printers in those early days knew little of visual hygiene.

Very few textbooks before the 1830's contained pictures, orher than the pictures illustrating the letters of the alphabet, as was done in the *New England Primer* and some early spellers. Then in the 1830's, when the textbooks in several fields began to appear in series, usually only the lower ones would contain pictures. One author was a marked exception; namely, Peter Parley (S.G. Goodrich). He wrote textbooks in a number of fields in the 1830's and 40's, and nearly all of them contained many pictures. Some authors, particularly in history and geography, included a considerable number of horror pictures. Beginning in the 1850's the physiology textbooks began to have more pictures than was true in other fields. Calvin Cutter's *Physiology* in 1852 contained more than 150 engravings. Other physiologies soon followed a similar practice. Some even included coloured pictures much earlier than was true in other fields, particularly showing the blood vessels and other physical characteristics. Coloured pictures did not appear commonly in readers or in other textbooks until the 1890's.

Directions for Teaching. Since the early American teachers were very poorly prepared for teaching, it was rather common for textbook authors to include teaching suggestions in their books. It must be kept in mind that the earliest popular pedagogical textbook, *Lectures on Schoolkeeping*, by Samuel Read Hall, was not published until 1829; and that the first public normal school, at Lexington, Massachusetts, did not open until 1839. So many early textbooks contained rather extensive and detailed directions for teaching the subject or using the text. In some instances these reflected peculiar whims of the authors.

The directions were presented in several ways or places. Most commonly they appeared in the preface, the introduction, or in a section addressed "To the Teacher." In some instances, and particularly in arithmetic books, the helps were presented in the back of the book. In some arithmetic books approaches for the solution of the problems even appeared in the back.

Where the skills were to be taught by a particular system, such as in penmanship, art, and music, many pages of detailed teaching instructions were common. In fact, in art and penmanship entire teachers' manuals of instructions were common. In music these instructions were usually very detailed and technical. Even in a geography textbook by Cummins in 1818, fourteen and one-half pages were devoted to teaching suggestions.

Learning and Teaching Aids in Textbooks. There have been marked changes in the practice of including learning and teaching aids in textbooks. With time there has been a steady increase in their inclusion. Table 3.2 shows how many textbooks in certain subject fields included them. Unfortunately it would require a too extensive and complex table to show how the earliest textbooks differed from the later ones in this regard. However, a detailed analysis of the studies from which this table is constructed would show that the earliest books rather commonly would contain only either a preface or an introduction or both, and sometimes a table of contents and an appendix. Early grammars and geographies rarely contained even a table of contents. Indexes and references were not too common until the latter half of the nineteenth century. Except for the very earliest books, some sort of visual aid—an illustration, picture, table, chart, graph, or map—was rather commonly included, although often only a few. The use of coloured pictures was rare until just before 1900. Notes and glossaries never became common. The use of questions was not universal, but the practice was somewhat constant throughout in all fields. Not only did the later textbooks include more learning aids, but these aids improved in form and usefulness.

TABLE 3.2

Number of Old Textbooks Containing Certain Lasted Learning and Teaching Aids

Aids	*76 Grmrs. Before 1850*	*49 Geog. 1784-1845*	*97 Geog. 1840-1890*	*54 Am. Hist. 1795-1885*	*87 Jr. H.S. Am. Hist. 1886-1954*	*70 Civics 1793-1890*	*62 Physiology 1800-1900*	*Per Cent*
Preface	71	41	84	47	53	66	59	85.8
Introduction	21	22	37	26	28	18	23	35.3
Table of Contents	27	20	48	44	86	57	61	69.3
Questions	32	36	90	36	77	44	52	74.1
Notes		26	61	19		32	52	57.2
Summaries		10	3	10	47	4	15	21.2
Illustrations	2	17	81	38		16	57	49.6
Tables		33	63	15	74		23	59.6
Maps		31	80	22	87			76.6

References		11	16	10	72	72	26	35.1
Index	6	5	11	17	83	47	38	41.8
Glossary		6	34	4		6	31	24.4
Appendix	29	16	48	29	86	51	25	57.4
Pictures		21	88	39	86		57	83.4

SOME PECULIARITIES

Printers and Publishers. The earliest American textbooks were not printed by one particular publishing house, as is common today. The absence of early copyright laws, railroads, good roads, and efficient mail service, prevented large scale publishing by particular firms. Thus the earliest books were produced by local printing shops. In the early colonial period the Boston area printed most textbooks. Later, possibly partly due to Franklin's influence, Philadelphia led in book production. Eventually New York City took the lead.

Before copyright laws became effective, local printing shops were not only the printers of books, but also the sellers of them. Any printer could secure a copy of a popular book and reprint it for local sale. In many cases more than one local printer would reprint the same book in the same town. For example, the 36 different copies of Lindlay Murray's *Readers* of different dates and titles in the writer's collection were printed by 22 different printing shops, nine of them in Philadelphia. To prevent this practice Noah Webster attempted to get the federal government to pass an early copyright law. Since he failed in this, he succeeded in getting a number of states to enact such laws. Thus he was able to collect royalties from the local printers in the states reprinting his books. These royalties aided his family to live while he was writing his dictionary. It was not until after the development of railroads that large publishing houses developed which were to sell and deliver books over the nation.

Advertisements in Textbooks. Even before 1800 a number of textbooks began to contain advertisements listing textbooks in other subject fields for sale by the same printer. In the beginning only a few printers did this. For example, in the different editions of the Murray *Readers* only a few of the printers included advertisements. But beginning in the 1830's this practice became more common, and for several decades after 1850 most of them did.

The 1853 edition of Murray's *English Exercises* printed by a Philadelphia firm contained 25 pages listing textbooks for sale, together with signed recommendations for them. In 1872 Martindale's *Human Anatomy, Physiology, and Hygiene* included 14 pages of advertisements. This practice lessened after 1880.

Testimonials and Recommendations. Even more common than the practice of including advertisements in textbooks, the earliest ones contained recommendations for the text in which they appeared. Usually these were written by very prominent persons. For example, Nicolas Pike, before he published his *Arithmetic* in 1788, secured recommendations from four college presidents and from Benjamin West to be printed in the book. Daboll's *Arithmetic* (1802) included recommendations by Noah Webster, John Adams, and several others.

The prize example of including numerous endorsements was in John Jenkins' *The Art of Writing* in 1813. It contained endorsements by 220 persons and recommendations by 109. However, it should be stated that the signatures of many of these appeared in groups. Many were signatures of very famous Americans. For Pittsburghers it may be interesting to know that one of the editions of Joseph Stockton's *Western Calculator*, which was first printed in Pittsburgh in 1819, contained 25 individually prepared recommendations in the back of the book. Among them were Western Pennsylvania's most prominent persons of that day, chiefly ministers, lawyers, and teachers. Sanders' *Spelling Book* (1838) contained recommendations or endorsements by 55 persons.

Interestingly, as the practice of including advertisements in textbooks increased during the middle of the nineteenth century, the practice of including recommendations and endorsements decreased. No doubt, this was true because of the development of large publishing firms. In most cases the advertisements would include a description of the purposes and merits of their books, making separate recommendations less essential.

Great Variation in Content. The content of old textbooks in most fields during any particular time varied more than is common today. Evidently the chief reason was the absence of the existence of professional societies or organizations, such as the American Historical Society, American Mathematical Society, and so on, which now more or less help determine the content of the textbooks in the respective subject fields. Before the organization of these societies each author could largely determine what his text would include and what omit. So individual whims and interests of the authors greatly determined the nature of the textbooks. In other words, the authors could be more independent.

Long Titles of Textbooks. A large fraction of America's earliest textbooks had very long titles. These titles often involved both the purpose and a description of the book. One marked example of this practice was Noah Webster's Reader. Its full title was, *An American Selection of Lessons in Reading and Speaking Calculated to Improve the Minds and Refine the Taste of Youth. And Also to Instruct Them in the Geography, History, and Politics of the United States. To Which Are Prefixed, Rules in Elocution, and Directions for Expressing the Principal Passions of the Mind. Being the Third Part of the Grammatical Institute of the English Language.*

4

LEARNING MATERIALS: AUDIO-VISUAL AIDS

TELEINSTRUCTION AND INDIVIDUALIZED LEARNING

APPROACHES TO THE SUBJECT

The purpose of this paper is to contribute to the tasks of clarifying and extending design strategies and practices for effectively using available and emerging telecommunication technologies for instigating the formal learning of college students.

The new cryptic term, *teleinstruction*, conveys the concept of the use of equipment, processes and procedures which provide instruction or the stimulation of learning at a distance from the original source of the stimulus materials. The operations can be simultaneous or sequential and involve recordings and time schedules.

THE MULTI-MEDIA APPROACH

Closed-circuit television (CCTV) is only one type of a very wide array of equipment, apparatus, instrumentation and procedures for providing communications for the instruction of individuals at remote points. Radio and broadcast television, on-line and shared-time computer arrangements, dial access materials and telephones can be used for purposes of tele-instruction. This extended concept should make a useful contribution to this important seminar on *Using Educational Media to Individualize Instruction* and to the design and use of instructional systems.

The problem that confronts us, and which we shall attempt to resolve, is to show how the so-called "mass media" and other associated and complemental technologies can be used in new patterns and varied configurations to provide some of the required conditions for formal instruction and the educational development of college students.

Rapidly advancing thinking holds that the designing of optimum conditions and general systems of information for learning by students in colleges and universities requires the use of planned and tested ***combinations of media***. The correct instructional uses of closed-circuit television, for example, currently may require books and periodicals, audio communication, tutorials, seminars and direct lectures, laboratory "experiments" and field experiences. This list does not exhaust the possible means and methods that may be needed for designing the complex requirements for optimally stimulating academic learning.

The multi-media system of instruction is widely accepted, and wise knowledgeable people have long since ceased to display the pathological syndrome of *single medium fixation* which was so characteristic of educational media innovators of the 1940's, 1950's and the early 1960's. Nevertheless there are still at this late hour fashions of Media. The current one can probably be labelled "computer aided instruction" (CAI). Programmed instruction and teaching machines were CAI's immediate predecessors, and closed-circuit and broadcast television were previous fashions. We are becoming rapidly more perceptive than formerly about media fads and fashions, and we calmly understand as each medium is proposed as the solution to learning strategies that "this, too, shall pass away."

REDEFINITION OF THE PROBLEM

There is an advance also of conceptual thinking about the media. They are carriers of information. They are empty channels and raw tapes, films and paper. The basic complex problem is to select the most *appropriate modes of communication* for learning strategies and put these into combinations. What kinds of proportions of modes are most effective for insuring specified learning results and performance changes for specified content units and for learners with known characteristics? When and where do we use print, spoken language (directly or recorded), graphic modes of communications, animation, art forms, and photography (both still and motion)? What kinds of print, and in what formats, best fit the requirements for optimizing the learning conditions? The same question can be asked about the other modes of communication. How do we use combinations of these modes in both simultaneous or sequential configurations? For what reasons or learning objectives should different modes and *combinations of modes* be used to provide high quality instruction? When do different modes summate, extend learning, increase generalization, and when do different modes produce interference with learning?

When we become more specific in the task of design strategies, the problem becomes that of selecting modes and mode configurations which summate, reinforce and strengthen the stimulus impact on students and which shape their conceptual skills and intellectual competencies. Those media and modes should be selected and used to *broaden* and *vary* stimulus conditions, to enhance the interests of students and to increase the possibilities for the retention and generalization of learned performances. It is most difficult to select mode combinations which do not have internal interferences or do not overload the neuro-sensory channels with information or exceed the optimum rate of stimulus presentations.

What are the relations of all of these questions to the problem of individualizing instruction?

This line of thinking points to some of the most fundamental problems of instructional communications, and indeed of the nature of knowledge, its origin and order, its growth and organization.

INDIVIDUALIZED AND SOCIALIZED LEARNING

Teleinstruction and individualized learning would seem to pose a dilemma, a clash of ideas and a conflict of concepts—How can the media and modes of modern technology be appropriately employed in learning strategies?

Education has many shrines where educators worship, and one of these modern shrines is *individualized instruction.* There is no inter-individual nerve net. Let us agree once and for all time that only individuals learn. Classes, groups, seminars, families. audiences and populations do *not* learn. Individuals alone learn, but most frequently they learn *in* classes, groups, seminars, families, audiences and populations. These groupings constitute important if not essential *conditions* which affect in many ways the learning of individuals.

Furthermore, it should be observed that there are factors in social conditions that affect learning positively by reinforcing, the learning, and there are other factors that affect learning negatively by interfering with or inhibiting learning.

Surely individuals to talk audibly or subvocally with themselves to good effect; they think, solve problems, test for better words or phrases, imagine new concept structures, create art objects and dream about the future. Surely, too, individuals do listen to others and learn; they engage in intensive and revealing dialogues, contend in debate and try their wings of logic in disputations. They observe models of intellectual performances and reject them or emulate them. In brief, learning is individualized and socialized. Only individuals learn but social factors provide positive and negative conditions which importantly affect the kind and rate of learning.

FOUR USEFUL GUIDELINES

There are four practical guidelines that may be useful in the planning and execution of learning strategies.

First, design and provide varied and balanced patterns of conditions for learning. Vary sizes and composition of learning groups. Vary schedules. Balance study in splendid isolation for depth with discussions in groups for brightness and interest.

Second, design and provide conditions for learning which are like or which simulate the future conditions under which the individuals will continue to learn during their whole life cycle. There is, partinent to our topic of *teleinstruction*, little prospect that the radio, the telephone, television, and motion-picture films will disappear as sources of information, instruction and entertainment.

Third, whatever the conditions of learning and learning technology, students need training in the strategies and skills for learning under the *special conditions* arranged or provided for formal learning. This proposition applies especially to individualizing learning and to planning for students to study independently.

Fourth, students should be taught in ways which lead them to become autonomous learners who are weaned both from their parents and teachers. The autonomous learner is freed from school requirements and restraints. He sets his own learning tasks, selects his own materials and methods, he achieves his own goals and reaps his own rewards.

TELEINSTRUCTION—APPARATUS

With these approaches now made explicit, let us turn directly to the question of how to use *teleinstruction media* and how at the same time to individualize optimally the learning conditions. The question could be stated to read: How are we to individualize learning optimally while using teleinstructional principles, means and methods?

Let us be very clear about the kinds of equipment, methods and content or messages that we are discussing and from which we can select patterns and combinations. The roll call is as follows: printed materials; recordings on film or tape, both audio and video; live transmissions ranging from telephone lines to multi-channel cables and from on-line computer to laser beams; and broadcast diffusions ranging from radio to continent-spanning communication satellites. It is proposed, furthermore, that many patterns of these *phynotypically different* but functionally similar media can be used to solve the design problems of maximizing the efficacy of instruction for learning. The design may include the special case of precisely adapted instruction for individualized learning.

ANALYSIS OF THE PROBLEM OF INDIVIDUALIZATION OF LEARNING

Essentially the general problem is to arrange for and adapt mediated instruction and conditions of media-mode uses to accommodate within the *tolerance limits* of individual differences which are essential and integral to learning. We are not to be concerned here with individual differences which are not highly contingent to learning operations. We are especially concerned with those adaptations and sets of conditions which affect learning to a degree of *practical significance* as well as *statistical significance.*

Ideally and theoretically we should include the *settings* or conditions for learning as well as the displays of materials for learning whether mediated by a teacher or through technologies. Individual requirements for learning are not unlimited. Tolerance limits can be found, it is assumed, and levels of difficulty, pacing rates and progression rates can be adjusted within these limits.

MANAGING INSTRUCTION

In addition to individual differences of students, there are other major components of the problem of individualized learning. Some of these are the following:

1. Arranging for optimized interactions of instructional materials with the personalized goals, values, interests and activated motives of students.
2. Determining the general and specific educational competency levels of students and adjusting the levels of possible interactions with the right *kinds* and *levels* of instructional materials and methods.
3. Designing and arranging the *places* where learning interactions are to occur between students and the stimulus materials, students and teachers, and students with students.
4. Scheduling, programming and pacing the patterns of interactions with the selected and designed instructional materials.
5. Programming the gradual transition from external control to self-regulated learning activities.

The regulation of interactions over time involves two main operations; scheduling or programming and timing or pacing. Programming a student through a curriculum or course is a gross operation extending over years, months, days and hours. Pacing is the rate at which an individual processes information provided by the instruction; the rate of perceiving, speed of reading, the rates of learning and understanding stimulus materials are processes that are included in pacing or fine timing. Pacing requires fine timing which may have an optimum rate range extending from microseconds for some kinds of foreign language learning, which involves matching and modelling phrases and sentences, to minutes for some kinds of problem solving or the mastery of complex concepts. Furthermore, pacing like scheduling can be self-regulated or externally controlled.

LEARNER ADAPTATIONS

The designing of instructional strategies includes another problem; namely, apportioning the kinds and amounts of adaptation demands or requirements between the *instructional materials and associated media* on the one hand and *the student* on the other hand. Effective instruction involves, among many other things, making appropriate and increasing demands on the student for increasing efforts to learn. When this is done, the student has many options of his own for accommodating to these demands. He can accept, reject or accommodate to them. Involved here are many styles of gamesmanship that are both understood and misunderstood by teachers and students. Students are not merely response mechanisms; they are persons who take action.

There is a problem here that we believe we discovered at PennState. We had been mystified over and over again by the finding that, regardless of the attempts to improve the instruction of courses, at least by greatly increasing the instructional energy input and by elaborating the instructional materials and methods, grades and test scores remained relatively constant. The results were reflected both in measurements of means and variances.

A condition that prevailed in our experiments was that we usually attempted to develop only one, and never more than two, of the four or five semester courses of the students' full course load.

It is known that students establish for themselves levels of performance expectancies, and these same expectancies are established for grades. Serious students also differentiate grade level expectancies for different courses in relation to the importance of a particular course to them. It is more important for students to achieve good grades, for example, in their majors than in their elective courses.

There is an additional set of factors which seems to be operating. *Poor instruction may be compensated for by good learning.* A condition for this to occur is strong interest on the part of students for a subject.

Now we are ready for the paradox and hypothesis: when instruction is importantly improved in one of a set of courses and learning is made easier for the student, the demands on the student are reduced in that course and the grade level expectancy can be achieved with less effort; then, the student channels his energies into the other courses of his total programme. Consequently grades and test measures in the improved experimental course remain as they were before the course was developed.

The most important conclusion that can be formulated, assuming that the hypothesis is correct, is that good experimentation in an operational educational context requires that the *total demand system* which operates on students be brought under control or included in the experimental design strategies.

It is interesting to observe that our definition of an adequate sampling of content has changed from lesson or instrutional units in 1948 to full courses in 1958 and now the entire work load of students in 1968!

PATTERNS OF USE OF TELEINSTRUCTION

The patterns of use of telecommunications equipment and technology for instruction in colleges and universities are only part of the full strategies of instruction. From 1954 to 1964 we at Penn State planned, developed, used and generally evaluated about twenty-five permutations and variations of patterns of use of telecommunications.

These studies have been reported in four major reports and a sound motion picture. I propose to review some of the main developments and suggest how some of these patterns can be used to accommodate to the goals and interests of students and their individual differences and also used to provide flexibility of instruction. Other patterns of use require adaptations that students themselves can make. There are patterns of production and patterns of use that cannot be recommended. There are those that remain to be developed, perfected and accepted by educators.

Initially we used the basic and primitive method of originating instruction from a large classroom with fixed cameras connected by means of cable to a series of small and moderate-sized classrooms. The instructors lectured, performed demonstrations, asked and answered questions and otherwise conducted the class as they would have done before the introduction of television. The television equipment and operating personnel were intentionally made inconspicuous and unobtrusive.

This basic feasibility study which was done for the Fund for the Advancement of Education provided comparisons between (1) *direct instruction* in a class of several hundred students with fixed cameras and (2) transmitted and cathode-tube displayed instruction in classes ranging in size from about thirty-five to sixty students.

The classes with television receivers were monitored first by faculty members, then by graduate students and later by undergraduate proctors. Finally, monitoring in classrooms was reduced in most courses and discontinued entirely in some courses. We made every effort to encourage students to *accept increasing amounts of responsibility for managing their own learning and for other classroom behaviour.*

Otherwise there was no more or less individualization of learning for students than in traditional college courses of instruction even though the students were one TV cable length removed from the instructor. Here a teacherless classroom was a new learning condition for many students. They needed to adjust to this condition.

It was clear from these early experiments that the fields of perception and information displays were importantly selected by the camera opertions. Objects and processes were enlarged or magnified, and the view of the instructor and what he displayed, including blackboard work, was improved for students conventionally seated from the center to the back of large classrooms. Thus, demands on students to select and react to instructional elements may have been reduced while viewing conditions were improved. Interferences of the large classes were reduced in the classrooms with television receivers.

The next set of variations which we introduced was renovating a classroom and remodelling it to serve as a place where instruction could be originated. In this "origination room" or studio there were several variations which differed from the pattern just described. The instructor could have with him in the studio small groups of students *who could give immediate reactions* to his lecture or questions, or raise representative questions which might have been asked in larger sections or by students not in the origination room. It another variation the instructor could lecture in the studio without students but direct his instruction to the movable cameras and the camera operators. This pattern made it possible to have more and better instructional materials such as charts, titles and graphics, as a result of more space and maneuverability of the television cameras. Later when slide and film chains were added to our equipment, these media could be used also by the instructor.

On the reception side we used a wide range of classroom sizes and solved many problems of arrangements of television receivers and speakers in classrooms that were not designed for the uses of "new" media. The objective was to have good viewing and listening contitions in all of the varied classrooms Television was used as a justification for renovating old classrooms.

It was in developing a third set of conditions of learning that we gave the most attention to providing for adaptations and *variations of conditions* for student learning. The first step was to determine that the whole course of instruction need not be channeled over television and that the academic *time-credit accounting system could and should be changed.* Scheduling of segments of some courses was changed to provide time for lectures, both straight verbal and illustrated; lecture-demonstrations; proctor-led discussions; practicum sessions (e.g., in accounting); and regular and special laboratory work in sciences. In addition, of course, there were the regular assignments of text materials, reference sourses, library work and other study. What we began to realize at this stage was that closed-circuit television could be made flexible and varied cross courses and curriculums and within a course of study.

Flexibility and variations of instructional technology, methods and even goals and levels of attainment are very important even if they are not ideal conditions for *individualized* learning.

The instructors in originating studios without students expressed the need for means of talking with students. Realizing the problem of *passivity of television viewing* and the need for active responses and "feedback" to the instructors, we developed the "Telequest" means for studio-classroom and classroom-studio intercommunication. With the "Telequest" sub-system, either the instructor or a student in any of the classrooms (and there could be fourteen of these) could initiate a question. The question or comment could be heard by students in all fourteen interconnected classrooms. Then, there could follow a discussion between the instructor and an individual student or several students in any of the classrooms.

The "Telequest" arrangement provided a means for the instructor to query individual students, and thus to introduce an element into his instruction which increased the alertness of students in television classrooms. This had a beneficial effect on class attendance even when rolls were not checked.

Some instructors provided times when students could seem them, but the students infrequently used these periods set aside for them. This problem raises a cluster of questions about how "feedback" on learning can be provided and used to improve instruction and the conditions for student learning.

Stephens College has very successfully adapted the telephone for mediating the "Telelecture." We tested this method at Penn State for reaching out long distances for information that is current and for outstanding people who could not have been otherwise brought to students in formal class instruction. Thus, two further developments followed.

The closed-circuit television and "Telequest" systems were interconnected with the telephone systems so that up to 400 or 500 students located in fourteen classrooms could listen to conversations and discussions by leaders in relevant fields and by specialists in subjects of interest. Students on signals could query the remote guest telelecturer. Conference telephone arrangements made available to students in a course in economics the opportunity to hear management and labour leaders at a state capital in a strike situation and in a legislative debate on proposals for new labour laws. In political science, leaders of contesting parties were invited into the closed-circuit course by means of telelecture discussions.

The second major development during the early stages of experimentation was on the distribution side of the television operation. We reasoned that if it was practical to transmit instruction from one campus building to another then why couldn't we reach out to the expanding number of Commonwealth campuses. This we did as a test case by installing a microwave link between University Park and the Altoona campus.

In the pre-videotape era we also experimented with kinescopic recordings of instruction. We undertook to produce two core-of-course sets of instruction for the Air Force. We helped the Dage Bell (now Raytheon) Company perfect an inexpensive kinescopic recorder and used a strategy that opened up television instruction to many and varied patterns of use and flexibility for individualized learning or study in small groups. The strategy is that of recording the *central* and most *important parts* of *courses*, those parts that are appropriate for the medium, and those that have the "longest half-life" or slowest rate of antiquation, along with the greastest consensus of experts about both the content and methods.

The recorded core-of-course development provides flexibility of scheduling and actually requires planned supplementary work on the parts of students and teachers in the learning situations.

The effects of the developments can be to provide specified places and roles for both students and teachers. Thus, the *displacement effects* of the televised "master teacher" can be greatly reduced or perhaps entirely eliminated.

The next development which became possible by linkage of classrooms at University Park with Channel 10 Altoona was to simultaneously broadcast courses of instruction while the same instruction was being given to formally organized classes at University Park and at the Altoona campus. Here we challenged the course-credit-fee structure of higher education. Courses in philosophy, sociology, economics, history and meteorology were distributed by both closed-circuit arrangements and by broadcast methods.

We determined by a well-conducted telephone survey of population of people of the broadcast area that about 35,000 people viewed and listened fairly regularly to the course in sociology. However, less than 25 persons were interested in credit for the course. Most of the 35,000 were *individual* viewers. Thus, we opened up the formal classrooms of the University and invited the public to see and learn what transpires at the very heart of the University's instructional programme. Sensitive administrators viewed as public relations issues instruction in such subjects as comparisons of religions, political issues, comparative economic systems, and instruction of the physiology of reproduction. Actually there was less than one-tenth of one per cent of negative comments. The economics professor received almost a thousand letters of appreciation.

Agreements were proposed to the colleges in the broadcast area in Central Pennsylvania that they use the teleinstruction without cost during the experiment and keep records of the results. There were few professors who would accept instruction originated by another in another university. This reaction deserves further discussion and constitutes one of the main barriers to the development of levels of utilization that justify the costs of producing high quality programmes of instruction.

What did this development show? That we could move instruction of some kinds to people rather than transport people to already crowed campuses. It showed that a very small percentage of the adult population is interested in courses for *credit.* Finally, it showed that it is difficult to share or exchange instruction among institutions.

There is much to be done and much promise in instructional broadcasting that can lead to individualized learning. Neither management strategies for instructional broadcasts nor those for use in homes have been as fully developed as they might be. There are needs for an instrument development for the home which will do the following: provide the means for informing viewers *immediately* of the correctness of incorrectness of their responses to questions, problems and issues; make permanent records of the learners' responses which can be transmitted to the place of origination of the instruction; make, on a pre-scheduled timing, a record of a unit of instruction that can be studied when it is best and most practical for the learner.

In addition, there need to be developments in producing and testing printed materials for coordinated study with televised instruction. There are no real technical barriers to the use of telephones for feedback from home-viewed instruction to points of origination. And finally, radio and television can be harnessed together. This could be modeled after the successful demonstrations of two-way radio made by the Albany Medical School, that an adaptation could also invole television components.

We at Penn State demonstrated two other adaptations of televised instruction before attempting to apply programing procedures to courses for use over the media. First, we developed a variation of the Pyramid Plan for use with large television-instructed sections in sociology. This involved the organization of several hundred students in a closed-circuit television course into small groups of twelve to fifteen individuals. The groups' discussions were led by selected and coached *under-graduate* students. The focus of the groups' dialogues was on the issues and problems raised by the professor over television and on those that were of interest to students themselves.

The other adaptation of television during this phase was to install receivers in dormitories. This method of use was at a later date tested thoroughly at the University of Illinois and found to be acceptable. The next step, obviously, is to provide television sets for student dormitory rooms which make some of the best carrel spaces available on university campuses. Further advances in dormitory design using individual rooms in the same manner as is now done in modern hospitals, will make it possible to individualize learning by having in the living-study room arrays of equipment which include sound systems, small television receivers and dial access capabilities for sound tape and film clips. In the building but not in the individual rooms, there could be on-line terminals for accesses to Computer Regulated Instruction (CRI).

In summary, we have in this section traced one exploratory development of *teleinstruction,* and thus we have described how technology has progressively become more varied and flexible, and therefore, more useful in *individualizing instruction*. By developing patterns of distribution of instruction over space, by scheduling and time-sequencing, by creating new patterns of course arrangements, the instruction has become more pliable and adaptable for both instructors and students. What remains is to deal with advances in providing pacing rates that are optimized for the differences in learning rates of individuals and to demonstrate how branching and differential levelling may be accomplished.

PACING RATES OF MEDIA

There is a pervasive belief in educational circles that pacing rates should be adjusted to each individual learner. When it is said that the student should be allowed to proceed at his own rate, two very different conditions may be involved:

1. the rate or schedule at which a student progresses through a course in terms of hours, weeks or months, and
2. the rate of learning which may include speeds of perceiving, reading, conceptualizing, choosing, solving problems and responding.

The independent study plan at Bucknell University releases the student from regular class attendance and permits him to regulate his own rate of progression through the course. The more microscopic pacing rate is not controlled. The Bucknell condition provides, however, possibilities of great economies. The problem would seem to be that of preparing students for accepting the unusual responsibilities for managing their own study time. It should be observed that after instructional materials are prepared and made available the students may need to make little demand on their instructors for their time and help.

We at Penn State have conducted research and development work in an attempt to apply programming principles with the "new" media, including closed-circuit television (CCTV). The critical problem to be solved was that of the rate of presentation and the rate of development of the instructional materials, lessons and courses. We solved this problem by determining the normal rate of work of samples of the target audience of students using preliminary versions of programmed instruction in algebra and grammar. After these empirical tests, pacing was adjusted to the several formats used in the project. Experiments were conducted with different pacing rates, both slower and faster than the learner based norms. Students adjusted their work rates to the controlled rates. There were no significant differences in test scores among the —80, —90, *100*+110 rates.

Two concepts resulted from these studies. First, it became doubtful whether or not the self-pacing rates of students are the optimum rates. Second, pacing that is slightly faster than an individual's normal rate over a whole course may favourably increase the perceptual cognitive response speeds of learning.

Results of the studies and analyses of pacing rates of instructional displays gave us confidence to proceed with programming materials for filmstrips, motion-picture films, film loops and for closed-circuit television.

Programmed instruction was originated "live" in television studios by especially planned mirror techniques, precisely paced on the basis of information collected from sample groups of students and distributed to classrooms where experimental groups, randomly assigned, observed and responded to the frame-by-frame materials. Student responses were made on "response schedule sheets" which paralleled the televised instruction. Reinforcement was given in either the written or the verbal mode at a time estimated to be after students had made their responses. Thus administered, the test scores for students who were instructed over closed-circuit television were not significantly different from the scores made by students who were instructed by the programmed book, filmstrip and teacher-presented versions of the course.

There was an incidental finding which relates to individualized instruction. It is generally known that some programmed books may not maintain the interest and motivation of students. This was found to be true with the Penn State programmed grammar course. Student assistants and observers proctored the evening sessions, and the students complained about the lack of availability of instructors and the dullness or absence of appeal of the course material. Reacting to these opinions and attitudes, we *paired students* randomly and required each pair to use the same programmed booklet and to complete one answer sheet. The pairs of students were asked to agree about the responses to frames or answers to problems and to accept the same unit test score. Complaints about the lack of attention from instructors ceased, as did complaints about dullness of rather finely programmed material.

It will be observed that programmed courses administered by media permitted the instruction of classes and multi-sectioned courses. Also, it is proposed that these feasibility demonstrations present the very real possibility that the procedures can be adapted and developed for uses with the broadcast media and further adaptations made for indvidualiz-ing instruction.

INDIVIDUALIZED INSTRUCTION BY MULTI-VERSIONS OF INSTRUCTIONAL MATERIALS

Instructional film research led to the development of production procedures for making multiple film versions. The experimental films differed with respect to defined variables either in the commentary and sound or in pictorial characteristics. All materials for the versions were "shot" or processed on a planned schedule and then edited together to meet the requirements of experimental designs.

This development demonstrated a means for producing instructional units for target audiences of trainees and students who differed in significant learning characteristics. Versions could be produced at low, medium and high levels of difficulty or in rates of context development. Thus, it was suggested that instructional film units could be adapted so as to accommodate to limited ranges of individual differences.

An extension of this methodology involves the production and use of "single concept" films, either 8 mm or 16 mm, which present usually in silent form the core-of-a-unit or the core-of-a-course of instruction. This method then provides varied opportunities for individualized adaptations to be made in the situations of use. This arrangement has the advantage at some levels of instruction of schools and colleges of providing essential and defined roles for teachers and instructors. They are not as clearly displaced with core-of-unit or core-of-course materials as they are by full courses of media-presented instruction.

Dial access tapes and films are yet other adaptations of mediated instruction for different individuals. It should be observed that pacing rates are fixed in most dial access materials but that the rate of progression through a course of study, the selection of what units to study when and the amount of repetition and review are under the control and judgement of individual students.

In conclusion, the theme that has been developed is (1) that individualized instruction has both limitations and advantages, (2) that the varied characteristics of individualized instruction such as pacing rates and rates of progression through courses of study, or the levels of relative difficulty, need to be defined, and (3) that many adaptations can be made in media programmes to provide new and significant means for *teleinstruction and individualized learning.*

MEDIA, FACILITIES AND LEARNER OPTIONS

It has often been suggested that learning is *always* a singular act, even when the setting for learning is not private. The plausible argument can be made that even in a group setting where all learners receive the "same" stimulus material, say a 16-mm motion-picture film, each of the learners will gain something different from the experience. In part this is because each learner is unique in the readiness he brings to the experience, e.g., his maturation, and prior educational development. It is also evident that ethnic, cultural or socioeconomic backgrounds, physiological impairments, and emotional disorders will have important effects upon his learning ability. The diverse effects of personality traits, motivation, attitude, and self-image will also differentially influence each of the learners.

Lastly, and rather obviously, sheer environmental or situational differences are important, e.g., some learners may be sitting near the projector noise, or in a corner with a poor angle of vision, or too near a heater or ventilator. Any of these many factors can radically alter the perceptual and cognitive capacities of each learner in the group.

Education has traditionally recognized these differences among individuals in the group and has evolved a grading system to reflect these differences. Through normative grading it establishes an acceptable level for the "average" child and then reminds the slower learner of how poorly he is doing by giving him low marks. If such a child does not soon become convinced of his incompetence and "turn off" it is little short of miraculous (Bloom, 1968). Instruction, to the extent possible, should be geared to the individual rather than the group.

What can media do? Properly used, and within the information transmission parameters suggested by Travers (1964), the media can be adaptive to the needs of the different learners and can, through their multisensory nature, provide a broader communication base line. Potentially, a wider variety of learners can benefit from the intended instruction (Twyford, 1969).

Just as the use of media may facilitate communication in the *group instruction mode,* it is also clear that media can have a similar function where communication takes place in the *individual learning mode* (Allen, 1969). Indeed, individualization *cannot* be accomplished unless there are more sources of information (message origination points) than the teacher in the classroom. Media, with their reproducibility and enduring nature, can carry a large portion of the instructional load.

It must be recognized that existing types of media vary in their appropriateness for use in group or individualized situations. This chapter takes the position that to the extent, possible, within cost constraints and local administrative limitations, media should be selected for their flexibility and applicability to specific learner needs and not to meet the needs of hypothetical "average" learners in the group (Torkelson and Driscoll, 1968).

GROUP-PROCESS MEDIA

To set a base line or reference point for comparison, four of the media which seem particularly suited to the advancement of *instructional* goals are described in Table 3.1. (It should be noted that the messages carried by any of these media are here *presumed* to be a valid use of the learner's time and that the messages generally facilitate his grasp of the content when contrasted with oral or written methods.)

TABLE 4.1

FOUR MEDIA ESPECIALLY SUITED TO GROUP INSTRUCTION

1. Television (Broadcast, 2,500 Megahertz, and closed circuit)

(*a*) *Key Instructional Benefits*

Increases the potential teacher/student ratio. Allows a greter audience to share an immediate "live" event. Permits a proportionately greater amount of time to be spent by the instructor in preparing and rehearsing his presentation. Allows special effects and other unusual instructional "assists" to be carried in a single communication channel. Encourages bridging of great distances, which enables expertise to be broght to remote locations. Can be recorded and played back repeatedly to amortize the cost of the original production.

(*b*) *Limitations for Individualization*

Cost of the system precludes its operation to meet an individual need. (Video tape recorders and video-active carrels are variants of television which may become economically viable for individualized learning in the context of self-performance evaluation.)

2. 16-mm Motion Pictures

(*a*) *Key Instructional Benefits*

Permits unique control (through photographic, animation and editing techniques) over the spatial and temporal aspects of the message, and this is equally true with both the picture and sound tracks. Can be readily projected to physical dimensions proportionate to group size. Can be used interchangeably on many machines, often negating the need to transport the equipment from place to place. Can be repeatedly interrupted or replayed as judged necessary by the instructor. Represents a wealth of "ready-made" topics to enrich instructional presentations.

(*b*) *Limitations for Individualization*

Acquisition and maintenance costs for equipment and film (particularly multiple amounts of each) are prohibitive for broad—based individualization applications. Difficulty in the operation of equipment and limited access to the films currently preclude much use by young learners.

3. Overhead Projection

(*a*) *Key Instructional Benefits*

Instructor is given extraordinary variety of control over the rate and form of stimulus presentation. Permits alteration of sequence, partial disclosure, and a number of other "ideal" instructional techniques. Focuses learner attention to a high degree while room lights are on. Permits continuous instructor—student eye contact. Is well suited to local development of instructional material. Enlarges the image readily without consuming much room space. Is "affordable" for every classroom.

(*b*) *Limitations for Individualization*

The projectuals (projected materials) can almost always be viewed directly by an individual *without* the need of a machine. Excepting the multicell transparencies, most images could be reproduced more cheaply in paper form and still be effective for individuals.

4. Group Response System (Edex, etc)

(*a*) *Key Instructional Benefits*

Provides the instructor with immediate feedback. The proportion of the group that "got the message" is known and not surmised. The presentation can be multimedia, and rather complex, and yet be preprogrammed for automatic display. Personalized and immediate scoring, as well as the accumulation of scores over time, is facilitated.

(*b*) *Limitations for Individualization*

In some manufacturers' versions no provision is made in the equipment to give the learner feedback on the correctness of his answer. Some other manufacturers' versions provide such feedback to the student but lack the automatic cotrol features for preprogramming of multimedia presentation. Cost of the equipment is quite high and programming is too complex to encourage message development for direct use by an individual.

To review the general point indicated above, certain media may be highly appropriate to group instruction but have drawbacks for facilitating individualization. This does not negate their value or suggest that their use be discontinued in appropriate situations.

As one rather obvious example of a "quality" message which had important learning value to heterogeneous groups (with little reference to their individul differences) one can cite the initial moon landing. The television medium reached a group of watchers as diverse as can be conceived, *all of whom "learned" but not all of whom learned the same thing.* In other words, though the event was a "constant" it was viewed differently by scientists, first graders, the astronauts' parents, and so on. In this instance, there was little to be gained by deliberately "individualizing" the experience in order to meet the special interests of the various viewers, simply because the immediacy (and the suspense) of the event was paramount for all.

A particular meassage, such as the moon landing cited above, need not be *exclusively* group oriented, however, even though that was its original intent. For instance, videotape replays of the landing or the astronauts' movements would yield considerable additional data to a lunar scientist who quite likely missed important details in his first viewing.

MEDIA FOR INDIVIDUALIZED LEARNING

When we consider the special requirements imposed on media (and implicitly on the messages carried by them) by emphasizing the meeting of an *individual* learner's needs we introduce a number of considerations which have historically been bypassed in the development of school audiovisual collections.

Table 4.2 gives the four examples of media which are probably better used in individualized contexts than group contexts. *These are given only as illustrations and in no sense are the only media that are well suited in this regard.*

TABLE 4.2

FOUR MEDIA APPROPRIATE FOR INDIVIDUALIZED LEARNING

1. Computer-Based Learning

(*a*) *Key Benefits to Facilitate Individualized Learning*
The medium has the inherent characteristic of giving the learner a sense of dynamic interaction and of *controlling* his learning to a large degree. It has a high potential for enhancing a self-competitive spirit in the learner. It allows a high degree of sophistication in the selection of appropriate "next steps" in the learning material by taking full advantage of the principles developed for use in programmed learning. In particular, the programmes can be made adaptive through the computer's ability to "generate" instructional material according to complex decision rules

which take into account the learner's previous responses *as well as* his present one. The computer makes feasible the precise and simultaneous measurement of learner progress along any of a number of continuums, such as time taken to respond, adequacy of response, etc.

(*b*) *Limitations for Individualization*

At the present time, computer terminals cannot be considered economically feasible as learning stations for the vast numbers of individual learners in the schools today. Rather, for the foreseeable future, the computer will be used to *support* individualized learning and will not be in the classroom. It will be used primarily for its prescriptive and evaluative functions but it will not be used to present materials and interact (via terminals) with the learner.

2. 8-mm. Motion Pictures (Hand-held and Table-top)

(*a*) *Key Benefits to Facilitate Individualized Learning*

Control over cues on a temporal basis (motion) is a crucial ingredient to the learning of certain concepts and processes, and the 8-mm. motion picture represents the most economical means for facilitating these types of learning. A wide variety of 16-mm. films can be adapted (edited) and reproduced for use in the less expensive 8-mm. format. In addition, however, certain types of projectors provide the learner with control over *stopping* the film for the study of individual frames, or the opportunity to control the *rate* of viewing and listening. Since many 8-mm. projectors accept cartridges or provide automatic rewinding, operation of the equipment as well as storage and handling of the films is simplified. The 8-mm. motion-picture medium presents a unique opportunity for local production by teachers, thus enhancing the relevance of the curriculum to the children's own lives. Finally, the children can find in the 8-mm. motion-picture medium a creative outlet for self-expression.

(*b*) *Limitations for Individualization*

Relative to the ***duration*** of their use (typically two or three minutes) commercially available 8-mm. films are costly. (Locally produced 8-mm. films tend to be somewhat less costly, provided the camera original film is used and prints are not required.) To realistically appraise their initial cost, it is also necessary to consider the *longevity* 8-mm. films will have, provided students use them with reasonable care, and to think in terms of amortized cost over their useful life. A further consideration is their impact value, since two minutes of viewing film that is unusual and memorable can be a rich educational experience.

3. Audio Card Readers

(*a*) *Key Benefits to Facilitate Individualized Learning*

Increments of instruction contained on each card are usually quite short, lasting only a few seconds. Each card is separately inserted and played, facilitating repeated use by a learner. The sound is reinforced by visual material imprinted on the card. Learners can sequence the cards to suit themselves and few learners in the classroom listen to each of the cards to the same extent. Blank cards can be recorded to meet local (or individual) instructional needs.

(*b*) *Limitations for Individualization*

Most versions of the card player are far too expensive (i.e., $200 or more). This is unfortunate since not only are they mechanically simple but they typically do not produce sound of high fidelity quality. A cost approaching $30 per unit would enable a greater number of machines, and hence cards, to be shared among the children. The method could then become a mainstay of individualized learning at the primary grades rather than an adjunct.

4. Electric Boards

(*a*) *Key Benefits to Facilitate Individualized Learning*

The electric board is a self-check device which allows presentation of information, asks questions, calls for the matching of the correct response to each question, and gives immediate feedback on the correctness of the response. In a sense, it is a battery operated, audiovisual version of the matching question format used on some tests. As such, it invariably generates considerable interest on the part of learners. They view it as fun and also as a way to demonstrate their mastery of the content. The electric board lends itself *only* to manipulation by one learner at a time. However, others can watch, thereby participating vicariously. It is readily adaptable, as a technique, across subject matters and grade levels.

(*b*) *Limitation for Individualization*

Electric board devices are typically set up as a semi-permanent display, available to learners as a kind of informal adjunct to instruction. Often they are relatively large (poster-sized) and are affixed to walls. In order for the technique to be integrated into the mainstream of learning it is desirable that (1) the electrical connections between question and answer be easily and frequently varied to ensure that the content rather than the wiring pattern is learned, (2) items included should be organized and interrelated so that the self-test becomes informative to the learner in a diagnostic way, and (3) results of the students' self-cheks are accumulated so that the elcctric board (like other materials for self-instruction) can be modified and improved in a systematic way.

Acquistion Considerations

In the past, the purchase of equipment and materials has generally been predicted on amortization and maintenance schedules which assume occasional *teacher* use. This assumption is wholly inappropriate to individualization. As alluded to previously, individualization of a school programme will almost certainly require a *different pattern* in the types and amounts of equipment and materials that are made available. Since it is implicit that the students will be operating the equipment, it is a virtual certainly that some items need to be in greater supply than currently are available in most schools that are group oriented. Of course, the initial capital outlay for equipment and materials can be lessened if equipment and materials can be reassigned from existing school resources. It should *never* occur that the introduction of individualization should be expected to succeed by using *only* the existing school resources. This would certainly be a case of "the tail wagging the dog."

As individualization is introduced to a school it very often begins with one class, under one teacher, or it may begin with several classes at a particular developmental (grade) level. In the next year a second developmental level or more is added, until eventually the phasing from experiment to adoption is accomplished and the whole school is operational with the new educational approach. When adoption is in its early phases, the provision of equipment and materials must be predicated on the notion of essentially self-contained rooms. Later, when levels and classes begin to lose much of their identity because of the different rates at which the students in the school are progressing, it is no longer economic to duplicate resources in each room. It is better to develop a readily accessible resource room and/or learning center within the school with only the more frequently used items remaining in the separate rooms.

Let us assume, for purposes of illustration, that a student-teacher ratio of 30 to 1 exists in a classroom and that an individualized programme which allows self-pacing, and which is both print and nonprint (multimedia) in nature, is introduced to the room on a "pilot" basis for the school. It is a virtual certainty that by the end of the first few weeks the 30 students will be well dispersed along a continuum of study. At any given point in time they will be requiring different instructional materials as well as various types of equipment. How, then, can one establish the *number* of items that must be purchased in order to allow continuous study? The answer is not easily obtained. One answer is to "overbuy" amounts and then introduce them into the learning environment *as needed.* Unfortunately, this iterative approach to the problem is rather costly and not too practical to implement.

Another way of answering the problem is to estimate the need as a function of five variables.

Variable 1: Estimate the number of students that might be using the same type of equipment at any given moment according to chance. In our example of a multimedia programme a child may be using texts, work sheets, audio cassettes, filmstrips, motion pictures, manipulative objects, records, and educational simulation games, plus some kind of learning guide which prescribes the objectives and relevant activities. Thus if the 30 students were equally dispersed (by chance) among these 10 alternatives then only 3 of the 30 students would need to work with cassettes and cassette recorders at a given time.

Variable 2: Estimate the proportion of the overall curriculum which is distributed or carried by the different media. Most often the print materials are the prime medium by which the learner masters concepts and nonprint materials are used less frequently. If, in our example, the print materials were used predominantly then the chance-based estimate that three cassette recorders were required could be reduced proportionately, and perhaps only two would be needed.

Variable 3: Estimate the typical duration of time that each type of item will be in use by a student before he releases it to the next student. Continuing with the example of cassettes, it may be established that the average playing time for cassettes in the classroom collection is 15 minutes. If allowance is made for setup time and/or rewined time, another 5 minutes might elapse for a total "in use time" of 20 minutes. In this classroom, where two machines are planned, the average waiting time would be about 10 minutes, even if they were being run steadily throughout the school day. The question to be answered, then, is whether a delay of 10 minutes is tolerable for a learner who is ready for the lesson material provided by a cassette but finds the two machines are busy. In most cases, it isn't likely that a 10-mintue delay would seriously hamper the child's progress, but other considerations may contradict that assumption. For instance, materials may have been specified in *sequence* for important pedagogical reasons and he might not be able to continue study while he waits. If such were the case and the student was forced to wait *without* staying busy then his idleness may lead to some form of classroom disruption or simply to a general loss of initiative and sensitivity to the specified learning tasks. In this case, let's assume that our learners are quite young and impatient; we consider this factor to be important enough that we would want no more than a 5 minute wait. Four cassette recorders would now seem to be required.

Variable 4: Estimate whether coincidence of need for a given item actually requires more units of that material or whether a single copy can be shared when several students simultaneously require it. The same equipment or materials may be needed by several students at the same time, even though the students have advanced to different levels in the curriculum. Or, as is more commonly the case, several students may reach the same point in their studies at the same time. If coincidence of need is expected to occur when cassettes are the medium being used for learning then the availability of a listening post with multiple earphone jacks is preferable to either the use of the cassette loudspeaker or the purchase of additional machines. Therefore, we might decide to lower our estimate from four cassette machines to three, but acquire at least one listening post.

By contrast, if coincidence occurs when texts are the medium for learning there is clearly a need for the purchase of more copies. In another example, work sheets would probably not need to be increased in quantity because these are likely to be consumed on a one-for-one basis and it is immaterial whether this consumption occurred simultaneously or not. Other items, such as large study prints, may simply be viewed by more people at the same time and no additional purchases would be required.

Variable 5: Beyond the basic complement of materials and equipment judged necessary (variables 1-4 above) there is a requirement for additional "spares." Spares are necessary to assure progress when loss or breakdown of the basis items occurs. These backup items need not be in the classroom but should be in the school since they need to be available on short notice. Generally, spare items should be acquired in proportion to the number of basic items that have been purchased, except in the case of particularly "destruct-proof" materials. At least one of each type of equipment item should be obtained for backup purposes and more than one if that type of equipment is heavily used.

Also, since machines which are appropriate for individualization are often small and portable it is not unusual that students will want to borrow them, along with the cassettes or other materials for home study. Because this practice is to be encouraged, enough additional machines should be purchased to ensure that the regular school programme is not impaired when some are inadvertently left at home. Certain items, such as a highly portable cassette recorder, are susceptible to theft because of their general desirability and some loss should be anticipated.

As compared to the implementation of individualization in a single classroom, there are operational advantages and savings which accrue when a schoolwide individualization takes place. For one thing, the number of "spare" items required does not rise appreciably by adding more rooms of students. For another, the pooling of less frequently used equipment and instructional materials in the school learning center enables a much fuller utilization of them than if the same items were duplicated in a number of separate rooms. For this economy to be realizable, however, it is essential that maximum student mobility and self-responsibility be encouraged and that browsing as well as will as formal study be permitted.

GENERAL CONSIDERATIONS IN EQUIPMENT SELECTION

While curiosity may be harmless in its less intent, it is not always harmless in its effect. At the middle and upper grade levels some damage can be caused by students who loosen screws or otherwise disassemble the equipment in order to see how it works. Machines that discourage disassembly (with hidden screws, etc.) are to be preferred. Considerable care should be exercised that the equipment will not present a hazard during its operating left. To minimize the chances for accidential fire or electrical shocks to exploring fingers, only UL approved equipment should be purchased. It is evident that the students should be taught how to operate the equipment rather than being left to their own ingenuity in discovering how it works. Damage to equipment is *not* typically a result of yourthfulness per se. More often it is a result of carelessness or a lake of understanding of proper operating procedures. To prevent inadvertent breakage, purchasers should avoid equipment having delicate plastic knobs or switches that are mounted in an elevated or unprotected position.

As implied above, students of all school ages (including first graders) can be taught to operate equipment. Naturally, the simpler and the more clearly marked are the controls, the easier and quicker this training can be accomplished. Fortunately, simplicity in equipment is often a concomitant of inexpensiveness. For example, cassette tape recorders are preferable to open-real recorders not only because they are easier to manipulate but also because they tend to be less expensive.

A Note about Cost versus Quality

A major consideration in equipment selection is its cost per unit. In that regard, established (audio-visual) buying patterns for group instruction are simply inappropriate for individualization. Traditionally, school district and college audio-visual centers have stockpiled expensive, heavy duty equipment which they then loan out on a daily basis to teachers. They expect to absorb this high initial cost by amortizing it over a 7- to 10- year period. To make these machines last for 10 years, however, they must receive regular maintenance and "overhauls" in addition to any short-term repair to correct unexpected malfunctions.

An alternative to this approach is the purchase of lower cost, shorter life equipment. This course of action may well be dictated by sheer economic realities in instances where many machines must be acquired in one school year in order to implement a new programme of individualization.

A realistic appraisal of the costs required to maintain a technical service staff should be taken into account, since all school districts should have their own staff of technicians. It is quite possible that warranty coverage provided at the time of purchase may be adeqaute to cover defective merchandise for the first year. Leasing, with an option to buy, can be a further way of ensuring against mechanical "lemons." The lower cost of some machines lessens the inevitability of major maintenance overhauls since these may require man-hours of effort disproportionate to the costs of a replacement item. If a $40 piece of equipment is at the end of its fourth year of use and is showing wear, it may possibly be regarded as "disposable" rather than invest four or five hours of a technician's time in a major overhaul. (Incidentally, "disposable" equipment items need not be thrown away. They can be used for parts, or, in the upper grades, many students have an interest in repairing them for their own use or in stripping them for components to be used for other projects in which they are engaged.)

In selecting low cost equipment for purchase some concessions *may* have to be made. It does *not* follow that quality standards (for picture and sound) should be ignored, but rather that they should be applied selectively according to the context; e.g., learning needs. For instance, one should ask whether:

1. The message (materials) cannot be effectively understood (used) unless *high* fidelity is present.
2. The equipment has the operating features necessary to meet *specific* educational requirements, for example, an instant stop button on a record player can allow time for notetaking.
3. There is evidence of faulty *workmansihp* in creation of the product such that damage or wear might be disproportionate to the amount of use.

To reiterate, simplicity is one way to lower costs, but this does not necessarily imply a reduction of standards for quality. For instance, filmstrip previewers at about $17 each are perfectly adeuate for individual viewing and represent only a small fraction of the cost for the much more complex filmstrip projectors that are intended for group use.

The general desirability of learner control over the form and rate of message presentation leads to certain engineering options, which may be cost beneficial. As an example, an 8-mm., sound, motion-picture device has recently been developed in the form of a battery-operated, hand-held viewer. The device uses a variable speed motor (to compensate for loss of battery power) which has the beneficial effect of giving the learner control over the *rate* at which the views the films. This feature makes possible more flexibility and variety of use than is present in current 8-mm. desk-top projectors and does so atless cost.

STUDENT ACCESS TO RESOURCE MATERIALS

It is quite likely to be the case that students' enthusiasm and success in individualized learning will be directly related to the case (or frustration) with which they obtained and use learning materials. As a general rule materials should be located where they will be most readily and frequently used. New technology has introduced the possibility for materials to be *remotely* stored and accessed, but for most schools individualization can be accomplished by a reorganization of materials in open stock for *direct* student access.

Open-Stock Materials

Book materials should be on open shelving and tapes, films and other nonprint materials seem best stored in cupboards. The materials should be filed according to type of media, with labels readily discernible to help the student match the material to identifying code numbers as specified in his learning guide. Colour-coded stripes laid diagonally across the edges of materials enable quick checks for completeness of the collection at the end of a school day and facilitate the proper return of the materials by students.

A considerable amount of time is usually consumed in preparing and cataloging these open-stok materials collections. Since the teacher should avoid becoming a stack clerk, she may seek the assistance of librarians, teacher-aides, parents, or students in setting up the collection. Further, she should develop an attitude of participant-citizenship among her students in order to maintain the collection, for the materials are quite literally each learner's key to academic success.

Remote Resources

The idea of remote access materials was first exemplified in the schools with the concept of the language laboratory, intended for the learning of second languages. It soon became apparent that a *learning* laboratory would be a more appropriate term since a number of content areas could be contained in the laboratory's tape collection. Later, lockstep listening (from a master tape deck) was replaced by a dial-demand capability (from a bank of tape recorders). It should be noted that then, and only then, did individualization begin to replace the group process because each learner could be served separately. The dial-access approach has subsequently proliferated and has reached new levels of complexity. Presently some versions offer the student direct control over television channels as well as audio channels. By an automatic process of accessing and dubbing of computer stored "instruction" at ultrahigh speeds, the individual learner can "call up" a particular segment of material and in seconds be studying from his own personal copy. Thus, if another individual "calls up" the same segment he is not forced to listen in on a partly elapsed presentation, as was true in the earlier laboratories, but starts at the beginning, being delayed no more than the minute or so it would take him to open his printed study materials and settle down to business.

The use of student terminals which are on-line to computers extends the technological continuum beyond the dial-access resource system just described. While many differences exist, just three will be noted here. First, the computer terminal often offers more student-input options. For instance, it may use a keyboard, touch-panel, or light-pen controls. Second, the range of data-base information available to the learner is extraordinary, since the decision rules programmed into the computer cause messages to be *composed* for the learner based on his response pattern. Thus, two learners who start with a particular computerized instructional segment are almost certainly *not* going to be receiving the same material throughout their study period because their different responses have helped to formulate subsequent computer-generated messages. Third, the capability for computer control over remote display devices at the student station, such as motion-picture cartridges, slide projectors, etc., increases the variety of communication channels which may be used to inform the learner.

The dial systems and computer networks both represent a heavy capital outlay for "hardware" *and* for the "software" (materials) which are to be remotely accessed. High operating costs and maintenance costs can be expected as well. It is probable that further improvements in technique and lower costs for terminals, lines, and central processing units will be achieved in the next decade. However, we are not likely to see widespread adoption of either approach in the *typical* classroom across the country unless per student costs are kept in reasonable relationship to the present operating costs of group-oriented instruction.

As can be seen in the preceding paragraphs, a dependence on sophisticated hardware as a means of introducing individualization is likely to be costly. For the near term, an alternative is to use existing types of audio-visual hardware (or slight modifications of it) in new ways. To the extent that costs can be kept low, then individualization will be affordable on a "normal" school tax base and replication of successful programmes will be facilitated. The present challenge, then, is to introduce individualization by way of a plan which uses equipment and materials functionally and with economic feasibility.

Updating the Materials Inventory

The process of keeping learning materials updated and relevant represents a difficult and complex problem, No simple techniques can be suggested which will prevail across the many present forms of individualized learning that exist in the schools, but at least one principle warrants mention.

New editions of printed materials typically represent either a change in pagination or format, or they may be a rewrite, deletion, or addition of content. If the school chooses to save its old editions *and* purchase some new ones (and use of both editions appears likely), the learner should be directed only to those specific learning activities that are appropriate to his edition. This may seem obvious to the point of absurdity but it is nevertheless quite crucial. Inefficiency of teaching will arise from having to make minor corrections in instructional references (to page numbers, etc.,) during classtime and inefficiency of learning will arise if the child cannot quickly find the information he needs.

Facilities Design and Centralized Learning Centers

Any school can individualize its educational programme *without* the benefit of new buildings, unusual floor plans, centralized learning centers, or private study carrels. On the other hand, the presence of these features in the learning environment can facilitate individualization to a great degree.

Obviously, the learner requires space for carrying out his learning activities. Upon occasion he may need privacy (for instance, in test taking) and access to a carrel is quite helpful. On other occasions he may need table space in order to experiment with science apparatus or to use audio-visual equipment. On still other occasions he may want to interact with classmates and a large carpeted area could provide an ideal learning space. Facilities should be designed for maximum flexibility of use from the *learner's* point of view.

As has been alluded to earlier, the school which commits to individualized learning should not try to make all the classrooms fully self-contained in terms of materials or equipment. This would not only be too costly but it would also inhibit the resourcefulness of those students whose learning patterns are characterized by divergent thinking and high activity levels.

A more practical approach is to designate a centrally located portion of the school as the learning center, make it functional in design for ease of access to equipment and materials, and encourage its use by the students. The learning center *can* be a focus not only for student activity but for adult learning as well. If this is the case in a given school, it could be advantageous to make it accessible from the outside when the remainder of the school is closed. The concept of keying facilities design to learning rather than to teaching is equally relevant to the renovation of old school buildings and to the building of new ones.

Three factors should be kept in mind when locating a learning center in the school. First, the notion of centrality may be considered either in terms of nearness to most classrooms or in terms of proximity to the heaviest point of student traffic. Both approaches have merit but probably the former has more application in elementary schools while the latter has more application for secondary schools and colleges where students may "move" to science labs or other departmental facilities.

Second, the learning center should be designed and/or located in a way that will permit its economical enlargement as growth needs occur. All too often where growth was not anticipated the costs of major remodelling will be so great that it is "easier" to compromise the educational programme, with the inevitable result that the "tail has once again wagged the dog."

Third, the utilization-oriented learning center should be bordered by ancillary rooms where teachers and students can prepare instructional materials such as displays, models, and recorded tapes, production supplies (film, card stock, inks, etc.) and Production equipment (dry mount press, thermal or diazo copy machine, lettering aids, etc.) should be available at all times.

Ideally, the learning center should be designed to give a feeling of openness, comfort, and aesthetic appeal. Carpeting, non-glare lighting and the nesting of study spaces, book shelves and other furniture will do much to enhance this effect.

Through proper design, classrooms can also be given a feeling of openness. One way is to group them in sets of four or six, equip them with folding partitions (typically kept in the folded, pushed-back position) and locate them around a commonly shared area (i.e., floor space) in which materials and equipment are accessible to all. Carpeting and proper lighting in the classrooms will have a salutary effect on the students' attention to their learning tasks and their feelings about the school.

Learning Stations and Furniture Arrangements

Individualized learning is characterized by the behaviour of students and not by the physical appearance of any *particular* type of learing station or precise arrangement of furniture in the classroom. This is not to suggest that the nature of the learning station or furniture arrangement makes no difference, but rather suggests that these factors can vary considerably according to programme goals and budgetary constraints, yet still provide an effective setting for learning.

Individual study carrels have been adopted fairly widely at the college and high school level, and especially in courses for which the content can be precisely defined and articulated into an orderly series of preplanned exercises. "Built-in" carrels (i.e., where standard desk-top equipment is built in for ease of use and to enhance security) may be located as convenient in the room or school. Dial access and computer systems also use carrels but rely on installed wiring and are necessarily in a more permanent room arrangement.

Small tables, often having the shape of a triangle or trapezoid, with detached chairs, have been adopted rather widely at the elementary and middle school grade levels. The tables can be thought of as modular units, permitting the addition of components such as dividers and book shelves. The shape of the tables encourages their use for various individual and small group situations and allows great flexibility in room arrangement. Testing can be occurring in one part of a room with the tables drawn apart; elsewhere the tables might be nested to provide a larger work space where students can "spread out," and still elsewhere they could be clustered to constitute a "media" corner where audio and visual devices are readily available. Typically these audio-visual clusters will be located around the periphery of the room to meet the need for proximity to electrical current: Any long power cords stretched across aisles to reach wall plugs represent a hazard both to the youngsters and to the equipment. A second reason for peripheral placement of equipment is to minimize any distraction resulting from operating noise.

MEDIA AS A MEANS FOR PROVIDING LEARNER OPTIONS

While researchers ase working on the problem (Briggs, 1967; Gagne, 1965) they have not, as yet, been able to establish highly generalizable or functional ground rules for matching the different media to individual learning styles. Nevertheless, there are few educators who would deny that "true" individualized learning should permit some student control over the form of the instructional material as well as its content. As indicated previously in Table 4.2, by four selected examples, various media appear to have logical applicability to individualized learning. In the future, accumulation of empirical evidence may enable a better matching of the appropriate medium to past student performance, assuming that alternative materials are actually available that cover comparable content (Flanagan, 1970; Rhetts, 1970). This process may well be accomplished by analysis of relevant message characteristics (e.g., spatial or temporal cue relationships), followed by a determination of which of the media can effectively transmit these message characteristics, and then suggesting the appropriate mediabased learning experience to those students for whom relevant perceptual abilities and interests have been evidenced previously.

Lacking clear guidelines for matching media to learning styles at the present time, the educator should strive for a reasonable balance of method/media alternatives. He must be alert against excessive parsimony, that could lead to boredom, and overabundance, that could confuse learners with meaningless choices.

In Summary

The equipment and materials that the learner utilizes are critical elements in an individualized learning system. Their function as carriers of information is well established, their motivational nature is readily evident, their relevance to the needs of different learners having particular perceptual abilities or disabilities is generally accepted, and their usefulness as vehicles for the building of self-reliance and responsibility in learners is being demonstrated currently at all educational levels (Hoban and Van Ormer, 1950; Lumsdaine, 1963; Reid and MacLennan, 1967; Weisgerber, 1968).

Not all equipment and material is equally appropriate for use in individualized learning contexts. Some types of equipment which have had high acceptance for group instruction (television, 16 mm film projectors, overhead projectors, and group response systems) seem inappropriate for a broad-based approach to individualized learning. For the most part this is not due to inherent deficiencies in these media but rather to the prohibitive costs which would accrue if their *use* was shifted from relatively few teachers to large numbers of individual students.

New assumptions must be developed regarding many traditional audio-visual and library practices. Ready access by the learner becomes a paramount consideration and affects the number of items purchased, their location, maintenance, and replacement schedules. Engineering and construction of the equipment should stress simplicity and should minimize the opportunities for student operators to disassemble or damage the machines through natural curiosity or deliberate tempering.

Configurations of study spaces within the school and classroom vary considerably depending upon such factors as the proportion of the school engaged in the individualization process and the opportunities available for planning of school learning centers, classrooms without permanent walls, and other flexible design characteristics. Resources for learning should be located in both the learning center and the classroom. Quite often they are clustered in particular study areas within these settings in order to localize machine or audio noise, to permit the items to be left in a "ready to use" status, and to facilitate supervision and assistance by the teacher.

Finally, learning should involve the learner in some control not only over *what* he studies but *how* he studies it. Ample provision should be made in the school programme so that the mastery of objectives can be accomplished in alternative ways, accommodating diverse perceptual abilities, interests, and needs. One obvious way to provide alternative learning methods is through the use of various media. It is reasonable to expect that the process of matching learners with appropriate media and materials can increasingly take into account the students' perferences as a result of the empiric evidence which continues to accumulate in various national projects, such as Project PLAN, which are focused on individualized learning.

5

PROGRAMMED LEARNING

Introductory Overview

Most of the work on programmed instruction seeks to apply knowledge of the learning process. The empirical facts have been known for some time, but only recently have they been quite seriously applied to the development of instructional devices and procedures. This relationship to scientific underpinnings offers the potential for teaching many subject matters much more effectively than they are taught at the present time. In addition, the efficiency of these new techniques can be evaluated more severely and precisely than has been possible with other teaching methods. When the question "Does this textbook or lecture teach effectively?" is asked, it is frequently answered on the authority of the textbook writer, editor, or lecturer. However, when this question is asked of programmed material, it can be answered by a detailed analysis of whether the behaviour of the student is up to the standard of achievement established by the programmer.

The success of programmed instruction depends upon the construction and arrangement of the subject matter material. This material must be built in such a way as to present learning tasks and experiences to the student so that he performs activities that contribute to learning objectives. Sometimes machines can facilitate the presentation of material to students and can provide appropriate ways for them to respond. However, whether programmed instructional procedures require machines or are in textbook form, the construction of the programmed instructional sequence is the important concern. It is primarily the development of these instructional sequences and their subsequent use in schools that involve the interaction between the science of learning and teaching practice.

The essential task in teaching is to get the student to behave in certain ways, and this behaviour must be appropriate to, or appropriately controlled by the subject matter content. This means, for example, that given a certain arithmetic problem, the student responds with certain solutions, or given a particular passage in a foreign language, he behaves by translating it correctly. The arithmetic problem and the foreign language words are the subject-matter "stimuli" to which certain student behaviours become attached. As a student goes through an instructional sequence, more and more appropriate and skillful behaviour becomes attached to finer and finer subject-matter distinctions. In this way, student behaviour is shaped from initial unskilled behaviour to subject matter competence. Instructional programming is concerned with the techniques of how one goes about this.

There is another aspect of human behaviour which must be considered as a basic premise in teaching. This is the fact that each individual has a unique history which shapes his individuality. Teaching can be most effective only if it adjusts to the singular requirements of each learner: Ideally the teacher and the learning environment should guide the individual actions of the student. The teaching of champions in sports results from the interaction of one man and one coach. The teaching of a skillful scientist results from the interaction of a graduate student with the individual professor in his laboratory. In the face of large-scale education and with the use of mass media, the skillful subtleties of the master teacher and the individualization of student instruction are often lost or reduced to an average method. Programmed instruction is attempting to increase the adaptive advantages of individual student-teacher interaction at the same time that the advantages of mass education are preserved. The present very early beginnings are only more or less successful in accomplishing this ideal.

Programmed instruction, then, is concerned with the selection and arrangement of educational content based upon what is known about human learning. It is a process of constructing sequences of instructional material in a way that maximizes the rate and depth of learning, fosters understanding and the ability to transfer knowledge to new situations, facilitates retention, and enhances the motivation of the student. It is an explicit process; it is what an effective teacher does intuitively. As this process is studied, the hope is that an effective instructional programmer might eventually be able to structure subject-matter instruction so that it develops according to definable rules that comprise a practicable teaching technology.

Instructional Objectives

A first and very important consideration in instruction is *what the student learns.* The primary objective of the teacher's work is to produce, definable changes in student behaviour and to bring this behaviour under the discipline of the subject-matter. For example, after instruction the student can make the response "8" to the expression "5+3." In this context the lesson to be learned from the experimental psychologist is a methodological one. In order to be appropriately developed, the learner's responses should be specified unambiguously in terms of tasks which he needs to perform. Such terms as "understanding" and "knowing" are amenable to experimental study and to instructional manipulation only when they are specified in terms of actual subject/matter situations and observable student performance. While progress in the science of learning has been made in the experimental laboratory by such precise specification of behaviour, there appears to be a general reluctance among educators to submit student behaviour to analysis in precise terms. It is necessary that the objectives of instruction be defined not by such statements as "to acquire a basic understanding of earth-sun relationships," "to be able to solve problems in algebra," or "to understand the concept 'noun,'" but rather by such statements as "to differentiate correctly between such terms as 'revolution' and 'rotation,'" "given a linear algebraic equation with one unknown, the learner must be able to solve for the unknown without the aid of reference tables or calculating devices," or "to identify nouns by designating them in a series of words, distinguishing nouns in a sentence, or using nouns correctly in writing sentences and phrases" (Lysaught and Williams, 1963).

In work of programmed learning it has been found convenient to make distinctions between *initial behaviour, intermediate behaviour*, and *terminal behaviour*. Initial behaviour consists of the behavioural repertoire the student brings to the instructional situation. Terminal behaviour comprises the specified final set of accomplishments with which he is to leave the instructional course. The initial behaviour brought to the instructional situation is the raw material out of which the terminal behaviour will be shaped. It is therefore necessary to specify not only the eventual objectives of instruction but also the behaviours with which it is assumed that instruction will begin. The instructional materials or subject-matter to which the student responds at the beginning of instruction are used to guide his responses in the direction of the subject-matter situations with which he should deal at the end of learning.

In the course of the instructional sequence, between initial repertoire and terminal repertoire, the student performs activities which enable him to reach the terminal behaviour or degree of subject-matter competence specified by a particular lesson. The student activity that the teacher uses for this purpose can be called intermediate behaviour. The teaching process seeks to use this intermediate behaviour to reach desired educational objectives. This process is greatly helped by the detailed specification of the behaviour that the teacher wants the student to perform. For each stage of learning, the subject matter stimuli (for example, words, symbols, and formulas) to which the learner can respond, and the kind of response which each of these requires (for example, solving problems, writing, or building a model) should be specified. In teaching mathematics, for example, is the student to solve problems, apply his knowledge to new problems, prove theorems, or all three of these? The construction of a learning programme can differ radically as a function of the criterion behaviour chosen. Furthermore, the activities the student performs must be specified in terms of observable behaviour so that when such behaviour occurs the teacher or teaching device can supply appropriate feedback, such as confirmation of the correct answer or correction. The necessity for the precise specification of behaviour is hampered at the present time by an inadequate systematic terminology that educators can use to describe student behaviour and also by the lack of psychological knowledge in analyzing complex behaviours. However, within the limits of present knowledge it is possible to apply concepts from the psychology of learning which permit more instructional guidance than is usually available in present classroom learning environments.

The topic of instructional objectives and what the student learns cannot be dismissed without mentioning those important extra-subject matter behaviours that are described by such words as "paying attention," "learning to learn," "curiosity," "concentration," and so forth. These also require explicit definition in terms of observable student behaviour so that the teacher can recognize them, work with them, and subject them to manipulation by appropriate instructional procedures.

A programmed instructional sequence, then, takes into account the initial repertoire with which it begins and the terminal subject matter competence which the student is to achieve. Getting from initial behaviour to skilled performance requires the manipulation of intermediate behaviour, and the remainder of this overview chapter introduces several of the concepts currently employed in the construction of programmed instructional sequences for accomplishing this.

The Transfer of Stimulus Control

First to the considered is the transfer of student response from the stimuli of the initial repertoire to the appropriate stimuli required for subsequent performance. This refers to the procedure by which the behaviour of the student becomes "attached" to subject matter content. Generally speaking, the process takes place in the following way: At the beginning of a learning sequence, the student is asked to make responses that are already familiar to him. As the learner proceeds to perform subsequent subject matter activities that build upon but are different from these, instruction takes place. In the course of performing these intermediate activities, the student transfers his original responses to new subject matter content and also attaches newly learned responses to new subject matter. This gradual transfer of behaviour to new situations is what happens, for example, in Susan Markle's example of teaching vocabulary in a programmed sequence shown in Fig. 5.1. Here the word "around" is already in the student's repertoire and it becomes attached to or controlled by the new term "circum." This "around-circum" combination is then manipulated so that new combinations take place and new behaviour is brought into the repertoire of the learner.

Sentence to be Completed	*Term to be Supplied*
1. The prefix circum (think of "circle") means "around." The circumference of a circle goes——the outside.	around
2. Circumstances are events going on————you when something happens.	around
3. A person who sails around the world————navigates the world.	circum
4. A cautious person looks around carefully before doing something; he is————spect.	circum
5. Which of these airplanes would fly farthest? ———— Least?———(a) interstate, (b) circumglobal, (c) transcontinental.	(b), (a)

Fig. 5.1: Part of a Programme in Secondaiy School Vocabulary.

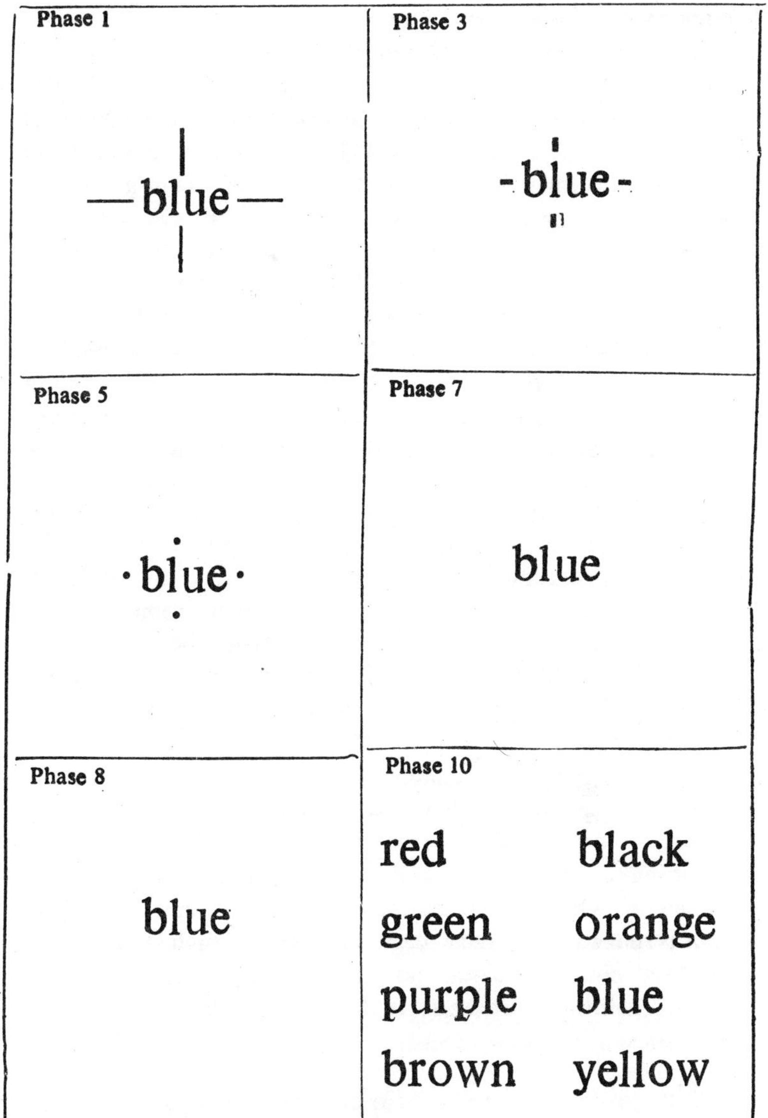

Fig. 5.2: An Illustration of the Use of Prompting in a Programmed Instructional Sequence. Note: The blue colouring in the original progrmme is represented here by the shaded portions of the figure.

Prompting and Guided Discovery

A second concept used in programming is called "response prompting," or, in certain instances, "guided discovery." The instructional procedure can begin by using only those responses which the student has available. The teaching task is to get the learner to make small changes in his responses which guide him toward the terminal performance. In a classroom and in a programme, the instructional material provides a variety of situations which assist the student in making these small response changes. In other words, the instructional material prompts behaviour which can be used to guide the student toward more complex behaviour. For example, a young chemistry student learning the Greek prefixes for number might initially be prompted by having to complete such statements as: "A *mono*cle is a lens for use in only—eye". Or to teach the prefix for ten he might be presented with the statement "The *deca*logue is another name for the—Commandments" (Skinner, 1959). In a programme in elementary physics the following statement might be used to help the student remember the meaning of the word "incandescent" after it has been introduced to him: "A *can*dle flame is hot; it is an—source of light." The response the student makes is the word "incandescent."

The use of prompting enables the learner to make, with a minimum of errors, the new, low-strength responses that he is learning. Prompting serves to make the occurrence of a response more probable and makes possible the design of an instructional sequence in which each learning step makes more likely the correct response in the next step. The use of such prompting, of course, must be based on the student's repertoire at a particular point in learning so that existing behaviour can be used to prompt out new behaviour.

While prompts serve to enrich the student's learning by helping him discover new responses, they are also necessary crutches which must be eliminated so that eventually the student responds to the subject matter content alone. Prompts therefore must be "vanished" in the course of the intermediate behaviour that leads to the level of subject matter competence desired. As instruction proceeds, prompts are gradually withdrawn so that the student learns to perform and discover new knowledge without artificial prodding and with only the information or stimuli he will have available when he is to demonstrate subject matter mastery. The concepts mentioned so far can be illustrated by a short instructional sequence used for experimental study (Taber and Glaser, 1962). Figure 5.2 shows illustrative frames from a 74-frame sequence designed to teach eight colour names to kindergarten children. The figure shows the portions of the progrmme cycle for the word "blue"; this cycle was interspersed with similar cycles for other colour names. Specifically, Figure 5.2 shows how the word "blue" was taught through the programme. The squares in the figure illustrate the form in which each of the eight coluor words appeared in phases 1, 3, 5, 7, 8, and 10. A child pronounced each of the eight words 11 times, and the order in which the words appeared varied from phase to phase. Consider this sequence in relation to the concepts introduced so far. First, there is a strong initial behaviour: saying "blue" in the presence of the *colour* blue. On the other hand, saying "blue" in the presence of the *word* blue is a weak or nonexistent response. The point of the programme is to bring the oral response "blue" under the guidance of the word blue. The colour itself initially prompts out the oral response in the presence of the to-be-learned word blue. The prompting crutch, the colour itself, is progressively vanished so that the oral response comes strongly under the guidance of the word blue. This restricted example serves primarily as an illustration of prompting and of the transfer of stimulus control. The technique, in general, is applicable to a variety of situations. For example, a frame in a number-reading programme may appear as shown in Figure 5.3. Perhaps

7

7 SEVEN 7

7

Fig. 5.3: The Use of Prompting in a Number-reading Programme

elementary reading training could be carried on with such words as "dog," "cat," and "dance" when the words are associated with pictorial representations of the real object or with figures illustrating the action referred to by a verb.

Gradual Progression

A principle implied in all that has been said so far is that a gradual progression of steps is employed in getting the student from his initial repertoire to the terminal repertoire. When developing complex performance, a programmed sequence first works with any available behaviour which is the slightest approximation to the terminal behaviour. In the course of instruction the student is guided by small changes which are in the direction of the terminal repertoire and is permitted, in a sense, to discover the next steps. In the course of this gradual progression, the attempt is made to make the student correct as often as possible, and complex behaviour is built up through a graded series of steps. At each step the programmer asks what behaviour the student must have before he can take the step and what general subject matter relationships or relationships to the student's behaviour will facilitate making the progression from initial behaviour to the speeified terminal repertoire. The steps in the sequence are presented to the stedent only when he can encounter them with a high probability of success.

Reinforcement

A concept central to programmed instruction is "reinforcement." This is a concept about which there is much theoretical debate among psychologists, who are concerned with its various interpretations. On an empirical level, however, the influence of reinforcement procedures upon learning has been established. Reinforcement refers to the fact that the consequences of an individual's actions serve to modify and maintain his behaviour. New behaviour is learned or old behaviour changed when the learner's actions produce a consequent event, such as a reward. Put another way, when an event that follows the learner's activity results in an increase in that activity, that event is said to be a reinforcer, and the process involved is called reinforcement. For example, when a parent makes sure that a child's desirable performance is followed by a cookie, the parent has provided reinforcement. Or, when the teacher makes sure that a child is permitted to perform an interesting exercise only when he has mastered some basic facts, he is in a sense providing reinforcement. The concept of reinforcement points out that individuals are influenced by the consequences of their behaviour. Such events as praise, promotion, good grades, and wages which follow behaviour can, therefore, serve to reinforce or strengthen preceding and on-going activity.

In the world in general, reinforcing consequences occur naturally as a function of the environment and society in which a person lives. In the classroom, the instructional process deliberately arranges behavioural consequences so that appropriate learning will occur. Programmed instructional procedures are set up to take advantage of the operation of reinforcement. One principle in designing programmed instructional procedures, then, is that provision should be made for specific reinforcement to occur. It is also necessary that reinforcement follow a response a sufficient number of times so that the response becomes strong and well learned. Practice without reinforcement is not very effective.

It is also known that the delay of reinforcement may result in little or no learning. In the design of programmed instructional procedures, this fact has been taken seriously so that the student gets almost immediate consequences of his work. In school learning, a major reinforcing event for the student may be "knowledge of results," that is, knowledge of whether or not the response he performs is considerd correct. In many programmed learning techniques, such confirmation is immediately forthcoming upon completion of the student's response. The utilization of this fact of learning in educational technology is very dramatic in view of the frequent delay of reinforcement that occurs in many classroom procedures. However, it must also be pointed out that knowledge alone of the fact that he is performing correctly may be a less effective reinforcer for the student than being permitted to engage in further and more complex activity. His learning programme can be arranged with this in view. Being able to move on, to get into and discover the fine details of the subject matter without being incorrect, frustrated, or punished for being wrong may be the most potent reinforcing consequence in a programmed instructional sequence. There seems little doubt that a significant aspect of educational technology is the management of reinforcing operations, and much research and development work is being carried out on the nature of effective reinforcing consequences for different subject materials at different educational levels and on the factors which affect the use of reinforcement.

Reinforcement must also be provided not only for subject matter knowledge *per se*, but for associated behaviour. Effective reinforcement can teach a student to learn to concentrate and pay attention to the subject material. When immediate reinforcement is forthcoming it appears that a student will be more likely to learn how to concentrate on specific features of a presentation. This is to say that the constant application to the subject matter which a programme demands may not permit the development of competing habits of distraction; less controlled methods of teaching, however, may allow such behaviour to occur more frequently.

Generalization and Discrimination

An important learning phenomenon that needs to be considered in instruction is that of "generalization." The term generalization refers to the fact that a student learns to respond to similar elements in different learning situations. He learns, for example, to recognize that all words with certain characteristics belong to one class called nouns or that all mammals belong to a class called vertebrates and many other creatures belong to a class called invertebrates. In addition to responding to similar elements in different situations, an individual also learns to make appropriately different responses to different stimulus situations. For example, he learns to discriminate between nouns and verbs. When a young child, on the right occasions, says "dog" and "cat," he has learned to discriminate between these two classes of animals. When he calls a strange cat that he has never seen before by the right name or when he says the word "cat" to the picture of a cat or to the sound of a cat purring, he has generalized within the class of stimuli that have something to do with cats. When an indvidual has learned to make discriminations so that he can respond selectively to different stimuli and when he has learned to generalize these same responses to a variety of situations, he has learned the concept. In the same way that the child learns the class concepts cat and dog, the older child learns the class concepts noun and verb, and the still older child learns the concepts light and sound.

The following example from the psychologist's laboratory indicates the kind of procedure used in many programmed instructional sequences to teach the student to make the same responses to all stimuli falling within a class concept and to make different responses to different classes (Mechner, 1965). In teaching a child who does not know colours the concepts of red and blue, objects are selected, some red, some blue, and some other colours. First, the child is shown successive sets of three objects, two red ones and one not red. Each time these there objects are presented the question is asked, "Which is not red?" This is repeated a number of times with only two blue objects. In this way discriminations are established between red and not red, and blue and not blue. The child might then be presented with two objects, one red and one blue and asked "Which one is red?" or "Which one is blue?" The number of nonred and nonblue objects could then be increased so that only one out of a number of objects is red or blue. In order to carry out training for generalization, objects with a variety of characteristics would be included in the sequence of colour discrimination training—large and small objects, dark and light ones, rough and smooth ones, near and far ones, square, triangular, and irregularly shaped ones, etc. This would prevent the responses "red" and "blue" from being attached to stimuli other than the appropriate ones. With the properties of the objects varied, the child would learn to generalize among objects in which the common characteristic is colour. In this way the child is presented with a series of progressively graded experiences by which he acquires the concepts of redness and blueness. Of course this is again a simplified example, and this process could be extended to the learning of many colour names or concept dimensions having multiple categories.

While this process seems clear cut, it requires ingenuity to apply when the concepts to be discriminated and generalized become very subtle, for example, when the concepts classic and neoclassic art are to be taught. For this purpose it might be necessary to develop careful and lengthy discrimination and generalization training sequences. If students are to learn these concepts, it might be necessary to teach preliminary discriminations and concepts such as composition, subject, texture, form, and colour tone. Another problem in teaching advanced complex concepts comes about when the classes themselves are imprecise and there is general disagreement among experts. It is difficult, for example, to teach the concepts of good and poor art unless one can define, at least among a particular community, instances about which experts would agree. It also may be highly desirable for an instructional course to leave the definition to individual determination and taste.

Understanding

Discrimination, generalization, and concept formation get close to the common-sense notion of understanding. When teaching machines and programmed instruction are discussed, teachers frequently remark: "Yes, the student seems to be learning, but does he really understand?" The answer to this question is related to the important fact that the educational technology underlying programmed instruction equates with behaviour such terms as concept formation, understanding, and reasoning. This is so because the actual behaviour that the student performs in the course of instruction is the only tangible evidence available that he is actually understanding and reasoning. It is up to the designers of instruction to provide problem situations which simulate instances in which the student must show understanding and reasoning. When such problems are devised and the student's behaviour is observed and measured with respect to them, then it can be said that his performance is an instance of behaviour which shows understanding or reasoning. The reply, then, to the question of whether the student really understands is, "Tell me what kind of behaviours, perhaps some test performance, that you would like the student display so that you will know that he understands." When such terminal behaviours can be specified, it is the task of instructional technology to determine what combination of educational experiences will rusult in this behaviour.

In general, it seems that continuous variations of the stimulus context in which the student responds result in the terminal behaviours which are defined as understanding, concept formation and utilization, and reasoning. These variations are set up so that the student gradually receives and discovers new information, learns to make progressively finer discriminations and appropriate generalizations, and also learns to apply his responses to a wide variety of situations. This process helps to enrich the student's breadth of learning and is an operational way of defining the development of understanding. Programmed instructional sequences can provide a series of well-organized examples leading the student to develop abstractions and complicated concepts. As pointed out by Skinner, "An important goal is to 'enrich the student's understanding' by inducing him to permute and recombine the elements of his repertoire" (Skinner, 1959, p. 65). The goal of instruction is really not concerned with the learner's response to any one situation. The objective is that the student acquire not a uniform and explicit set of responses about a particular concept, but rather a repertoire which is applicable in a variety of situations. He can therefore use the concept to solve problems, to describe a concept to others, to modify it for certain purposes, to build a model of it, to discover related concepts, and so forth. This terminal behaviour can be defined as reasoning with, or understanding, a concept. Appropriately programmed sequences which can be employed with other kinds of learning experiences can provide the variation which contributes to the growth of understanding.

Empirical Development

An essential aspect in the construction of a programmed instructional sequence is that constant feedback about its effectiveness is obtained in the course of constructing a programme. If a student does not learn, the attitude of the programmer is that something is wrong with the programme and he attempts to modify it. The analysis, editing, and revision of this instructional material are based upon measurement of the student's performance, and the teaching procedure is modified on the basis of information obtained from the behaviour of the learner. Each successive revision that is made in developing a programmed instructional sequence helps to ensure that the student's performance is brought closer and closer to the defined terminal behaviour.

The work to date on teaching machines and programmed instruction is based upon the philosophy that the process of teaching and learning can be made an explicit subject matter for experimental scientific study and can form the basis for the development of a technology of teaching. As knowledge of the learning process increases, teaching can become more and more an explicit technology which can itself be definitively taught. The belief that teaching is primarily an art with which the gifted teacher has to be born and which defies precise description thus gives way to the conviction that teaching consists of techniques and procedures which can, in large part, be made communicable or teachable. This is not to say that the talent of the superior teacher can be replaced. On the contrary, it seems clear that outstanding performance in teaching, as in any profession, is achieved only by those who, in addition to a firm grounding in a communicable technology, bring to their practice a high degree of creativity and inspiration. This certainly must remain true in teaching as well as in medicine, law, architecture, engineering, physics, or musicianship. At the same time, however, the highest achievements in any profession seem likely to be realized only when they are built upon a well-developed underlying technology.

SOME DEFINITIONS AND OPERATIONS IN LEARNING AND INSTRUCTION

From the point of view of the psychologist, learning involves the modification of behaviour. The instructor's goal is to change the nature of the student's behaviour with respect to a given subject, event, or object. His teaching techniques are all attempts to increase the probability that the student will make a particular kind of response to a certain subject matter. When the student has learned to add, for example, his response to "5+7" has changed from any number of inappropriate statements such as "5 cross 7" or "5 ex 7," and inappropriate activities such as scribbling or singing, to the appropriate response, "12". As a result of having learned to add, "12" is a response to "5+7" that has become highly probable or exists at high strength. Put another way, the stimulus "5+7" has come to control the student's behaviour.

The primary contribution of the science of behaviour to training and education is the premise that behaviour is guided in this way by specifiable circumstances. While many of the characteristics of behaviour and principles of behaviour modification were first observed in the laboratory, it is the task of the psychologist interested in instruction to consider their application to human behaviour outside the laboratory. This chapter and the next describe some behavioural principles which are useful both to the psychologist studying the behaviour of his subjects and to the educator modifying and guiding the behaviour of his students.

A major reason for including a discussion of basic principles in this book is that the technology of programmed learning is still relatively undeveloped. It is highly probable, therefore, that the techniques of programming will change to a much greater extent than the underlying principles on which they are based.

DATA AND RESEARCH ISSUES

This chapter presents some examples of the use of programmed instruction in a school system and in an industrial organization. It also discusses general research and development issues that have grown out of the use of programmed instructional materials. A greater variety of examples of results from the use of programmed instructional materials have been reported in numerous articles and books, for example, Hughes (1963), Margulies and Eigen (1962), Coulson (1962), Glaser (1965), and Ofiesh and Meierhenry (1964). Discussions are also available of pertinent issues in programmed instruction and in the application of psychological findings to educational practice, for example, Lumsdaine (1961), Glaser (1962), Hilgard (1964), Dececco (1964). These references provide a broad coverage of work and thinking in the field.

Use in a School System

As a part of a study reported by Glaser, Reynolds, and Fullick (1963), commercially available programmes were introduced as instructional materials in the curriculum of the elementary grades. Prior to the selection of programmed material, teachers, school administers, and university researchers met to discuss available programmes, methods of using them, and procedures for collecting detailed data on their effectiveness. Some of the results obtained during the course of the school year are described below.

The programmes employed were available from reputable programmes publishers. These publishers provided some evidence that the programmes were constructed according to good programme development practices. This evidence was frequently on an informal nature, since most programme publishers at the present time do not provide manuals giving detailed programme use and validity data. To a large extent this omission is a function of the newness of programmes, and manuals similar to those accompanying nationally standardized tests will probably be made available in the future. Standard criteria which publishers can follow in the development of a programme manual are being developed by a national committee (Joint Committee on Programmed Instruction and Teaching Machines, 1963; Lumsdaine, 1965). The common type of programme on the school market is the linear programme in which all students go through the same materials and no provision is made for branching sequences. In the study to be reported, all programmes used were linear in format.

The subject matters taught were selected on the basis of the availability of programmes, subject matter requirements for the particular grade levels involved and student-teacher-community acceptance as determined by the school administrators. The programmes were considered as representative of the subject matter normally taught at the grade levels in which they were introduced.

The teachers involved were chosen on the basis of their interest in trying out programmed instructional materials and participated in the development of the procedures to be used; one teacher at each grade level prepared a manual for all the teachers involved. This manual consisted of a day-by-day plan of specific classroom activities. The exact manner in which a programme was to be used was described and the use of related materials for nonprogrammed instruction was specified.

In assessing the outcomes of instruction, three types of measures were employed at various times, namely, programme tests, teacher-made tests, and nationally standardized tests. Programme tests are achievement tests which the programme publisher considers an adequate sample of student performance to measure the objectives taught by the programme. Teacher-made tests are developed in cooperation with thc classroom teacher and consist of items representative of the expressed educational objectives of classroom instruction. Nationally standardized tests are those commercially available achievement tests used by schools to assess their instruction and compare themselves with national norms. All three of these types were employed in the various studies reported, although they may not be described in the illustrative data presented below. Where the programme test not considered an adequate test of overall classroom objectives or of the programme itself, it was supplemented by a teacher test or by a nationally standardized test. When a nationally standardized test was used, agreement was obtained from the teacher and school administrators that this test was an adequate measure of their own course objectives.

Measuring Student Mastery. In this connection, some general remarks can be made about the measurement of instructional outcomes. If a definitive test is established to indicate mastery of course objectives, then the objectives of instruction are to teach so that students attain such mastery. This means that in succesful instruction many students will obtain perfect scores and the distribution of scores obtained for a class will be skewed with a ceiling imposed by perfect test performance. If two different instructional treatments are given to two different groups and both groups show many students with near perfect test scores, the problem is to distinguish which treatment represents the more effective instruction. Factors other than student achievement must be considered, such as time taken to attain mastery, etc. If achievement is the measure of concern, then the percentage of students obtaining a perfect score, the average level of mastery, or the gain in mastery from pre- to posttesting can be used. A question might always remain, however, with respect to how much more knowledge would have been exhibited by students if the test did not have a mastery ceiling. For example, if the objective of a course of instruction is to teach students addition and subtraction with single-digit numbers, a mastery test would measure just that skill—addition and subtraction with single-digit numbers; however, it is justifiable to ask to what extent students can extrapolate and transfer their knowledge to two- and three-place numbers. The tests employed in the school studies reported here were, for the most part, tests with mastery ceilings and were used to assess the attainment of specific mastery objectives. Sometimes tests of more general objectives were employed which did not display ceiling effects. There were usually nationally standardized tests which are constructed so as to give a wide distribution of scores.

First Grade Arithmetic. In the beginning weeks of first grade, an exploratory study was conducted to determine how well very young students could work independently on programmed instructional materials. The programme used taught the students to write and to recognize the numberals from 1 to 10, associate numerals with number of objects, and to discriminate between numerals. Students worked for approximately 20 minutes each day. A pretest measuring the programme objectives was given prior to beginning the programme, and the same test was given to each student as he completed the programme. Each student progressed through the programme at his own pace. The distribution of completion times, shown in Fig. 5.4, ranged from 8 to 25 days, indicating that the slowest student needed a little more than three times as much time to complete the programme as the fastest. Pre- and posttest scores are shown in Fig. 5.5; this figure shows two frequency distributions of test scores. The numbers on the vertical axis refer to

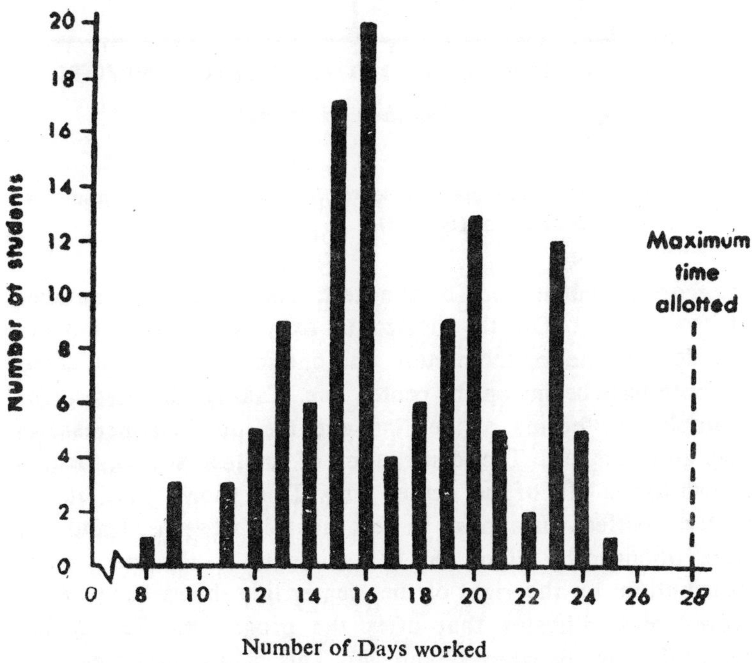

Fig. 5.4: Number of days to complete introduction to numbers programme (N=121; total possible correct=40).

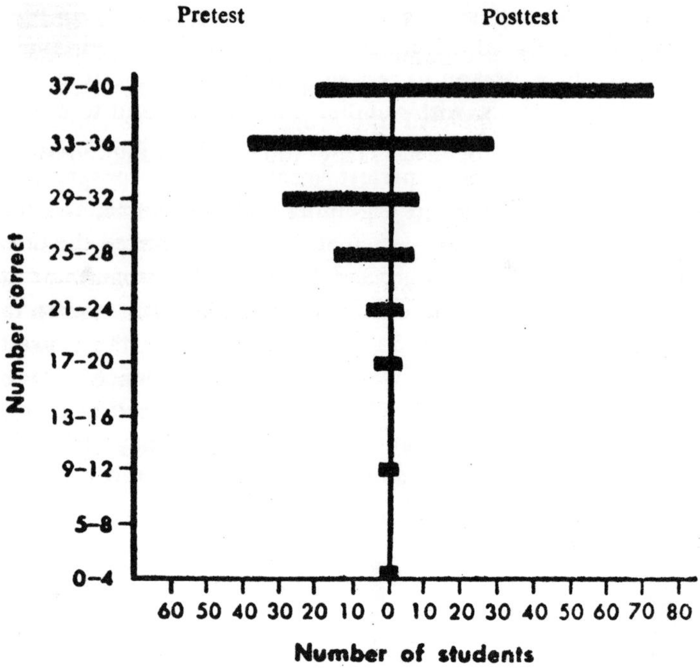

Fig 5.5: Pre- and posttest scores on introduction to numbers programme (N=121).

the score a student made on the test. The score is the number of items correct. On the horizontal axis, two sets of numbers are plotted, one for the pretest and one for the posttest. Zero for both tests begins on the center line. Taking the pretest, for example, zero begins at the line, and the numbers increase as they go to the left. The distribution of pretest scores, then, is shown to the left of the center line. This shows that, on the pretest, perfect or almost perfect scores, between 37 and 40, were obtained by 20 of the 121 students in the study. The distribution to the right of the center line shows the posttest scores and indicates that after the programme 75 students received scores between 37 and 40. This figure indicates that these students were successful in learning the material taught by the programme. However, many of them knew much of the material to begin with. Fig. 5.6 shows a scatter diagram of time to complete the programme and final score and indicates that there was little correlation between these two factors, that is, the students who completed the programme in the shortest period of time were not necessarily those who achieved the highest posttest score.

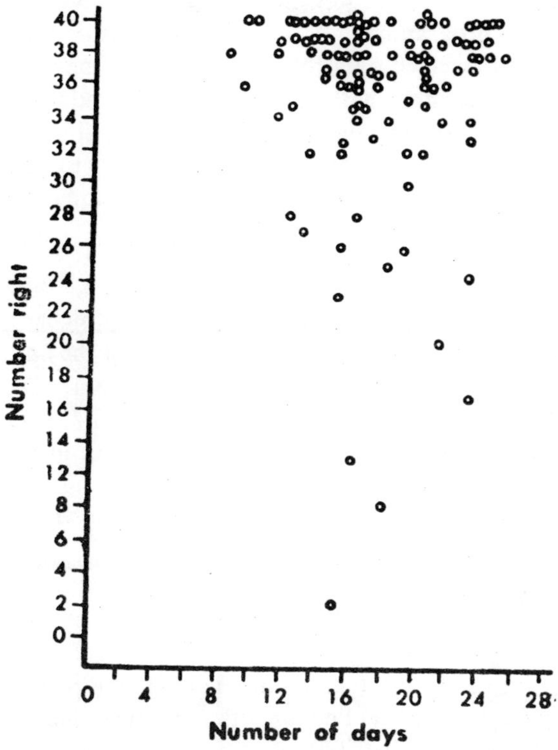

Fig. 5.6: Scatter plot of final test scores and number of days to complete introduction to numbers programme.

Later in the semester students in this same group used a programme in addition and subtraction. The programme was used in an experiment designed to study procedures for co-ordinating teacher instruction and programmed self-study activity. The programme taught single-digit addition and subtraction facts, and classes were scheduled for two 20-minute periods of arithmetic instruction per day, one period in the morning and one in the afternoon. One group of students (the alternation group) received alternating teacher and programmed instruction. The students worked on the programme by themselves through an assigned number of frames during the morning, and in the afternoon the teacher reviewed the material covered in the programme. A second group (the total programme group) received only the programme during both daily sessions for the first half of the study, working on the programme in both morning and afternoon until is was completed; following this the teacher reviewed all of the addition and subtraction facts during both daily sessions for the remainder of the study.

Test results show that the "alternation group," which was intially higher on the pretest, scored significantly higher on the posttest, but that the two groups were equal in the amount of learning gained during the course of the programme. Data for the "total programme group" are shown Fig. 5.7. The distribution marked *interim* shows scores on a test, identical to

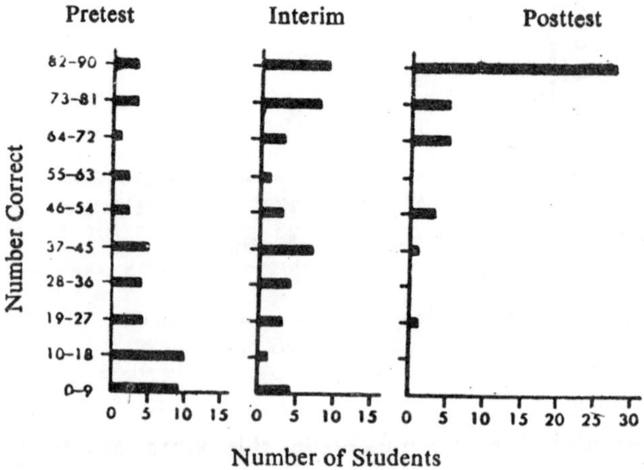

Fig. 5.7: Pre-, and post-, and interim test distributions for addition and subtraction, total programme group (N=43).

the pre- and posttests, given to this group immediately after they completed the programme and prior to teacher instruction. These scores point out that this programme did not teach as effectively as could be expected, and that while some students attained mastery with it, the role of the teacher, as indicated by the posttest distribution (after both programme and teacher instruction), insured proficiency in the subject matter for many more students.

Fourth Grade Arithmetic. At the fourth-grade level, students were given a programme which taught multiplication and division facts through operations with two-place numbers. Over a six-week period, students worked through the programme at their own paces during 45-minute sessions on Monday, Tuesday, and Thrusday Friday. The programmed material was divided into ten sections, and as the student completed a section he was given a written test. If he failed to achieve a score of 70 per cent on any section he was required to go through the programme again and pass a retest at the 70 per cent level. Wednesdays were set aside for teacher instruction periods, and at this time the teacher presented review and practice materials relevant to the parts of the programme which most students had completed.

Fig. 5.8 shows pre- and posttest results when this required mastery level procedure was used. Pretest data indicate that some students knew much of the programme while others may not have mastered the prerequisite behaviour necessary to profit from the programme. However, posttest data indicate that this was a fairly effective proceduce for using the programme and that 96 per cent of the students reached a level of at least 65 per cent mastery.

After completing the multiplication and division programme, the participating classes were divided into two groups. One followed the arithmetic curriculum that was currently being used by the school system for the remainder of the school year. The second group was given programmed instruction in fractions. This constituted an acceleration of the arithmetic

Protest Posttest

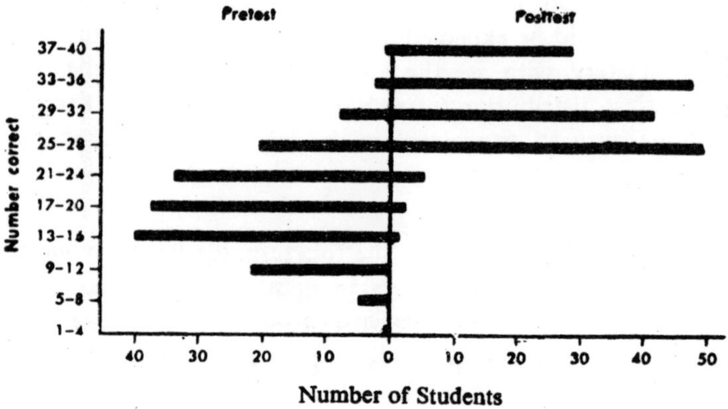

Fig. 5.8: Pre-and posttest scores on multiplication and division test (N=173).

curriculum, since fractions was normally not a part of the fourth-grade subject matter in the school participating in the study. The two groups were matched on Otis IQ and previous arithmetic achievement: Fig. 5.9 shows pre- and posttest distributions for the fractions group; Fig. 5.10 shows posttest score

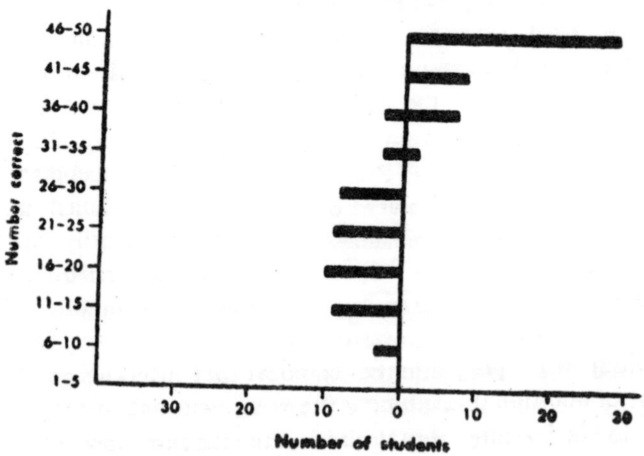

Fig. 5.9. Pre- and posttest scores on fractions test (N=45)

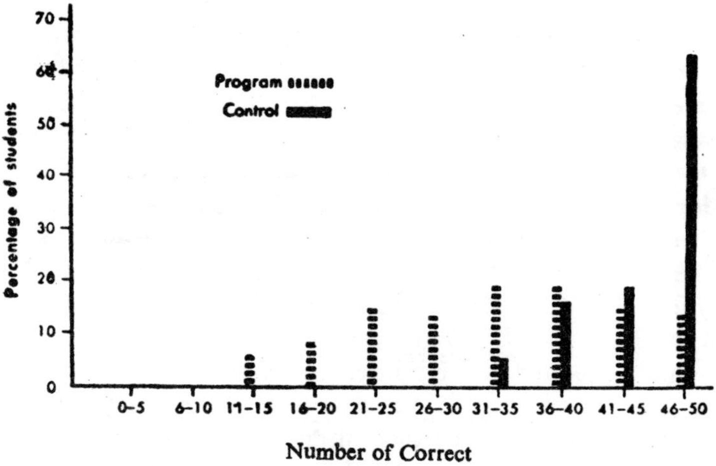

Fig. 5.10: Posttest scores for fractions programme group and control groups following regular curriculum.

distributions on the fractions test for the group taking the fractions programme compared with the group that followed the regular curriculum. Both of these figures would indicate that the fractions programme was an effective teaching device. At the end of the school year, both of these groups were given tests in multiplication and division, and in fractions. Test data indicate no difference between the two groups in multiplication and division performance, indicating that the fractions group, which spent less time on multiplication and division, reached an achievement level equal to that of the other group. On the fractions test, the fractions group did much better than the other group, as could be expected. In general, it seems that the eight weeks of arithmetic periods spent by the fractions group in learning additional advanced material, necessarily taking away learning time from the regular arithmetic curriculum did not detract from their learning of the usual fourth-grade arithmetic topics. This strongly suggests that extension of the curriculum with programmed material produced a significant amount of additional arithmetic learning without being detrimental to the learning of material in the standard curriculum.

Fourth Grade Spelling. Six classes in the fourth grade received programmed instruction in spelling, using a programmed text which taught 354 new words. All classes worked on assigned frames during scheduled 20-minute class periods on Monday, Tuesday, and Wednesday of each week. On Thursday the teacher directed review and enrichment periods, and on Friday students received a written test of words covered during the week. Pre- and post-instructional spelling competence was assessed in this study by means of both a test designed specifically for the programme and the spelling section of the Iowa Test of Basic Skills, a more general, standardized test. Fig. 5.11 shows pre- and posttest distributions on these two tests. These data indicate that 65 per cent of the students achieved a score of 90 per cent or higher on the specific programme test and in addition were quite successful on the nationally standardized test. The performance of a control group receiving traditional spelling instruction was also measured with these two examinations; this comparison showed no differences in the performances of the two groups on the Iowa Test. However, the control group was less successful than the programme group on the programme test. This test contained many words which the control group did not encounter in the course of their

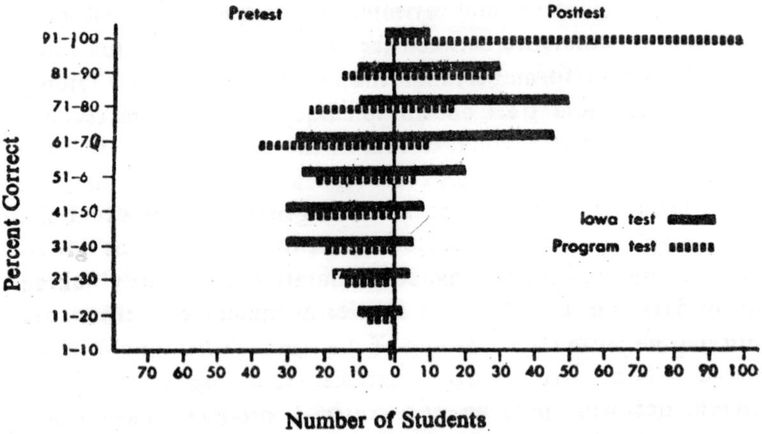

Fig. 5.11: Pre- and posttest distributions on spelling section of Iowa Test of Basic Skills and programme test (N=169).

regular fourth-grade instruction. While this explains the lower control group performance on the programme test, it also indicates that the programme group, by being required to do so, was able to learn additional spelling words.

An Example from Industry

Holt (1963) reports a study in which basis electricity was taught to trainees at the Bell Telephone Laboratories. One group (C) was taught by the standard lecture-discussion method; the other (X) was taught the same material through a programme designed specifically for this course. The primary objective of the study was to compare the effects of method C and method X on the proficiency of telephone technicians being trained in basic electricity. The comparison was made on the basis of a criterion test taken immediately after training and again six months after completion of training. This test consisted of two parts: (1) a facts examination consisting of 75 multiple choice and completion items, and (2) a concepts examination designed to measure the trainees' ability to manipulate electrical concepts in "situational" type test items.

Before beginning the study it was determined that both determined that both groups were equivalent on measures of intelligence, knowledge of basic electricity, pretraining in mathematics and electricity, and years of company service. The results of the administration of the facts examination immediately after training are shown in Fig. 5.12. The results of the administration of the concepts are shown in Fig. 5.13. The difference between the means of the two sets of data is statistically significant in favour of the self-instruction group. Fig. 5.14 and 5.15 show the scores of the two groups on these two tests six months after completion of training. These longer range data show that the statistically significant differences between the means of the C and X groups which were found immediately after training were maintained during the retention interval although the mean scorer of both groups dropped over the course of time.

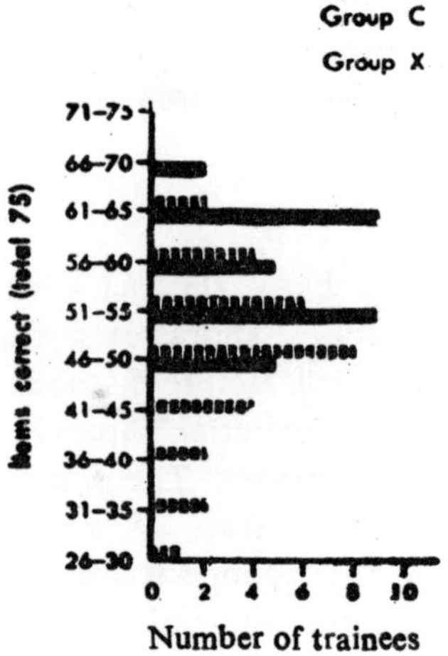

	C	X
Mean	48.6	57.6
S.D.	8.9	6.9

$t=4.5$ $p<0.001$

Fig. 5.12. Distribution of scores on facts examination immediately after training.

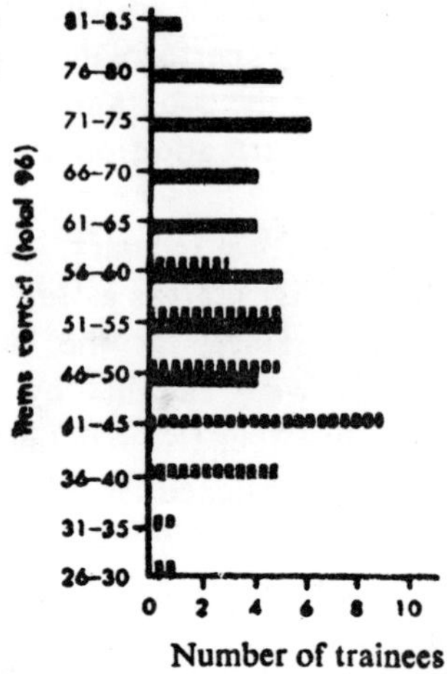

	C	X
Mean	45.6	63.7
S.D.	7.7	6.9

$t=8.08$ $p<0.001$

Fig. 5.13. Distribution of scores on concepts examination immediately after training.

For the most part, the illustrations of the use of programmes in schools and industrial training have considered programmes that are successful teaching instruments. It is true that there are many programmes available whose effectiveness has not been so carefully documented and may not yield results comparable to those reported here. However, it would serve little purpose to report the methods by which a poor programme can be implemented for instruction. Specifically, the above illustrations attempt to make four basic points: (1) The effects of programmed instruction can be usefully reported by comparing pre- and post test score distributions. The juxtaposition of such pre and post data can give a graphic account of the

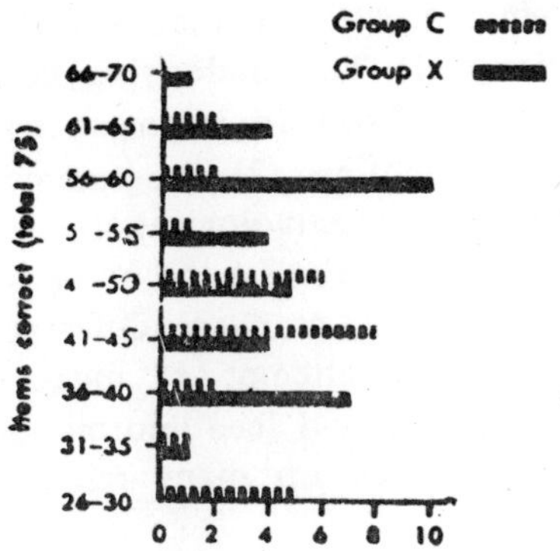

Number of trainees

	C	X
Mean	43.9	50.4
S.D.	9.3	9.7
	t=2.69	p<0.01

Fig. 5.14: Distribution of scores on facts examination six months after completion of training

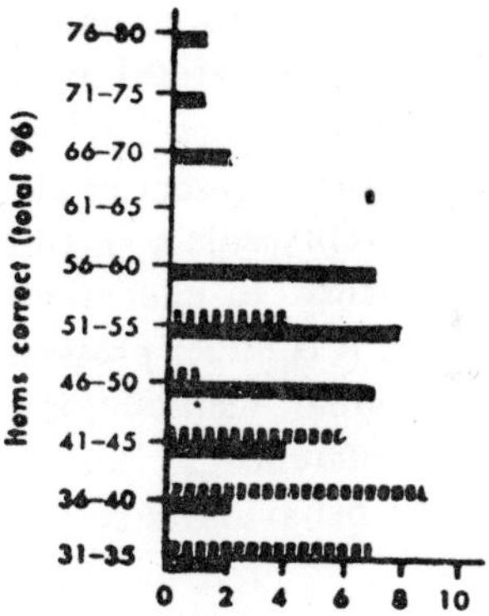

Number of trainees

	C	X
Mean	40.6	52.5
S.D	6.8	10.0
	t=5.51	p<0.001

Fig. 5.15: Distribution of scores on concepts examination six months after completion of training

degree of instructional success or failure. (2) In such evaluation, special attention must be paid to pretest performance (entering behaviour). It may be found that many students already know the material or do not have the prerequisites to begin learning it. (3) Also of special importance is the nature of the test by which a programme is evaluated. Different outcomes can be obtained depending upon whether one uses the test published by the programme publisher, a test made by the teacher, or a nationally standardized test in the general subject matter area. (4) In addition to subject matter competence, other behavioural characteristics of the programmes, such as its effect over a retention period, should be considered in its evaluation.

RESEARCH AND DEVELOPMENT ISSUES

With respect to programmed instruction, the thesis of this book can be summarized as follows: (1) The underlying concepts of programmed instruction are of primary importance in contrast to their present crude implemention. (2) Programmed instruction represents a small step in the technological application of science to educational practice. (3) As a technological application, it is under pressure to make a practical difference in instructional methodology. (4) The attempt to make a practical difference in human learning will feed information back to the behavioural scientist and open up many research questions.

Parametric Baseline Data

The first part of this chapter has presented some evaluative studies of programmed instruction. It is necessary to point out in evaluating an instructional procedure, however, that comparisons with the existing state of affairs may not be especially informative or helpful in further development. What is most useful are data on some absolute scale of just how much students actually accomplish in a subject matter, the rate at which they learn it, how long they usually remember it, etc. Just as an engineer can give some available figure on the amount of production and yield when certain techniques are used, it is necessary for edcators to obtain baseline information on student performance. This should be done, not in normative terms where performance is measured in relation to the group average, but rather in behavioural terms such as size of vocabulary, the kind of arithmetic problems that can be solved, etc. Such baseline data provide a mark for evaluation and a mark to exceed.

The idea being expressed here has been referred to as the carrying out of parametric studies (Carroll, 1960) because such studies would seek to define the parameters of the learning process and would allow us to state, for example, that a given person with a specified degree of aptitude and background would take so long to reach a specified degree of subject matter competence. The question of the evaluation of programmed instructional procedures force such studies.

Terminal Behaviour Analysis

While much time has been spent on the analysis of curricula and educational goals, less time has been spent in pinpointing the kinds of performances that students must display to indicate achievement of those goals. One reason for this is that not enough is known about the analysis of complex behaviour such as creativity and problem solving to allow the educator to be as specifie as could be desired. A second reason, however, is that the generality of instructional procedures has not forced the delineation of performance standards which are to be attained. In contrast, the development of a programmed instructional sequence requires the programmer to analyze the characteristics of terminal performance. It is perhaps this one thing, the behavioural specificity of objectives, that may account for the success of curriculum redesign based on programmed instructional concepts. Apparently less influential in the present state of knowledge are particular variations in the nature of response characteristics, for example, free response or multiple-choice, as the learner goes through a sequence. As much attention needs to be paid to the development of procedures for the analysis of terminal behaviour.

The notion of behavioural specificity for educational objectives need not necessarily imply that an instructional procedure trains all students to react in the same way under similar circumstances. Work is going on, and should be continued, with programmes that are designed to take students to the brink of creativity and to encourage problem solving in new situations (Crutchfield and Covington, 1963). It is conceivable that programmes which take account of past backgrounds can be designed to produce student heterogeneity rather than uniformity of performance.

Subject Matter Task Properties and the Learning Process

As points out that the requirement to carefully specify instruction in terms of human performance has forced the psychologists to consider the development of a taxonomy for behavioural description (Melton, 1959; Melton, 1964). A related problem that arises when one starts to build an instructional sequence is an analysis of the subject matter domain to be covered. In acquiring subject matter competence, both the structure of the subject matter, that is, its logical and epistomological arrangement, and the learning structure are involved. Learning structure dictates the kind of sequencing and ordering of subject matter stimuli and responses that have been discovered to produce certain kinds of behaviour, such as retention, concept manipulation, etc. The task for research and development is (a) to study the relationship between the characteristics of subject matter tasks and the properties of the learning process which are required in order to effectively teach the performance of these tasks, and (b) to incorporate these appropriate learning structures with the epistomological structure of the subject matter domain in order to produce a more ideal acquisition of knowledge.

Performance Limits of Learning

A further aspect of instructional objectives is the question of expanding the capabilities of human performance. Presumably, as educational techniques become more effective, more of the abilities of human beings will be tapped, and new levels of performance will be reached. The concept of guiding human behaviour, with its emphasis on shaping and extending behaviour beginning with available repertoires and proceeding to more complex objectives, can test performance limits. This can be done, for example, by teaching presently taught subject matters at earlier grade levels and by teaching aspects of behaviour which have been formerly classed as aptitudes.

Assessment of Entering Behaviour and Aptitude

The behaviour brought to the instructional situation by the student consists of the initial repertoire, aptitudes, and prior educational attainment with which the instructional process begins. It has been pointed out that the explicitness of programmes development requires the assessment of these initial behaviours so that they can be used as the basis on which to guide learning. With this necessity for specifying entering behaviour, the diagnostic assessment of subject matter prerequisites must become more and more precise. This raises the problem of developing an improved methodology for diagnostic achievement testing and of using this preinstructional information for guidance and motivation in the learning process. It may happen that for the purposes of a particular instructional course, the requisite entering behaviours may be diagnosed as not present in the student's entering repertoire. If such is the case, the student may be directed to acquire certain proficiencies before proceeding. The individual's entering behaviour may also recommend one instructional sequence rather than another. The practical question for instructional guidance is whether the present competencies of the student can be used to get him where he would like to go and whether he can get there at this point in this development. The probable outcome of the interaction between entering behaviour and the educational process or processes to be employed can be used for making a prediction about the probabilities for educational accomplishment. In this sense, aptitudes may be defined as the initial behaviours with which the instructional process must start. There is much to be done along these lines, since there has not been research which provides ready answers to the difficult problem of establishing relationships between aptitudes, including the general aptitude of measured intelligence, and the ways in which an individual learns.

The fact that a programmed instructional sequence can be used as an experimental "apparatus" makes it useful as a research tool in studies of individual differences. For example, experimental tasks can be taught to bright children and the behaviour with which they enter and leave the programme can be carefully identified. A group of retarded children with similar entering competence levels might then be brought to the same level of achievement as the bright students; this could be done by changing the properties of the programme required to accomplish appropriate instructional steps. In this way it may be possible to operationally identify the differences between the properties of the instructional sequence required for these different group of students.

As has been indicated elsewhere in this book, experimental work in programming has attacked the problem of constructing programmes to produce certain behaviours which might be classed as aptitudes, that is, the kind of behaviour measured on aptitude tests. For example, instructional programmes have investigated the teaching of musical pitch discrimination (Skinner, 1961), and spatial visualization, as in translating between two and three-dimensional figures (Brinkman, 1963). The concept of programmed instruction, with its emphasis on the development of behaviours in the individual, may permit research inroads into the analysis of behaviours which are usually not part of the school curriculum and may lead to a more regorous definition of "aptitude."

Instructional Sequencing

This book has indicated that the development of an instructional sequence is accomplished on the basis of some knowledge of findings from the science of learning plus a good deal of practical experience, ingenuity, and empirical testing. The basic structure of present day programmed instructional sequences is a progression of behavioural steps which takes the student through to the attainment of a complex subject matter repertoire. The nature of these instructional progressions in terms of both the stimulus materials displayed to the student and the way in which he interacts with and responds to them are a fundamental issue of learning research and instructional technology. Some of the aspects of instructional sequencing which have arisen in work on programmed instruction are discussed below.

Size of Step

An instructional progression consists of steps which bring the student closer and closer to subject matter competence. The apparent "spoon feeding" which steps seem to represent is often more apparent to the subject matter expert reviewing the programme than to the student taking the programme. Nevertheless, the nature of a step requires study because the meaning "step" and "step size" is, for the most part, ambiguous (Lumsdaine, 1960). For example, a step may be defined in terms of the probability of a correct response, small steps resulting in a high probability of correct responding as one proceeds through a programme progression. Step size may also refer to the ammount of material which the student must read before making a response or to the number of responses made before knowledge of performance is given to the student. There should be some optimal size "bite" which will be most efficient; such bites are probably different subject matters and for different entering behaviours. A teaching machine might be built which hunts in an adaptive way to adjust step size to an individual. At the present time, however, most programme constructers act as if uniform steps are the most efficient for both the programme builder and the student. The advantage to be gained by more individual adjustment is a matter for investigation.

As points out that there is no special rationale for the short two- or three-sentence frames currently in vogue. The same principles of learning might be applied to much grosser units if these were the most effective way to attain the desired terminal behaviour. Size of step cannot be considered in isolation from other properties of the step such as those considered below.

Providing Richness of Experience

It is an advantage for the student to have experience brought to him. As the amount of knowledge in a subject matter grows, the codifying and transmitting of well-sampled experiences become very important for the instructional enterprise. A rich programme should permit the student to work on a subject matter in a variety of contexts. Keen discriminations and the ability to differentiate and generalize between concepts can be guided in this way. For example, a thorough mastery of the concept "noun" occurs when the student works with material that requires the use of various kinds of nouns in contexts in which they must be discriminated from other parts of speech. As suggests how graded sequences should be able to teach discrimination and generalization between classes of concepts. Appropriate use of specific situations can provide the student with a repertoire which is applicable to a wide variety of situations. Research and development on programmed learning should accept as a major problem for investigation the study of the properties of student response to a graded sequence of instances which lead to effective use of the generalized and more abstract concept or rule involved.

The Form of Student Response

There has been much controversy on the manner in which a student should respond to a programme. For example, experimental studies have sought to contrast the effectiveness of constructed versus multiple-choice responses; no conclusive differences have been found. The assumptions of programming procedures do not make any one kind of responding any more correct than another—response mode is a function of the desired terminal behaviour. For programme construction, however, the form and encoding of responses can be an important matter, since some forms of response are easier to code, evaluate, and automate than others. The important research and development problem involved is the determination of the degree of generalization between different forms of response to subject matter stimuli. In the study by Evans (1961), for example, children could construct (write) numbers after making *only* multiple choice discrimination responses in which they circled the correct matching response or pushed a button to select the correct choice. This study indicated that learning discriminations in one response mode apparently permitted the student to monitor his own behaviour when different responses were required by the same stimuli.

Learning Rate

A great deal has been written about the fact that with present day programmed instructional techniques the learner can proceed at his own rate. This aspect has been proclaimed as one of the substantial advantages of programmed self-instruction. It is an advantage, especially if considered in the light of a deemphasis of lock step curricula and as a contribution to the notion that for different individuals equal educational attainments can take unequal amounts of time.

From another point of view, programmed instruction can provide an opportunity for *not* permitting students to go at their own rate and, in fact, pacing them so that they learn at a fast rate and learn to work at a fast rate wherever this is desirable. For example, under the pressure of an external or self-imposed deadline, an individual works rapidly and often produces a product that is equal or superior to what he would have done had he worked more leisurely. Little basic research work has been done on pacing during learning, and consideration of it can have both technological and scientific interest.

Response Feedback and Reinforcement

Although response feedback and reinforcement have been central concepts in this book, knowledge of the effects of these variables is quite incomplete, and investigation of the utilization of reinforcing feedback and the factors that influence it is a significant area of ongoing research. The influence of variables such as the amount, schedule, and delay of reinforcement, which have significant effects in the learning laboratory, need to be appropriately placed in the context of subject matter instruction. Furthermore, reinforcement is not an average matter, and the same instructional environment may have different reinforcement properties for different students. An interesting problem is the development of methodology whereby a learner can adjust an instructional sequence so that it is optimally reinforcing for him. Related to this latter problem is investigation of the nature of reinforcement that is produced as a result of prior performance, that is, response-produced reinforcement. The activities the student carries out in the course of learning can become ends in themselves and are "intrinsically" reinforcing, perhaps in the same sense that a student is reinforced when he is led to discover something and make what he considers an ingenious response to a situation. A major concept in programmed instruction is the presentation of a stimulus situation which has a high probability of eliciting desired performance; this provides the foundation for an intrinsically reinforcing state of affairs. In this sense the steps in a programmed sequence can be "peaked" to an optimum of difficulty, that is, made neither too easy nor too difficult. Such programming would provide a setting for a self-reinforcing learning step. When an instructional sequence is constructed for use with a large number of subjects, each step is not quite peaked for the individual learner and hence he may require confirming feedback. Programmed sequences can probably be made more intrinsically reinforcing if they are designed so that the individual can select a learning step which most likely assures him of making an appropriate response. The term "adaptive programming" has connoted this kind of adjustment to individual differences, and experimental work with computer-based instructional systems suggests that computer capability is a possibility for handling the adjustment to individual instructional requirements. The important problem for research and development involved here is investigation of the dimensions along which an instructional situation can be individualized, such as rate of learning, mode of responding, content of examples, etc.

A problem related to the above is the study of the nature of reinforcing events in various instructional situations. For example, recent work with programmed instruction in the primary grades suggests that for bright children the aspect of a programme which is most reinforcing is being permitted to go on to the next step. For these children, observing that their response is correct may not constitute a highly reinforcing event, since they have a history of being correct most of the time. With retarded children, on the other hand, the important reinforcing event in the same programme is the confirming feedback that tells them they are getting certain responses correct. For the retarded children, response confirmation is highly reinforcing, since they have frequently had a history of failure in the subject being taught.

Among experimental psychologists, much work has been done on the effect of the pattern and schedule of reinforcing contingencies. This work takes account of the fact that reinforcing events can occur in different frequencies and in different patterns in the course of learning. For example, studies have indicated that the behaviour of individuals matches the proportion of reinforcement to nonreinforcement of a learning task so that the probability of the response will approach the probability of reinforcement. To illustrate, if 90 per cent of English nouns encountered by a student form their plurals in 's' and 10 per cent with 'n,' the student would be expected to form the plural of newly encountered nouns with 's' about 90 per cent of the time (Estes, 1960). Such relationships require intensive investigation in the context of the science of learning and also for appropriate practical implementation. In general, as pointed out the concept of reinforcement and how reinforcers operate are central in learning and instruction, and the variables involved require extensive analysis.

Measuring Learning Outcomes

The concept of programmed instruction demands that programmes be accompanied by carefully prepared tests of instructional attainment. These tests serve two purposes: first, they present quite specifically a sample of the terminal behaviour that the programme was designed to teach. Secondly, they show, on the basis of previous programme tryout, what the expected achievement can be for a particular population of students. The final frames in a programme consist of samples of subject matter situations which the student must handle at the end of the instructional sequence; a relevant achievement test is then considered as representing another sample from the universe of subject matter content. In the context of programmed instruction, therefore, the development of appropriate achievement tests takes on special significance, and the requirements of programmed instruction force a re-examination of the general concepts of achievement testing.

Underlying the concept of achievement assessment is the assumption that there is a continuum of subject matter competence ranging from low proficiency to high proficiency. A student's performance occurs at some point along this continuum as measured by the behaviour he displays during testing. The standard with which an individual's performance can be compared consists of the behaviours which define the points along the underlying achievement continuum. Performance levels can be established at appropriate points in the course of instruction where it is necessary to obtain information about the adequacy of student achievement. The behaviours which define each level of proficiency can be identified and established as a criterion to define the subject matter skills that a student is capable of performing when he achieves a particular level. In this sense, performance measures can be "criterion referenced" in terms of specific accomplishment which occurs along a continuum of proficiency. In contrast to criterion-referenced measures, where the performance of an individual is compared with specific subject matter competences, achievement assessment in schools is most frequently expressed in terms of "norms" where the student's performance is compared with the performance of other individuals. In much of current practice, an individual's relative standing is the primary information required, and reference is not made to subject matter contant and associated performance criteria. "Grading on a curve" is a notorious example of the extreme of this practice. While normative information is certainly of practical use, measures referenced in terms of norms provide little information about the degree of student achievement in terms of what behaviour he can actually perform. Norm-referenced measures supply information that one student is more or less proficient than another but do not provide information about how proficient either student is with respect to the specified terminal behaviour of instruction. With increasing application of the concepts of programmed instruction, criterion-referenced scores should become more frequently employed, and the development of measurement procedures for these kinds of scores should be undertaken in a research and development effort.

Machines, the Marketplace, and the Profession

The history of the machine aspects of programmed instruction is an interesting story. The original programmes designed by Skinner employed simple mechanical devices to display programme frames and to receive student responses. Pressey's early work also used a simple mechanical unit. In one of the first national conferences on teaching machines, it was indicated (Homme and Glaser, 1959) that what was being accomplished by most existing devices could probably be accomplished by a programmed textbook format. This emphasis was warranted at that time to make the point that the programming of subject material was the essential ingredient and that the machine aspects, however desirable, were supplementary and useful only as they accomplished instructional functions to produce appropriate learning. Skinner made this emphasis explicit in his early papers while at the same time employing illustrative devices. However, this did not prevent a rash of commercial hardware from appearing on the market for which few programmed materials were available. A recent business survey in *Dun's Review* entitled "Programmed Learning: Return to Reality" (Buckley, 1964) discusses the disappointment of industry with teaching machines and programmed textbooks as a potential market, but also describes how programmed materials (essentially programmed textbooks) have been beneficial in industrial training. A further ominous portent is the fact that papers at professional meetings with programmed instruction in their titles are less numerous than they were a few years ago.

It is useful in concluding this book to consider the three aspects indicated above—machines, general adoption, and professional activity—in some perspective.

1. *Machines and Automation.* It has been repeatedly emphasized throughout this book that iustructional methodology must consider both subject matter properties and learning

characteristics. The stimuli for some subject matter can be displayed by print on paper, and the response to them can be made by a pen or pencil. The stimuli for other subject matter may require the display of sound and ideally the detection of correct vocal responses. The subject matter of reading, for example, might profit from a programmed talking typewriter (Moore, 1964). The learning of mathematical functions (Licklider, 1962), the prosodic features of speech (Lane and Buiten, 1964), the teaching of stenotypy (Uttal, 1962), and the teaching of pitch discrimination (Skinner, 1961), might require special display and response equipment for programmed instruction. In general, with the advances of modern technology in man-machine interaction and in the use of on-line computer functions (Coulson, 1962), only the most unimaginative can fail to see the significance of the "machine" in instruction. However, this hardware will not be on-the-shelf, available projection devices or simple all-purpose audio-visual aids but will be developed especially with consideration for the properties of the subject matter being taught.

2. *General Adoption*. It seems fair to say that, with only few exceptions, no publisher of programmed textbook materials has offered school systems an integrated, well-organized, graded curriculum series. What has been available, for the most part, are short sequences to be used at best as supplementary texts. Nowhere has there been a set of programmed instructional materials in which there is the continuity and coverage provided as there is, for example, in a basal reading series for the elementary schools. These reading series are replete with texts, workbooks, tests, teacher's manuals, and even associated hardware. As indicated in this book, production of a programmed instructional series with its emphasis on empirical development and the submission of evidence of effectiveness would admittedly be more expensive than the usual school textbook series, but probably very significantly less than the effort and expense devoted to the development of modern curricula going on throughout the country in many subject matter fields. After prototypes, production costs are usually drastically reduced. Programmed

instructional materials, then, probably have not had as widespread adoption as publishers thought would occur because the schools demand more useful packages than have been available.

3. *Professional Activity.* The implicit thesis of this book has been that probably the best thing that could happen to programmed instruction is that it become integrated into research and development in human learning and into educational psychology. This appears to be what is happening, except for a number of staunch enthusiasts who too early in the development of programmed instruction have attempted to separate technology from scientific research and would like technological practitioners to stand on their own. This of course is hardly possible or desirable at the present time. What appears to be happening, as indicated by the literature in the field, is that work in programmed instruction has raised many questions about the relationship between psychological knowledge and educational practice, and researchers have investigated these problems with primary regard for their particular disciplinary interests, assimilating the concepts of programmed instruction with no special necessity for setting up a special field labeled "programmed instruction". For the present, programmes will continue to be built for educational and research purposes along the lines indicated in this book, but with the increasing interest in the scientific bases of instruction that programmed instructtion has helped engender, the shape of things will certainly change. As this happens, the science of learning, educational psychology, and educational practice will develop a mutual relevance.

SKINNER'S THEORY OF TEACHING MACHINES

On of the differences between the natural and the social sciences is that in the natural sciences, each succeeding generation stands on the shoulders of those that have gone before, while in the social sciences, each generation steps in the faces of its predecessors.

Whether psychology is a natural science or an unnatural one may be a question, but given a practical psychological problem of training devices to solve, there is no question at all that we have a choice of two strategies here, the shoulder or the face.

If it is the shoulder, where should the constructor and the programmer of human training devices look in the scientific literature of psychology for experimental data relevant to his task?

Any answer to this question implies a theory of training devices. It is in this loose but yet important sense that the word theory is here used.

Skinner has a theory, if I read him rightly, and it says the appropriate reference class of experiments, the appropriate experimental paradigm, for construction and programming teaching machines is that of free operant conditioning. Others, in particular those using the memory drum, are held to be inappropriate.

Skinner's resolution of the shoulder-face question is, happily, the shoulder, but the shoulders are too ivy-league-ish—too narrow.

It is the counter-thesis of this talk, that existing teaching machines (and those likely soon to be built) represent complex admixtures of at least three basic experimental paradigms, free operant, controlled operant, and classical conditioning, and that of these, the free operant may be the least pertinent. Furthermore, of all the commonly used apparatuses for experimental study of learning that one which most closely resembles one of Skinner's teaching machines (the Write-in Model) is the memory drum.

Since there is something less than universal agreement on classification of learning paradigms, let me ask for a temporary convention in the use of the words "controlled operant, free operant, and classical conditioning."

All three refer to experimental arrangements of observable variables that a machine can handle. The common elements of all three include two stimulus events S_1 and S_2, occurring in that order, and at least two responses arbitrarily designated as correct and incorrect.

By "controlled operant" or "discrete trial operant" is meant those experiments incorporating the following acquisition features: (keeping the Graham-Gagne Runway experiments in mind will help you here).

The acquisition trial begins with the presentation of a stimulus situation S_1 which lasts until the subject makes a correct response—R. One and *only* one correct response R occurs per trial because the correct response terminates S_1. It also brings S_2, which in this case is a reinforcing stimulus. S_2 does *not* elicit R. The timing arrangements are partially subject controlled, partially experimenter. The time interval between S_1 and S_2 is subject controlled since S_2 is contingent upon R, but the intertrial interval, that is the S_2—S_1 interval is usually under the experimenter's control.

Acquisition is measured by S-R latency or the conditional probability of R given S_1.

Illustrative apparatuses for controlled operant conditioning include the runway, Miller-Mowrer Shuttle Box, Retractible Bar Skinner Box, the Single-door Lashley Jumping Stand, and also if correction technique is used, the Simple T-Maze, Discrimination Boxes and the Two-door Jumping Stand.

In the free operant or ordinary Skinner box situation, similar features are present with some exceptions. The initial stimulus situation S_1 is of prolonged duration, allowing many correct responses to occur, each one reinforced during continuous acquisition by the contingent reinforcing stimulus S_2. This of course permits a rate measure to be taken.

Both the free and controlled operant paradigms, then, display an SRS sequence, with the second S contingent upon R.

The big difference lies in the number of correct responses allowed per trial, only one in the controlled operant (since the correct response eliminated S_1 as well as bringing S_2), but *many* correct responses in the free operant.

What about timing differences? Is one self-paced and the other not? If one accepts Estes' analysis of the free operant, the animal turns S_1 on and off by himself, even though the experimenter leaves it on. Each reinforcing stimulus S_2 turns over the S_1 and the subject gets a fresh look at S_1. In this analysis, the free operant is self-paced, in the sense that the subject controls the intertrial interval, the time between S_2 and S_1.

This is to be contrasted with the controlled operant in which the subject waits for the experimenter to turn on S_1. It is not completely self-paced.

It is important to note here that if you accept this analysis and regard the free operant as self-paced, it is only so when the S_1's remain the same.

If the experimenter has a number of different S_1's to be connected to a number of different correct responses, free operant techniques can be used, but then it is no longer completely self-paced. The experimenter changes the problem. The inter-problem interval is not subject controlled, and it is this interval that we are usually interested in with teaching machines.

Now finally to the classical conditioning paradigm. The previous two paradigms were SRS sequences with a contingency. This one is an SSR sequence with no contingency. To fulfil the paradigm, the first stimulus S_1 must *not* elicit R as strongly as you would wish, whereas the second stimulus S_2 *must* elicit R, the correct response.

This is a highly operational, non-theoretical specification of the classical conditioning paradigm. It is not asserted that S_2 be an innate elicitor of R, nor even a strong stimulus. Whether such a paradigm always provides the necessary or sufficient conditions for learning is an empirical question not easily resolved, given the existing literature. It is, however, a paradigm that can be used in construction of training devices, and it looks operationally at least to be different from free and controlled operant conditioning, in not having a contingent S_2 and in requiring S_2 to elicit the correct response.

In the matter of timing, classical conditioning resembles the controlled operant in that the experimenter controls the inter-trial interval (the S_2, S_1 gap) but classical conditioning differs from both free and controlled operants in also giving control over the S_1—S_2 interval to the experimenter.

With these three paradigms specified in this way, let us take a look at three pieces of apparatus, a memory drum set up for paired associates, Skinner's Write-in Model teaching machine and Skinner's Arithmetic machine.

First the paired associates experiment. On the first trial around, there is ordinarily no anticipation. The subject sees the S_1 syllable and reads the correct associate. This fits the classical conditioning paradigm. It is an SSR sequence, no contingency, and all stimulus intervals under control of the experimenter.

On the second and subsequent trials, the possibility of operant conditioning enters. If the subject correctly anticipates the associate, he is reinforced by the match of his anticipated answer and the forced answer. Since this matching or knowledge of correct results, is contingent upon a correct anticipation, elements of a controlled operant are present.

If the subject gives the wrong response, the contingent reinforcement is not present, and the trial resembles an extinction trial of a controlled operant. The trial ends, of course, with a classical conditioning feature, a forcing of the correct response, elicited by the appearance of the associate.

If no overt response is given at all, the trial becomes a simple classical conditioning trial again.

Thus there are three kinds of trials possible with a paired associates machine, a simple classical trial, a controlled operant acquisition trial with a terminal classical feature, or a controlled operant extinction trial with a terminal classical feature. The timing of these trials is almost exclusively that of a classical conditioning, however both the S_1—S_2 interval *and* the S_2—S_1 interval are experimenter controlled. To my knowledge there are no animal experiments with trials at all like these, although I believe they might be arranged.

Consider now Skinner's Write-in Model learning machine. It presents a written question or an incompleted sentence or paragraph in an aperture, and then waits for the subject to write in his answer or completion. Following this the subject operates the machine to present the correct written answer to be compared with his own. The next problem appears when the subject indicates to the machine that he is ready.

We analyze the machine in the terms used before. As with the memory drum there are three kinds of trials, depending upon whether the subject makes no response, makes the correct response, or makes an incorrect response.

If no response is made, the trial looks like a classical conditioning paradigm or SSR. The question stimulus S_1 is presented. Then the answer stimulus follows, and elicits the answer response. No contingency, just a forced response like classical conditioning.

If the correct response is made, an instrumental or operant feature emerges. The correct answer given in anticipation of S_2 is reinforced by a maching of the correct results. This reinforcement is of course contingent, and makes the trial resemble the free *or* controlled operant. But since there is only one correct response made, this aspect of the trial looks most like the controlled operant.

If an *incorrect* response is made, the contingent matching reinforcement is absent and we have elements of a controlled operant extinction trial. The trial is terminated however with the forced response characteristic of the classical procedure.

The high similarity of these three kinds of trials with those of the paired associates memory drum experiment is obvious. Yet there is some difference. A difference in timing. With the usual paired associates procedure, all stimulus intervals are *experimenter* controlled. With the Write-in Model, in contrast, the S_1—S_2 interval is *subject* controlled (that is, the subject can give himself as much time as he wants before presenting S_2) and the interproblem interval is also subject controlled. It is indeed a self-paced device.

The subject's control of the timing of the S_2 stimulus is by no means new: it is a property of free and controlled operant procedures in general but the subject's control of the inter-problem interval is relatively novel. It is *not* found in either the usual controlled operant experiment, or in the usual free operant, nor of course, in classical conditioning. Some recent experiments on the role of observing responses in animal discrimination have incorporated an analogous type of paradigm. Wyckoff had pigeons turning on their own discriminative stimuli by stepping on a treadle. His work should be relevant to this machine. And other work may be relevant too.

Since there have been so many memory drum experiments done, and since it is no engineering trick at all to convert the usual memory drum to an entirely self-paced apparatus, like Skinner's Write-in Model, I would be surprised if a literature survey failed to turn up any self-paced paired associates data. Of course when a subject riffles through a deck of flash cards at his own time, the paradigm for this primitive machine is the same as that of Skinner's Write-in Model.

The last device to be inspected is a modification of one of Skinner's devices which we have also constructed and called the "Arithmachine." It presents visual material and allows the subject to make any of a large number of numerical responses, one of which is correct. The response is the movement of sliders and the turning of a crank. If the sliders have been positioned correctly, each slider position representing a number, the turning of the crank will bring reinforcement and the next problem.

The analysis. This machine operation looks much more like the controlled operant procedure than does the Write-in Model. The S_1 or question is presented, a response is waited for, and a contingency set up. If the response is correct, the subject is rewarded by the complete turning of the crank and whatever other reinforcing signals the experimenter wants. There are no forced responses of a classical nature at the end of the trial. The correct response not only brings reinforcement, it eliminates S_1, the question stimulus, thus allowing only one correct response per trial, the hallmark of the controlled operant.

Timing is not completely self-paced. The S_1—S_2 interval is subject controlled, but the interproblem interval is not. The problems come in massed sequence. As soon as the subject finds out that he has been right on the last problem, the new one stares up at him.

Strength of acquisition is inferred with this apparatus from latency or probability of response, as it is for the other machines mentioned. Free rate of operant response, in the presence of a prolonged S_1 is not taken here, nor is it a measure taken for any teaching machine that I know of.

This machine, in summary, embodies all of the elements of the controlled operant, and the literature on this kind of experiment may therefore be relevant.

In final summary, the original question is re-asked, where should the constructor and programmer of human training devices look in the scientific literature of psychology for experimental data relevant to his task. Any answer to this question implies a theory of training devices. If Skinner's theory says that the literature on free operant is most relevant, this paper proposes the counter theory that the literature of controlled operant and classical conditioning is also relevant but more so.

If Skinner's theory says that memory drum experiments provide an inappropriate model for construction of training devices, this paper proposes the counter theory that no other experimental device or procedure more closely resembles Skinner's Write-in Machine than a common memory drum paradigm.

Old Ebbinghaus's shoulders may not be ivy-league, but we ought to stand on them anyway.

PARADIGMS

(A) *Controlled Operant*

Trial 1 — Trial 2

S_1 R S_2 S_1 R S_2

Subject Controlled (S_1 R S_2) — Experimenter Controlled (S_2 … S_1 R)

(B) *Free Operant*

Trial 1 — Trial 2

S_1 R S_2 R S_2 R S_2 S_1 R S_2 R S_2 R S_2

Subject Controlled (S_1 R S_2) — Experimenter Controlled (S_2 S_1)

(C) *Classical Conditioning*

Trial 1 — Trial 2

S_1 S_2 R S_1 S_2 R

Experimenter Controlled (S_1 S_2) — Experimenter Controlled (S_2 … S_1)

A REVIEW OF THE LITERATURE ON CERTAIN ASPECTS OF AUTOMATED INSTRUCTION

The primary purpose of this paper is to review the fast-growing literature on the design and utility of automatic teaching devices. A secondary purpose of the paper is to suggest a number of hypotheses, the testing of which might further our understanding of the variables which influence the effectiveness of automated instruction in the classroom.

The plan of the present paper is as follows: First, there will be an attempt to provide a conceptual framework in which to place a discussion of automatic teaching devices. Second, a review will be made of the rather extensive literature on automated instruction. In this section, the writer will be concerned with two types of studies, (a) simple evaluation studies, in which the researcher compared the effectiveness of a given teaching device with the "standard" form of instruction and (b) parametric studies, in which the reseacher investigated one or more variables of which the effectiveness of the teaching device might be a function. Finally, there will be an attempt to summarize some of the current thinking as to how research in this area might best proceed and to suggest some specific hypotheses.

Some Principles of Learning

For almost one hundred years, psychologists have expended a considerable portion of their research effort toward an understanding of the learning process, chiefly by studying the variables which influence the rate of learning and forgetting. Out of this effort has come a number of reliable principles of learning which can be utilized to design an efficient learning situation.

Gagne (1958) has reviewed the literature on learning, on a very broad scale. His paper encompasses almost all of the known variables which influence learning and retention. Moreover, Gagne has discussed at some length the importance of using adequate measures of learning, which necessarily includes the problem of transfer from the classroom to real life.

Skinner (1954) and Gilbert (1958) have summarized those principles of learning which have led a number of workers to consider seriously the development of automatic teaching devices for use in the classroom. A rephrasing of these principles, couched in non-technical terms, might take the following from. Accompanying each principle is a brief statement showing how that principle is sometimes violated in the typical classroom.

1. *Learning takes place most rapidly if the student is actively engaged with the subject matter.* At the outset of training, some time might profitably be spent in watching or listening to someone else perform the acts to be learned, but the student will become proficient only if he practices the acts himself. This principle applies to verbal skills as well as to non-verbal ones. Unfortunately, in most classrooms the learning of most subject matter is thought of as being a spectator, rather than a participator sport.

2. *Learning is most effective if the student develops the skills and knowledge in a form which will readily generalize to the "real life" situation for which they are intended.* Usually, this means that the student must learn to construct correct answers to questions, rather than merely be able to recognize them. Thus, the responses which the student makes in the learning situation should be of the former rather than of the latter type. All too frequently, in the classroom of today, recognition is used as a criterion of learning.

3. *Learning takes place most rapidly if* immediate "*knowledge of results" is given for each response.* If the response is correct, the student should be so informed, just as soon as the response is completed. If the response is incorrect, he should know this, also. Even a slight delay drastically retards learning. Presently, our students must frequently endure long delays before they receive feedback of this sort.

4. *Learning takes place most rapidly if the subject matter is organized in a hierarchic form.* Lessons should begin with very simple problems, for which the student already has the necessary skills and knowledge. Gradually, the difficulty level may be raised until the desired level of proficiency is obtained. Care must be exercised so that at each point the student is given new information to be used to solve the next problem. Ideally, the

subject matter should be presented in steps so small that the success of the student on the next problem is practically guaranteed. Unfortunately, both textbooks and classroom techniques frequently ignore this principle.

5. *Receiving frequent "knowledge of results" keeps students working at the assigned task.* The hurdles which the student must surmount should be kept immediately before him and by making successes frequent, the student will develop a high level of aspiration. In the typical classroom, the student is studying to prepare himself for a far-off quiz or test. The result is that the teacher must spend a considerable portion of her time devising some artifical motivators, to keep the students working.

6. *Since learning takes place in individuals, the learning situation should be designed so that each student may proceed at his own pace.* For various reasons, some students learn faster than others and therefore, it is difficult to have them learn in groups. This principle does not necessarily dictate that students must work alone. It merely emphasizes the belief that if students are to learn in groups, the learning situation should be designed so that the fast learners are not impeded by the slow ones and the slow learners are not confused by too stiff a pace.

The list of principles given above is neither new nor exhaustive. Good teachers have known of theses principles for a long time and have endeavoured to utilize them as best they can, within the limitations of the present-day classroom situation.

But it must be recognized that the limitations imposed on the teacher by the present-day classroom situation are extremely severe. Many educators and psychologists have been impressed with the folly of trying to teach thirty or more children, simultaneously. Consider, for example, the teaching of the multiplication tables. While on student recites, the teacher is able to reinforce each of his responses. But the other children are merely listening and probably little learning occurs. Further, if the teacher uses the weekly quiz as a learning device, learning suffers from the long delay between the responses and the knowledge of results. Finally, if the class is working on the "five" tables, some bright students might more profitably be working one the "sevens" while some of the slower ones should still be working on the "threes." True, making the class more homogeneous with respect to mathematical ability might help, but this poses special administrative problems.

The teacher's inability to work efficiently with more than a very few students at a time has caused a number of psychologists to follow the lead of Sidney L. Pressey and B.F. Skinner in recommending a thorough investigation of teaching by means of automatic teaching devices. Presumably, each student would have the daily use of a machine for a period of time. Theoretically, at least, the machine could be designed so that its operation would be congruent with all of the principles of efficient learning which have been here reviewed.

Skinner (1958) has discussed some of the social and economic ramifications of his proposal to make wide use of automatic teaching devices in our educational system. Space will not be devoted to this topic in the present paper, except to point out that few if any workers in this field intend to build devices designed to replace the teacher in the classroom. At the very best, the devices can only hope to supplement the efforts of the teacher, by relieving her of the task at which she is probably least capable—delivering "knowledge of results" rapidly to her students for each response directed toward the subject matter. If effective, the use of such devices would free the teacher for tasks which she can perform well and for which no machine can replace her.

A Review of Literature

Porter (1958a) has recently published an excellent review of a portion of the extensive literature dealing with the many devices which have been suggested as being useful adjuncts to the teaching process. Further, he has developed a system of classification of these devices which promises to be quite useful. He has distinguished among three classes of devices.

Stimulus Devices. Stimulus devices are those which present some information to the learner, by way of one or more sense modalities. Frequently, they show how or under what conditions something is to be done. Examples of this class of device are: models, projecting devices, phonographs, braille, and the like. It should be pointed out that while these devices do present subject matter to the learner, they do not necessarily require any action on his part and thus learning is not assured For this reason, Porter suggests that they be thought of as teaching aids, rather than teaching devices.

Response Devices. Response devices are those which provide the learner with an opportunity to practice some activity. These devices are usually used to collect or manipulate data. Examples of this class of device are typewriters and desk calculators (as data manipulators) and the Classroom Communicator or the GSR secorder (as data collectors). Thus, a response device permits the learner to practice some activity, but it dose not necessarily provide him with subject matter on which to practice. For this reason, Porter suggests that response devices also be thought of as teaching aids, rather than as teaching devices.

Stimulus-Response Devices. Stimulus-Response devices are those which both present information to the learner and also require some appropriate action on his part. Further, such devices usually respond differentialy, depending upon the behaviour of the learner. Examples of the stimulus-response class of device are the Pressey multiple-choice apparatus, Skinner's device and the classical memory drum. It should be lipted that the stimulus-response device more nearly stimulus the role of the teacher by both presenting information to the learner and requiring some appropriate action on his part. Porter feels that these might properly be called teaching devices, since no human teacher is required to mediate relations between the machine and the learner, except to service or maintain the machine.

Further, Porter distinguished among three types of stimulus-response devices. First, there is the *simulator*, which duplicates the essential characteristics of some complex task and which requires appropriate action from time to time on the part of the learner. Ordinarily, this type of device does not provide immediate feedback. The electronic flight simulator is a good illustration of this type of device.

The second type of stimulus-response device distinguished by Porter is the *immediate reinforcer*, which not only presents the learner with a problem situation but also provides him with immediate "knowledge of results" concerning his answers. It should also be noted that this type of device is learner-paced, in that the machine's reaction is contingent upon the learner's behaviour. Pressey's multiples-choice device and Skinner's teaching machine are examples of the immediate reinforcer.

The third type of stimulus-response device is what Porter called the *pacer*. A pacer is a device which presents stimulus materials for a given interval of time and then provides the appropriate response, whether or not the learner has attempted to answer. The memory drum, so frequently used in psychological research on learning phenomena, illustrates this type of device.

Of the three types of stimulus-response devices distinguished above, the one which seems to offer the most promise for use in the class is the immediate reinforcer. Simulators ordinarily do not provide immediate feedback and the operation of the pacer is independent of the behaviour of the learner. Thus, these latter types of devices seem to violate one or more of the principles of learning referred to earlier. Hereafter. in the present paper, consideration will be given only to those stimulus-response devices which are of the immediate reinforcer type.

A word of caution might be added with respect to Porter's classification of learning machines. It is quite possible that a slight modification of a stimulus-device or a response-device might enable it to qualify as a stimulus-response device. Also, it is possible for both simulators and pacers to be reclassified as immediate reinforcers, if appropriate changes are introduced. Porter has classified particular devices in accordance with the design of the machine offered by its designer.

Some History of Automated Instruction

Perhaps the first attempt to develop an automatic teaching device was made in 1918 by English (1942). This worker constructed and tested a device by which soldiers rapidly learned to squeeze rather than jerk a rifle trigger. Knowledge of results war delivred to the soldier via a manometer attached to the trigger. However, it should be pointed out that the subject matter in this case was quite simple, consisting of a single habit.

Sidney Pressey (1950) is often credited with being the first to give serious throught to the widespread use of teaching devices in the classroom. Although, at the outset, Pressey was primarily interested in automatic testing devices, he soon discovered that students could learn by taking tests via his machines. Pressey and his students have published a good number of papers in which various designs of machine have been described and evaluated.

Besically, the type of device developed by Pressey follows the format of the multiple-choice question. The student is presented with a question and four options, only one of which is correct. He chooses an option and the device provides some immediate feedback. If the studant has chosen the correct answer, the machine presents the next question. If an incorrect option is chosen, the student must continue responding until he selects the correct option.

Three different recording devices were described by Pressey and his students. They developed a punch-board device, a system using chemically treated paper, and an electrical system. See Pressey (1950) for a more complete description of each.

The type of device developed by Pressey suffers from at least two defects which seem quite important. First, the student must merely recognize the correct answer among a number of options. In many cases this format is quite unlike the real life situation for which the skills are being developed and the problem of transfer arises. Second, the materials which Pressey presented were not arranged in any hierarchic fashion. The lack of carefully prepared sequence of information does violence to one of the principles of learning described earlier in this paper.

Recently, Skinner (1958b) developed a different type of teaching device which circumvents the limitations of the Pressey machines. Using the devices developed by Skinner, the learner must construct, rather than merely recognize correct answers to questions. Further, Skinner and his colleagues spent a considerable portion of their research time, in attempting to construct programmes of subject matter, beginning with simple problems and gradually increasing complexity only as the learner demonstrates that he is ready for it. For a good illustration of what is meant by a programme, see Skinner (1958a, pp. 3-7).

One of Skinner's machines is used to teach arithmetic. The learner constructs his answer by operating sliders, each of which represents a digit. In this way, the learner can construct answers up to four digits in length. For materials other than arithmetic, the learner writes out his answer. Then he may compare his answer with the correct one, merely by operating a lever. The reader can easily see that such a procedure introduces a source of error, since the learner decides whether or not his answer is correct. In some models, the machine provides for recycling of those questions which the learner had wrong on previous trials.

Parameters Influencing the Effectiveness of Automated Instruction

A good deal of the research on automated instruction has taken the form of evaluation studies, in which teaching by machine has been compared with teaching by the "usual" method. The present writer shares with Gilbert (1958, p. 29) the belief that while a certain amount of evaluation research is necessary in order to justify a continued interest in the basic concept of automated instruction, the major portion of the research effort should be devoted to an experimental analysis of the parameters which influence the effectiveness of automated instruction. This latter type of study will be discussed first.

A distinction may be drawn among three classes of variables of which the effectiveness of automated instruction might be a function. They are: characteristics of the device, of the programme, and of the learner. Each of these classes of variables will be discussed in some detail and an effort will be made to summarize the pertinent research findings.

Characteristics of the Device. The reader will recall that, earlier in this paper, a teaching device was defined as a machine by which stimulus materials are presented to a learner and which requires some response on his part in order for the device to operate. Further, the type of teaching device with which this paper is primarily concerned is one which provides immediate feedback to the learner. This type of analysis permits one to discuss the characteristics of the device within the framework of a three-fold analysis:

1. *Display or input characteristics.* So many specific devices have been used by workers as means of presenting the stiumulus materials that a complete classification of them is almost impossible. Suffice it to say that most workers have made use of mechanical, electrical, or optical components to present information to the learner. Two exceptions may be noted. Crowder (1958b) and Homme & Glaser (1958) have successfully presented stimulus materials in the form of a modified textbook. And Rath & Anderson (1958) have used the IBM "650" print out.

To the writer's knowledge, no experiment has been performed which compares the efficiency of different methods of presenting stimulus materials.

2. *Response or output characteristics.* Two basically different modes of responding have been employed. Pressey, and his colleagues, and some researchers in military establishments have made heavy use of the multiple-choice or recognition mode while Skinner and others have used the "free operant" or construction mode of responding. No study was found which permits the comparison of these two basic modes of operation.

However, Irion & Briggs (1957) have experimentally compared several variations of the multiple-choice mode of operation. The four modes compared were (a) *quiz mode*: in which the S chooses one of the responses by pressing a switch and the machine immediately indicates which of the responses was correct, (b) *modified-quiz mode*: which is identical to (a) except that a buzzer indicates that an incorrect answer was made, (c) *practice mode*: in which the S must press switches until the correct response is made, and (d) *single-try mode*: in which the S may respond only once and then the next stimulus item is presented.

Each of the four modes of operation was employed by different groups of subjects as they learned three types of tasks: serial learning, paired-associate learning, and problem solving. The dependent variables were the number of trials required to learn the tasks to a given criterion and a measure of retention, taken two weeks after learning.

In general, the relative efficiency of the four modes of operation was in the order: quiz-mode, modified-quiz mode, practice mode, and single-try mode. The amount of difference in efficiency was a function of the type of learning task. Later, Irion &

Briggs used different modes of operation within a learning situation and found no differences in amount of time to criterion.

3. *Reinforcement characteristics.* Little attention has been given to the problem of the optimal type and schedule of reinforcement to use as the means of maintaining the maximal rate of perforemance. Most workers report that sheer "knowledge of results" suffices to keep the learner working. Skinner (1958) reports that students work harder and longer when using the machine than they do when they merely read the textbook. The implication is that "knowledge of results" is an effective reinforcer, but it seems clear that various methods of providing feedback might very well influence the learner's performance rate. For a more complete discussion of this subject, see Porter (1957, pp. 134-136).

Characteristics of the Programme. Programming refers to the arrangment of the stimulus materials in the order of presentation which will maximize the rate of acquisition of the habits to be learned. Presumably, proper programming permits the gradual shaping of the learner's responses from low to high levels of approximation of the desired responses.

It should be noted that Pressey and his group gave little attention to the problem of programming, perhaps because the were primarily interested in developing testing devices and only secondarily interested in developing teaching devices. Further, it is likely that some types of subject matter require little in the way of programming at all (e.g., toruble shooting and the identification of objects such as enemy aircraft).

But for certain kinds of complex tasks, it is likely that efficient learning can take place only if the materials are carefully programmed into a hierarchy, extending from very simple to complex habits. See Gillbert (1958) for a more complete discussion of this point.

Several problems associated with programming immediately present themselves.

1. *Extrinsic Versus Intrinsic Programming.* Of those workers interested in teaching devices, Skinner was the first to give serious attention to the matter of programming. For a given subject matter, he attempted to construct a single programme, through which all learners would proceed. This type might be thought of as a straight-line programme. Later, Crowder (1958a, 1958b) described another type of programming which tailors the programme to the individual lerrner, depending upon his strengths and weaknesses (as reflected by his previous errors). Crowder's might be thought of as a branching programme. The branches would permit the learner to retrace his steps back through that portion of the programme which his errors indicate that he did not adequately learn. Crowder referred to his type of programme as *intrinsic* and he reserved the term *extrinsic* programme for the type described by Skinner.

For obvious reasons, the intrinsic programme would place a special burden on both the author of the programme and on the teaching device used. However, the use of an intrinsic programme might very well result in a more efficient learning situation. Unfortunately, no experiment has yet been done which compares the two methods of programming directly.

2. *Size of Step.* Skinner (1958) and others feel that the most effective programme is one which raises the level of the learner's proficiency by such small steps that the probability of the learner being wrong is so low as to be negligible. In fact, Skinner uses the percentage correct as a measure of the optimum size of step.

On the other hand, some have argued that the optimal size of step is the one which results in the most rapid learning to a given criterion and that this optimum can only be determined experimentally. Homme & Glaser (1958) investigated the effect of size of step upon frequency of errors and upon immediate and delayed retention. Using a single programme on elementary number theory, they varied the number of steps over four values: 30, 40, 51, and 67. Presumably, the greater the number of steps, the smaller the mean size of step. Independent groups of five Ss each were used. The results showed that the smaller the step, the fewer the errors and the greater the retention. However, it is conceivable that increasing the number (and therefore decreasing the size) of steps beyond 67 might have resulted in no further change in dependent variable performance. Further, the relationship between measures of learning and size of step might interact with characteristics of the programme employed. Clearly, further research is necessary before this important question can be answered unequivocally, but a start has been made.

3. *Rules or Principles of Programming.* Skinner (1958), Beck (1958), and Gilbert (1958) have described a number of rules or principles of programming. Although these rules or principles seem eminently logical, they appear to lack empirical support. Thus, they might better be thought of as hypotheses to be tested. Space does not permit a detailed discussion of these rules and the interested reader is referred to the appropriate references.

Characteristics of the Learner. A third major variable of which the effectiveness of automated instruction might be a function has to do with some characteristics of the learner. For example, one might hypothesize that the use of teaching devices might wipe out differences in achievement measures associated with intelligence or aptitude test performance. The findings of a number of experiments seem to support this hypothesis.

Porter (1958) found that the correlation between IQ and achievement in spelling was lower for a group of learners who were taught by machine than for a control group who were taught in the usual fashion. Ferster & Sapon (1958) reported similar findings on the relations between aptitude and achievement in a course in German. Finally, Lumsdaine (1958) showed that the advantage of active participation in a simple learning task decreases with increases in intelligence.

The experiments just cited might lead one to believe that superior students do not learn efficiently by machine. Pressey (1950), Briggs (1947) and Jensen (1949) have all reported data which show that bright students are quite capable of benefiting from the use of teaching devices.

Another characteristic of the learner which might influence the effectiveness of automated instruction is the level of anxiety of the learner with respect to the subject matter being taught. Porter (in a personal communication) has suggested that learners who are quite anxious or who have a low level of aspiration concerning the subject matter seem to be ones who profit a great deal from machine instruction. It seems reasonable to suppose that since the machine instruction provides for many reinforcements, the learner's degree of anxiety might be reduced and his level of aspiration raised. The result should be an increase in rate of learning, but this hypothesis has yet to be tested.

The Evaluation of Automated Instruction

A good number of studies have been located which can be used to compare the effectiveness of teaching by machine with teaching by the "usual" classroom techniques. A number of these studies were performed using one or another variation of Pressey's multiple-choice type of device. All studies conclude that there is something to be gained by using machine type of instruction. Usually, the advantage is expressed in terms of the superior performance of an experimental group (those using teaching devices) over a control group.

Porter (1957, pp. 137-40) has carefully reviewed most of these studies and has pointed to a number of defects. In many of the studies cited, little if any effort was made to equate the groups for initial proficiency with respect to the subject matter, for level of motivation, for the "novelty" effect, or for the amount of time spent in study. Further, although immediate reinforcer teaching devices were used in all of these studies, it cannot be said that these studies demonstrate the superiority of immediate versus delayed reinforcement since it seems clear that the control groups received *less* reinforcement as well as delayed reinforcement.

Several evaluation studies have been performed using Skinner's type of device in which the learner constructs his answer (rather than merely identifies it) and which presents the stimulus materials in a carefully arranged hierarchic sequence. Porter (1958) has shown that the use of such a device and programme for the teaching of spelling in second and sixth grade students renders them superior in spelling achievement to a control group.

Homme Glaser (1958) recently reported a study in which comparisons were made between groups who learned by using programmed textbooks and groups who used standard textbooks. Two types of subject matter were used: sections of a statistics course and a course in the fundamentals of music reading. In both cases, the experimental groups outperformed the control groups on achievement tests. No mention is made in this study of the procedures used to equate groups for initial proficiency, amount of time spent in study, and so on.

Holland (1958) and Ferster & Sapon (1958) have also reported the results of automated instruction, using college students as subjects. Holland had students learn sections of a course in psychology and Ferster & Sapon used the subject matter of a course in German. Control group data were not reported.

On the basis of this cursory review of the validity studies, one might conclude that we are still lacking in carefully executed experiments which unequivocally demonstrate the superiority of automated instruction over the "usual" classroom procedures. And too, one might say that we know even less about *why* automated instruction might prove to be superior. It is entirely possible that all of the validity studies are dealing with a "novelty" effect. However, Porter (1958) has shown in his year long study of spelling achievement that the second semester's performance of the experimental group was just as superior to the control group as was the first semester's performance. Such evidence would suggest that if there is a "novelty" effect operating in Porters's study, it is slow in disappearing. Nevertheless, it is very clear that a great deal of additional research is in order before we can be at all confident about the superiority of automated instruction over the "usual" classroom procedure.

A Few Hypotheses to Test

The review of the literature presented in the previous section of this paper provides a number of hypotheses which seem worth testing. This discussion of hypotheses might well be organized around the three major classes of variables of which the effectiveness of automated instruction is a function.

Characteristics of the Device. The writer shares the view expressed by Gilbert (1958a) that, for the present, most of the research on automated instruction might best be spent by studying relations between characteristics of the programme and rate of learning or amount of retention, However, at least three characteristics of the teaching device might profitably be examined immediately.

Hypothesis 1. The use of self-paced instructional devices yields more rapid learning and better retention than does group-paced devices and that this relationship holds for all types of learning tasks and for all types of learners.

Lumsdaine (1958) has suggested that group-paced devices might prove to be almost as effective as those which permit the individual learner to proceed at his own pace. Although there is good rationale for the belief that in most cases the self-paced device will prove to be the more effective of the two, this is still an empirical question. Further, the advantage of the self-paced device over the group-paced type might interact with both the nature of the task to be learned and with a number of characteristics of the learner. Finally, the advantage of the self-paced device over the group-paced device might not be great enough to warrant the accompanying increase in original and maintenance costs.

Hypothesis 2. The use of reinforcers in addition to "knowledge of results" will result in a higher rate of performance on teaching devices and perhaps render "knowledge of results" (as a reinforcement) more resistant to satiation.

As mentioned earlier in this paper, most researchers seem to believe that mere "knowledge of results" is sufficient reinforcement to keep students working. However, it is entirely possible that prolonged exposure to such reinforcement may result in an effect akin to stimulus satiation. Porter (1957) has warned of just such a "novelty" effect.

Moreover, it may well be that the use of other reinforcers in addition to "knowledge of results" might result in an increase in rate of performance. Skinner (1954, pp. 93-94) has suggested that approval from the teacher, being permitted to engage in desired activities, successful competition with other students, and even aversive stimulation might be used to augment the reinforcing properties of "knowledge of results."

Hypothesis 3. There is an indirect relationship between the amount of delay of "knowledge of results" and the rate of learning and this relationship holds for all types of subject matter and for all types of learner.

Pressey (1950, p. 418), in particular, has argued that the superiority of teaching devices over the more standard pedagogic practices stems from the fact that the devices minimize the delay between the learner's responses and "knowledge of results." But Porter (1957, p. 138) has pointed out that in several of Pressey's validating studies, the *amount* of "knowledge of results" varied simultaneously with the delay in "knowledge of results". Thus, we are left without knowing which of the two factors is the more important. Deese (1958, p. 199) reports a study by Saltzman which shows that a delay in "knowledge of results" can seriously hamper the learning of a rote verbal task. A delay of but six seconds resulted in a 50 per cent increase in errors.

However, it may well be that certain types of subject matter and perhaps certain types of learner might be able to withstand fairly long delays without affecting learning rate appreciably. Such information would be of some help to the designers of teaching devices.

Hypothesis 4. Having students learn to compose correct answers to questions results in faster learning, better retention, and more positive transfer to "real life" situations than does having students learn to recognize correct answers from among a number of options. Further, this relationship holds for all types of learning situations and for all types of learners.

Skinner (1954) contends that, for most learning situations, it is more desirable to render learners capable of composing correct answers to questions, rather than make them able merely to recognize them. There are good reasons for believing that Skinner is correct on this point, but once again, this is an empirical question. Further, the advantage of composition over recognition may interact with the type of task and with characteristics of the learner.

Characteristics of the Programme. As mentioned earlier in this paper, the writer believes that the usefulness of teaching devices is more a function of characteristics of the programme than a function of characteristics of the device, itself. For the present, many believe that programme writing is an art, which is perhaps another way of saying that we know little about the characteristics of the optimal programme.

However, some programme characteristics have already received some study. Crowder (1958b) has distinguished between extrinsic and intrinsic programme techniques. Homme & Glaser (1958) invested the characteristic called "size of step." Further, Beck (1958) and Gilbert (1958) have both written at length on a few principles of programming. Perhaps these principles might be put into the form of hypotheses worthy of experimental test. For these reasons, the following hypotheses are suggested:

Hypothesis 5. Intrinsic programming yeilds more rapid learning and better retention than does extrinsic programming. Further, this relationship holds for all types of subject matter and all types of learner.

Once again, the reader should keep in mind the fact that although intrinsic programmes might prove superior to extrinsic ones, the intrinsic type places a considerable burden upon both the programme writer and upon the teaching device, itself. One way of reducing the mechanical complexity of the device would be to use a programmed textbook, intrinsically organized. Crowder (1958a, 1958b) has already put this idea to use.

Hypothesis 6. The rate of learning via automated instruction is a function of the size of step employed in the programme. Further, if properly measured, the optimal size of step is a constant for all types of subject matter.

When a student is taught a given subject matter, it is assumed that he starts off at a given level of proficiency and, after training, ends at a higher level. Now, one may attempt to go from the lower to the higher level by presenting the learner with relatively few or many steps. Further, assuming that the steps are roughly equidistant, then size of step is negatively correlated with the number of steps. Thus, both number of steps and size of step might be variables of which the rate of learning is a function.

Skinner (1958, p. 5) feels that steps should be so small that errors are rarely if ever committed. In fact, some workers feel that the percentage of errors is a measure of the worth of an item. Items which result in more than a minimum number of errors are viewed with suspicion. On the other hand, some workers feel that some percentage of error might well be built into the programme and presumably this would be done by increasing the size of step in order to obtain the desired percentage of error.

The question of the optimum size or number of steps in a given programme is obviously an empirical one, to be answered by experiment. Homme & Glaser (1958) have shown that increasing the number of steps (and thereby decreasing their size) resulted in more efficient learning. However, it is entirely possible that Homme & Glaser did not vary the number of steps in the programme in an asymptotic function or even in a decrease in learning efficiency. Clearly, this variable is worthy of careful examination.

Finally, the writer believes that subject matter currently thought of as being difficult may simply be material which is programmed in very large steps. If a technique could be developed which would permit the measurement of size of step in units which provide an equal-ratio scale, then one could test the hypothesis that the optimal size of step is a constant for all types of subject matter. Unfortunately, the writer knows of no such technique.

Characteristics of the Learner. As mentioned earlier, several studies have shown that the amount of improvement shown by students is relatively uncorrelated with their intelligence and/or aptitude for the subject matter. Such data must be interpreted carefully. They do not imply that students with low intelligence or aptitude profit more from automated instruction than do "bright" students. Rather, these findings merely state that the amount of profit is independent of such factors as intelligence and aptitude.

Researches would do well to continue to search for characteristics of the learner which are correlated with amount of improvement. For such information would probably give us hints about the optimal design of the programme, the type and schedule of reinforcement, and of the teaching device, itself.

Hypothesis 7. The rate of learning via automated instruction is a function of level of anxiety and/or level of aspiration of the learner with respect to the subject matter.

Porter has noted clinically that one benefit of automated instruction seems to stem from the fact that some learners become less anxious about their performance on the subject matter after they have used a teaching device for some time. Such an observation suggests that immediate knowledge of results and perhaps a high percentage of correct responses might be more beneficial to learners who are anxious than to those who are not.

Notes on Difficulties Inherent in Research on Automated Instruction

Porter (1957, pp. 137-38) and Gilbert (1958, pp. 29-32) have discussed some of the difficulties inherent in research on automated instruction. Both workers feel that most evaluation studies presently available simply do not meet the necessary criteria of excellence which permit us to state categorically that automated instruction results in performance superior to instruction via the "usual" techniques. Most studies simply lack sufficient experimental control. The experimental and control groups differ in so many respects that it is impossible to tell which of the differences in treatment account for the differences in performance.

The chief difficulty seems to stem from the inability to control the subjects' previous experience with, and aptitude for, the subject matter to be learned. Most studies have used regular students as subjects in classrooms at all levels of education. Further, the subject matter employed is usually standard material. Finally, many of the studies have employed such large numbers of subjects that it is practically impossible to learn much about what is taking place while an individual is learning.

The writer suggests that at least some research time might be devoted to the careful observation of small numbers of subjects while they are learning materials with which they are totally unfamiliar. The classical non-sense syllable or objects frequently used in concept formation studies recommend themselves. Zeaman (1958) recently discussed the use of the latter type of material within the context of automated instruction.

If, for one reason or another, the researcher desires to do research in a real classroom, he might give thought to the teaching of relatively discrete skills which are subject matter for only one or two years of schooling. For example, at the elementary school level one might easily programme the teaching of "telling time" or the use of roman numerals. Such instruction rarely interacts with other types of subject matter. At the collegiate level, the teaching of parliamentary rules might be more easily programmed than the teaching of algebra, philosophy, and the like.

Further, ease of programming is not the only benefit which might obtain from the use of subject matter described above. Since such material is relatively discrete, the techniques used to teach in will not interact with the learning of other subject matter.

TEACHING MACHINE DICHOTOMY: SKINNER Vs. PRESSEY

Even though the field of teaching machines is not very old or very large, there has already developed what appears to be a relatively major dichotomy. On one hand we have the historically older faction headed by Sidney Pressey at Ohio State University, which emphasizes multiple-choice devices; and on the other, a newer faction headed by B.F. Skinner at Harvard University, which emphasizes construction of response devices. Numerous theoretical and practical considerations (amount of error permitted and methods of programming) enter into the dichotomy.

The common characteristics of teaching machines may be described simply. These are devices which tutor the student without assistance from a human instructor. They require the student's active participation. He must respond to questions which may be interspersed with graphic or verbal subject matter, or with other techniques as the Socratic method or "vanishing" (gradually removing part of a word or phrase until the student responds without a cue). Two basic principles are involved: (a) *complete variability in rate,* rate being determined by the student's responses which permit individual differences, and (b) *immediate knowledge of results,* i.e., the device "rewards" the student with the answer immediately after he responds.

Types of Questions and Learning Theory

The first major difference between the two schools is the type of questions preferred. Pressey prefers the multiple-choice type of question, partly because originally he envisioned his teaching machine as also an automatic testing device. He states (1926) that permitting the student to make more than one error per question (his "degree of ignorance" per question) greatly increases the spread and significance of the total score. Learning theory at that time was strongly influenced by associationism. Pressey referred to the laws of recency, frequency, and effect, but was also willing to use questions which called for "insight."

Skinner prefers that the student construct his answers rather than relying upon recognition. On his arithmetic machine (1954) the student responds by moving digit-marked sliders to indicate the correct answer. The constructed-response type of question is in line with Skinner's emphasis on the principle of operant conditioning in which characteristic learning is controlled by rewarding the student after he has made the correct response. Skinner attempts to structure the situation so that responses lead step by step toward the desired goal, thus shaping behaviour through successive approximations.

Amount of Error Desirable

Skinner would avoid the structuring of wrong answers in programming questions for his teaching machine. "Why cause any learning at all between the wrong answer and the right question?" he asks. He would be happy if every student got every question correct.

Pressey, on the other hand, is willing to allow some error. Although specific amounts of error are seldom mentioned, Pressey would say (and most psychologists would agree) that the number of right responses should greatly exceed the number of wrong.

Supplement or Replace Other Teaching Methods?

Although perhaps a debtable point, the dichotomy extends to the instructional uses planned for the two types of machines, Pressey's devices having been used more as supplemental adjuncts to courses and textbooks, and Skinner's as replacement for texts and classroom instruction. For example, Porter (1958) used a simple write-in machine to supplant spelling instruction; "No spoken instruction was given." By contrast, Pressey (1950) used multiple-choice questions with self-scoring punchboards to supplement regular instruction in educational psychology. [Incidentally, results of both studies favoured the experimental groups. Neither Pressey nor Skinner would eliminate teachers, both being interested in making more efficient use of the teacher's time in class.]

Is Intelligence Strictly Quantitative?

To Skinner, the difference between a bright and a dull student is largely one of quantity of learning. If teaching steps are small and understandable, a poor student can learn the same thing as a bright student; he just has to work longer. And when students find concepts difficult, Skinner believes (1958), the instructor has not presented the steps in small enough or correctly ordered units. In planning curriculum, the programmer must discover and properly order the units of information, or steps.

While Pressey does not deny the truth of Skinner's quantitative concepts of intelligence and learning, his experiments are structured as though "superior" students were, indeed, different (Briggs, 1949; Jensen, 1649). Crowder (1958) actually presents more and different steps for poorer students. Pressey places no stress on the smallness of the learning steps or the ordering of presentation.

Practical Applications

While both sides of the dichotomy envision wide use for their devices, actual hardware and experimental studies are rather scarce. Pressey showed an actual multiple choice testing and teaching machine at the 1924 American Psychological Association meeting. And, from time to time variations have appeared, such as Peterson's chemo-card in 1931 and Angell's punchboard study (1949) in which 81 matched pairs of chemistry students used punchboards on regular quizzes. Angell and Troyer later developed a commercial punchboard which Science Research Associates published for a time. Pressey's 1950 study of over 1000 students ushing punchboards led to the production of the punchboard for use in the Navy (Hill, 1955).

Besnard, Briggs, and Walker (1955) developed for the Air Force several large multiple-choice devices for trouble shooting. Electronics trouble-shooting research has produced numerous other multiple-choice devices, such as the Tab Test (Glaser, 1954), Trainer Tester, and Automat. Also, Skinner has a small battery of disc-type write-in machines which were used by Holland (1958). The Navy Special Devices Center has recently constructed a small battery of similar machines. Skinner has a slidertype of arithmetic-spelling machine produced by IBM. Also at Harward, Porter has several of the very simple write-in machines mentioned earlier.

Dichotomy in Non-Mechanical Devices

A new development is not to use machines at all, but to use books and paper devices. Although lacking some of the control of machines, these devices provide flexibility of rate, unit presentation, and immediate knowledge of results. Yet non-mechanical devices fall into the basic dichotomy discussed here. An example of a new multiple-choice paper device is

Crowder s (1958) scrambled book, in which a bit of information is followed by a multiple-choice question. The student answers the question by turning to the appropriate page; the answer page tells whether the choice was correct, and why. If the answer was wrong, further instruction is given, followed by a new question. If correct, the next problem is presented.

Ferster and Sapon (1958) describe a cardboard device which requires free response. A cardboard sleeve contains a slot which exposes one line of a question on a printed paper slip. The student writes his answer on a scrap of paper moves the cardboard down one line to expose the answer, scores himself, and proceeds to the next question. Another device is that developed by Homme, Glaser, and Evans (1958), a programmed textbook" to which the student makes numerous subjective responses. He is given the answer on the next page, thus providing him with knowledge of results.

Summary

We have seen that in the field of teaching machines there is a dichotomy of opinion with respect to response mode, step size, amount of error desirable, learning theory, views on intelligence, and the supplementing of traditional instructional methods. What we need now are a lot of good experimental studies, both theoretical and applied in nature.

6

EDUCATIONAL FILMS AND INSTRUCTION

INTRODUCTION

We assert nothing new when we state that television and film can teach and that they are capable of serving as substitutes for, or supplements to, more traditional modes of teaching. Nonetheless the search continues for criteria concerning when teaching with television or film should be chosen over live teaching, for guidelines to the selection or production of appropriate programmes or series, and for techniques for integrating television or film most effectively into the educational experience of the student. This chapter will review the information we have obtained thus far and demonstrate again that, as with all decisions about teaching, there is no substitute for careful, sensitive consideration of the characteristics of the students, the teaching goals, and the variety of available teaching techniques.

In much of this chapter television and film will be treated as though they are equivalent media. Many researchers have done so when they have investigated the ability of one or the other to communicate information, compared live and mediated instruction, and examined ways to integrate television or film into an educational environment. It is worth noting, however, that television and film are not fully interchangeable media. The artistic formulas differ; for instance, film makers are much freer to present wide panoramas and crowd scenes than are television producers. Economies of scale cannot be as easily or completely achieved with film as they can be with television by increasing the audience size. Scheduling of television and film differs in that television is most often broadcast at a specified time to a presumably large audience, while film is most often shown to a small audience at a time the teacher chooses. Finally, the technical means for producing the images differs between the two media, and this may produce differences in the information processing skills required of the user. Where appropriate in this chapter, these differences will be considered, but for the most part television and film will be considered as equivalent, alternative delivery systems.

The chapter is divided into six sections. The first presents five types of content, or messages, that television and film convey and evaluates their effectiveness in conveying them. The second discusses the processes by which students learn from television and film. The third relates these processes to the evaluation of existing programming or the production of new material. The fourth considers the utility of television and film in teaching, and the fifth discusses the ways in which television and film may be most effectively integrated into ongoing educational activities. The sixth section summarized the chapter.

CONTENT THAT TELEVISION AND FILM MAY CONVEY

Television and film are most often given the explicit educational goal of conveying cognitive information to students. Recently they have occasionally been used intentionally to teach social and emotional content. There is a growing recognition that television and film can also be explicitly used to convey visual and cognitive processes, that television and film programmes carry with them effective implicit as well as explicit content, and that choosing either of these media as an educational agent communicates to students ideas about appropriate and useful modes of learning. This section reviews what is known about the educational impact of television and film in these five content areas.

Teaching Cognitive Content

The earliest—and still most prevalent—use of television and film in education was in the communication of cognitive content to students. Current cognitive programming encompasses a wide range of topics and intended audiences. Individual programmes and series are available in nearly all, if not all, the traditional areas in which we educate children from preschool to high school graduation: mathematics, history, science, art, social science, government, and so on. Material for college students and adults does not span all the areas in which they may wish to be educated, but nonetheless a wide range of material exists. Most television and film material is apparently geared for "the average student." Generally this means a middle-class white student in an urban or suburban community. Recently, however, there has been some programming for more specialized audiences, such as inner-city blacks. Hispanic groups throughout the United States, and Appalachian whites. I expect that this trend toward production for both general and more specialized audiences will continue.

Much educational television has been produced by local and state agencies intimately linked with the school system, while most educational film has been produced by commercial organizations. Educational television particularly is considered to be low budget, low quality, minimally entertaining fare. The introduction of "Sesame Street" (a television series for preschool children) in the late 1960s did more to change this view of educational television than did any of the other excellent television and film material produced either before or after. "Sesame Street" At present, educational television and film for every age group range from the groovy to the gruesome and from informed to ignorant.

Whatever their merits as entertainment or information, educational television and film can communicate their messages to students. Evaluations of instructional programmes viewed in class have repeatedly indicated that children, adolescents, and adults learn the cognitive content that is presented. Evaluations of the first and second years of "Sesame Street" indicate that programmes viewed at home or in class teach preschoolers a variety of cognitive content, and evaluations of "The Electric Company" indicate that programmes viewed in class can increase the reading skills of some elementary school children. None of these evaluations is, however, free from criticism and counterinterpretations. For example, the evaluations of the Educational Testing Service (ETS) of "Sesame Street" have been roundly criticized by a number of researchers who conclude that the gains from viewing that programme are considerably less than those reported by ETS and that "Sesame Street" may widen, rather than narrow, the gap between the educationally advantage and disadvantaged. Nonetheless, there is overwhelming support for the conclusion that a teacher can use television and film with relative assurance to communicate cognitive information.

The teacher may also be assured that, on the average, television and film will impart information as well as the average live teacher does. Innumerable studies support this assertion. In 1967, Chu and Schramm reviewed more than 400 comparisons of live and television teaching at all grade levels and in 1969 Dubin and Hedly reviewed nearly 400 comparisons of live and television teaching at the college level, including many of those reviewed by Chu and Schramm. Although these reviews deal for the most part with students in secondary school and college and with mathematics and science curricula, all grade levels and traditional areas of instruction are adequately represented so that broad conclusions may be drawn from the data. The evidence clearly supports the conclusion that television and film are as effective at teaching students from kindergarten through college as are live teachers. This conclusion is based upon summary comparisons of the results of all studies reviewed and upon comparisons of the many fewer studies researchers consider to be unambiguous comparisons of live and mediated teaching. There is a slight indication that television teaching may be relatively more effective with elementary school students than with older students, but there is no indication that television teaching is more effective in some curriculum areas than in others.

All comparisons of live versus television and film teaching run into problems. Experimentally, the cleanest comparison is one between the same teaching format and the same content presented by a live teacher and by television or film. In this situation the stimuli obviously differ only in the channel of communication. Thus, conclusions may clearly be drawn about the differential impact of these two modes of teaching. Such comparisons, however, restrict each medium to a limited range of teaching techniques; the live teacher cannot engage in an animated, responsive discussion with the students, and television and film cannot resort to slow motion. instant replay, or animation. The more nearly unique capabilities of each medium are not brought into play in presenting the curriculum.

Researchers have not yet characterized educational tasks and medium capabilities precisely enough to permit conclusions about which medium is better suited to which educational goal. In the late 1960s Allen rated the ability of various modes of instruction to teach various educational tasks, and Briggs, Campeau, Gagne, and May proposed a set of procedures by which educators could decide which medium to use for which educational goal. More recently such divergent thinkers as Salomon, Olson and Bruner, and Lesser have also sought to characterize media-specific capabilities. None of these efforts has been supported by abundant research, nor has any yet led to a clear specification of curriculun goals for which television and film are better, worse, or equally well-suited when compared with live teachers. As Schramm concluded after a thorough review of the efforts of the 1960s, teaching media may be interchangeable for most educational tasks. Until better information is available, prospective users of television and film must content themselves with the consideration of such commonsense questions as the extent to which achieving a curriculum goal depends upon dynamic visual images, student-paced instruction, verbal interchange, active manipulation of materials, or uncommon material or occurrences. Answers to questions such as these should help an educator decide whether to find a good classroom teacher or to look for television or film materials and evaluate the feasibility of delivering them to students.

Teaching Social and Emotional Content

While the bulk of instructional television material deals with topics traditionally classified as cognitive or intellectual, some recent series have dealt with social and emotional content. Such production no doubt proceeds from the increasing concern with social and emotional, as well as intellectual education in school. Examples of such series include "Ripples" (a perspective-giving series on urban children's lives) and the Emmy award-winning "Inside/Out" (a mental health series). Both of these were created for older elementary school children by the Agency for Instructional Television. "Sesame Street" includes segments designed to teach pro-social behaviour and recognition of emotions to preschoolers. "Mr. Rogers' Neighbourhood" focuses on preschoolers' social and emotional development. Several series for children between preschool and junior high, funded by the Emergency School Aid Act, deal with racial stereotyping and integration. The goals of these programmes differ somewhat from those with more traditional cognitive content in that producers often intend the programmes to be instigators of classroom discussion or influencers of social behaviour rather than simple communicators of information.

Social and emotional programming has undergone considerably less evaluation than has cognitive programming. Evaluation of the prosocial behaviour segments of "Sesame Street" indicates that they can promote preschoolers' understanding of the concept of cooperation, recognition of pictorial instances of cooperation, and prosocial behaviour similar to that portrayed in the programme and tested in situations similar to those portrayed in the segments. Preliminary evaluations of the emotional segments indicate that preschool children can recognize simple emotions when they are presented (for example, happy, sad, and mad) and may increase their ability to recognize them in other contexts. Recent evaluations of "Mr. Rogers' Neighbourhood" indicate that viewing the programme as part of a preschool programme can increase children's sharing, self-control, and positive interpersonal interaction. Informal evaluations of series such as "Inside/Out" indicate that students and teachers in the upper elementary school grades like the programmes, identify with the interpersonal and individual dilemmas they present, and find themselves provoked into challenging class discussions after viewing. More formal evaluations of the effects of these series have not, to my knowledge, been conducted, nor have comparisons of effectiveness been made between television or film teaching of these topics and more traditional teaching either in or out of class.

Teaching Information Processing Skills

Recently the visual and time-dependent aspects of television and film have been recognized as potential teachers of visual and information processing skills. Carpenter and McLuhan were early and notable exponents of this concept. McLuhan categorized media as "hot" (for example, film), extending a single sensory modality, well-filled with data, and requiring low participation, and "cold" (for example, television); low in data and requiring high participation. American culture was viewed as logical, linear, literary, hot, and troubled by its encounter with the cool world of television. McLuhan's ideas were presented with all the razzmatazz of modern life, perhaps overshadowing the important point that different experiential modes required different human skills and energies. His ideas excited the populace, but educators and psychologists originally did little to pursue them.

Unlike most of us who have remained locked into our literary view of television and film as communicators of intellectual, social, and emotional content, Bruner, Olson, and Salomon have each explored the information-processing skills required by various modes of experience. None of them has differentiated television and film as McLuhan did, but they have differentiated visual media, print media, and individual activity. Olson and Bruner, for instance, make a major distinction between "knowledge" and "skills" (or abilities). For them knowledge about objects and events is constituted by the "set of features that are more or less invariant across different activities," and skills are "the set of operations or constituent acts that are invariant when performed across different objects and events." These authors suggest that educators must be concerned with the acquistion of both knowledge and skills, for without skills children cannot easily acquire knowledge from teachers nor can they educate themselves.

Salomon has provided some experimental evidence that television and film do indeed promote information-processing skills. Films that explicitly modelled operations such as focusing on details and laying out solid objects could increase such skills in eighth and ninth graders who were initially less skilled, and films that required viewers to focus on details or mentally to lay out solid objects could increase such skills in eighth and ninth graders who were initially more skilled. Evidence for similar effects was found in a field study of the effects of "Sesame Street" on Israeli children between the ages of five and eight. There is also some evidence that live and film models can encourage more reflective or more impulsive approaches to intellectual tasks by elementary school children.

Developmental studies of children's understanding of television and film programmes indicate that there are age-related changes in their ability to process plot-line information correctly. Of course, one cannot know whether these changes result from general intellectual development or from the additional practice in decoding television and film presentation that comes with increasing age. The changes found, which could be due to acquiring skill in utilizing the medium, are in the ability to sequence main events in the plot, to retain plot-line connections that are interrupted by commercials, to understand both the main plot and subplots without confusing the two, to acquire the expectation that information will be presented linearly, to anticipate the next event in the plot, and to understand the depicted motivations and consequences for characters' actions.

We have some evidence that television and film can influence the information-processing skills of children and the suggestion that there are particular decoding skills that children learn when they use these media. We have no information yet about the relative impact of mediated versus live experience in influencing certain skills required by both, nor do we have a clear delineation of the different skills each requires. In the future we can expect more information on the ability of television and film to promote information-processing skills in children as researchers such as Salomon, Olson, and O'Bryan develop their current lines of work. For the present educators should be aware of the fact that television and film require and promote information-processing skills that differ somewhat from the skills required by conversation, lecture, and reading.

Implicit Teaching

One factor that most students of instructional television and film overlook and that most students of entertainment television and film explore is the implicit curriculum of a programme. The usual issues here are the social characteristics of the live, puppet, or animated people presented in a programme and the ways in which these people interact with each other. In general, programmes are much more likely to feature males than females and to portray males as sources of authority and expertise. Similar statements can be made for comparisons between whites and minority groups. For example, a recent film strip designed to facilitate growth in moral judgements featured a black male youth group leader and a white male boat captain. No women were visible or active in this world. The social interaction of the two men conveyed additional information in that the black youth group leader repeatedly deferred to the "wisdom" of the white boat captain in making decisions about the activities of the children, even when these decisions had nothing to do with the boat. There is evidence from studies of entertainment programmes and commercials that such portrayals influence children's opinions about men and women of various racial and ethnic groups, even when there has been no explicit intention on the part of the producers to impart "information" about social roles.

The evidence from studies of entertainment television and film is fairly consistent. Programmes made solely to entertain children and adults influence viewers' antisocial and prosocial behaviour, their reactions to violence, and their attitudes and ideas about national groups, American racial groups, sex roles, occupational roles, inter-personal interactions, and the American social system and its place within the world. If entertainment television and film can communicate these messages to viewers between the ages of three and forty, there is every reason to expect similar effects from educational television and film. It is up to researchers to provide evidence of the effects of educational television and film and to compare the influence of live and mediated experience on social attitudes and behaviour. Still, a sensitive educator should expect a programme or series to convey unintended, usually social, messages as well as intended intellectual or social information and should evaluate programmes on these bases as well as the more usual ones.

Teaching about Modes of Learning

The final type of message that television and film can convey is one about appropriate and useful modes of learning. When we use television and film to teach, we are also saying something to students about how we think they can or should learn. As yet we have very little research evidence about what this means to a learner. There are indications that students from elementary school through college like being taught by television, although college students prefer seminars to televised courses, and that teachers are less enthusiastic about television than are students. Teachers also worry that the current generation is deficient in speaking, listening, reading, and writing skills—those traditionally fostered in school—precisely because it has been acquiring the skills required for extracting information from television. But we do not yet have good evidence for whether students who have more television teachers have different skills and opinions of themselves as learners and of the learning process than do students who have more live teachers.

Educators must decide how much they want to suggest to students that less personal, active, and interactive processes are appropriate learning modes. This issue certainly encompasses more than television and film, since many forms of face-to-face teaching also require students to sit passively and absorb information given by another. Nenertheless it is an issue that is largely endemic in current television and film programmes. To the extent that television and film embrace commercial standards of excellence, educators must also ask how much they want to convey to students the impression that learning comes slickly packaged in entertaining, fast-paced modules. Such packaging may make education more palatable to the current generation of students, but it may not be the message that educators would like to reinforce.

PROCESSES OF LEARNING FROM TELEVISION AND FILM

Over the years we have acquired a great deal of information about the ways in which people learn from television and film and about programme characteristics that influence their learning. In general, different variables have been assessed by researchers interested in educational programming and researchers interested in entertainment programming, although there is some commonality in the conclusions one can draw from this material. In this section I shall review what is known about how people learn from both educational and entertainment programming, because I believe that the processes identified in one area will ultimately be shown to apply in the other as well.

Observational Learning

The first and most obvious point is that television and film learning results from relatively passive consumption of content chosen by someone else and presented at a predetermined pace. Increments in learning or performance may result from student activity during or after the presentation or from variations in the way in which content is presented. Still the principal form of learning must be visual and auditory encoding of material presented on a two-dimensional screen. Observational learning is the current popular theory that deals most directly with this phenomenon, although contiguity and associationist theories are also able to account for such learning.

Observational learning theory states that individuals learn by watching and listening to others in either live or mediated form. Furthermore, variables that traditional learning theory has identified as affecting learning when they are experienced directly also affect learning when they are experienced vicariously. In analyses of learning from television and film there is indisputable evidence for this position from studies of learning cognitive content from instructional television and film, cognitive content from public and commercial television, aggressive behaviour from commercial entertainment television and film, prosocial behaviour from "Sesame Street" and "Mr. Rogers," "facts" from Hollywood-made entertainment films in the 1930s, and racial and sex-role attitudes from entertainment television and film. Except for learning cognitive content for instructional television and film and aggressive behaviour from entertainment television and film, none of these areas has been explored with viewers from preschool through adulthood. Nonetheless, the obtained effects so consistently demonstrate the phenomenon of observational learning that there is no reason to doubt that they would also be found if viewers of all ages were studied in all content areas.

It is important to note, however, that the effects of viewing televised or filmed information may not be as unidirectional as most summaries would lead one to believe. Scattered throughout the literature are indications that some presentations elicit from some viewers effects opposite to those one would predict from examining the content. For instance, examples of nontraditional roles for women led third and fifth grade boys and girls and eighth grade girls to endorse less traditional roles for women, while it led eighth grade boys (who presumably are most concerned about their own masculinity) to a stronger endorsement of traditional roles for women. Similarly, viewing aggressive material can lead to increases in prosocial behaviour in middle class preschool children, even though it also leads to more aggression in most preschoolers. In angered adult males, viewing aggression sometimes leads to decreased rather than increased aggression, apparently because it recalls to them sanctions againt aggressive retaliations. Thus, material can occasionally lead to behavioural and attitudinal effects opposite to those predicted by a simple, unidirectional stimulus-response model. There is no ready explanation for this phenomenon, but the best guess is that it occurs when the intended message is received by an individual with a vital investment in a behavioural or attitudinal stance opposite to that suggested by the presentation. Most students, however, learn of accept what is presented, so that the old saw "What you see is what you get" is worth remembering in choosing or producing television and film materials.

Content Variables Affecting Learning

A number of content variables—other than simply what messages are presented—influence learning. The effects of most of these variables on learning from instructional television and film have been tested with only a limited range of subject matter and a limited age range of potential learners. Schramm has provided a very comprehensive review of this work, including about 150 experiments using instructional television or film. He indicates that fully 31 per cent of the experiments were conducted with college students, another 28 per cent with military personnel, and only 41 per cent with elementary and secondary school students and adults. In terms of subject matter, 26 per cent dealt with science, 16 per cent with military skills, 12 per cent with applied or practical science, and the remaining 44 per cent in decreasing percentages with psychological and social sciences, miscellaneous topics, language and literature. professional and semiprofessional skills, and motor skills. Schramm's review indicates that active practice and repetition of content most consistently lead to improved learning. The salutary effects of repetition have also been demonstrated in evaluations of "Sesame Street." Schramm finds other content variables that generally increase learning such as (a) feedback on correct and incorrect practice; (b) material that is clearly and sequentially structured; (c) relatively simple material without irrelevant, attention getting features; and (d) material that is made easily encodable by being written below the viewer's reading level, by being delivered at relatively slow rates, or by being overtly labeled on the sound track.

Some of these content variables have also been found to influence learning and performance from entertainment television and films. Repetition of the same or similar content increases learning or performance of aggression by viewers from preschool through junior high school and of social attitudes by children from seventh to twelfth grade. Clearly organized, sequentially presented plot lines are better understood, especially by younger elementary school children. Irrelevant, attention-getting aspects of a presentation will be learned by children, especially prior to adolescence, and may interfere with learning by fourth graders. Finally, codability influences adults' retention of complex patterns of movements, and children between four and eight remember social material better when they are helped to encode verbally as they view.

Other content variables have been found to influence learning of behaviour or of information through entertainment programming. Although they have not been examined in instructional programming, it is reasonable to assume that they would also be effective there. These variables include (a) the depiction of positive and negative consequences for an event, (b) mild arousal, (c) characters who are similar to viewers, (d) situations that are familiar to the viewers, and (e) more realistic portrayals. Studies of the first of these, that is, the effects of vicarious consequences on learning and performance, have recently been reviewed by Thelen and Rennie. From their summary and other work, there is ample evidence for the influence of vicarious consequences, including influence on (a) the performance of aggression by viewers between the ages of three and about eleven, (b) game playing strategies used by boys between the ages of eleven and fourteen, (c) strategies for leading groups used by children between the ages of nine and thirteen, (d) commodity preferences of six- and seven-year-old girls, and (e) recall of behaviour by first to third graders.

There is less evdience for the utility of the other four variables, but there is enough to warrant mentioning them here. Moderate arousal has been shown to facilitate observational learning of aggression and attitudes by elementary and secondary school children. Material filmed in familiar environments is better remembered by children between second and tenth grades than is less familiar material, and the actions of characters who are more similar (and hence also more familiar and relevant) to children between the ages of eleven and fourteen may be better remembered than those of less similar characters. Finally, there is some indication that children from preschool through adolescence learn, perform, or react more to material that is labeled as real than to material that is labeled as fantasy. These results have been found to occur for emotional responses to aggressive programming and for aggressive behaviour subsequent to viewing "real" or "fantasy" violence, but the latter finding should not obscure the fact that "fantasy" material also teaches.

Production Techniques Affecting Learning

A number of production variables do not seem to affect the amount of learning of cognitive content that results from viewing instructional programming. Again, Schramm has provided a thorough summary of these variables based on the same set of studies that were described at the beginning of the preceding section. Variables that he found not to matter, unless they impair the clarity of the presentation, include focus and size of the picture. Variables that matter only when they are relevant to the content being presented include colour, subjective camera angle, animation, and special pictorial treatments. Finally, some variables are never consistently related to learning: eye contact, background music, a multiplicty of camera angles or film techniques (these may even detract from learning), elaborate visual aids, professional production techniques, dramatic rather than expository styles, and humour.

While these conclusions are warranted from existing research, there are a number of reservations that educators should have about them. First of all, they are often based on one or two studies of viewers within a particular age group. One cannot be certain that the conclusion would be supported by future studies of the same age group and the same content, nor can one be certain that the conclusion would apply to age groups or content other than that studied. There are good reasons to believe that preschool and early elementary-school age children may learn differently than older students who again may learn differently than adults. Thus, age-and content specific results are necessary before one can be certain of an effect. Second, nearly all of the studies upon which these conclusions are based were conducted in laboratory or classroom settings, both of which increase attention to and retention of stimulus material. Consequently, some of the variables, such as commercial production techniques, humour, and animation, that do not affect cognitive learning in these settings might affect it in other settings where students are freer to reject unattractive material. The final caveat is that almost any variable can be shown to influence learning when it is applied in ways that are relevant to the desired and measured learning outcome. Once again educators need to decide upon educational goals before they can decide what variables will help programming achieve these goals.

DESIGNING OR EVALUATING PROGRAMMING

The preceding section has summarized much of what is known about content and production variables that seem to influence learning from educational and entertainment programming. This knowledge can be put to use in selecting programming to fulfil an educational goal or in producing new television or film material. In the discussion that follows, I shall apply the information to the selection of programming, but the principles apply equally well to programme production.

An educator's first responsibilities are to know the characteristics of the intended audience and the goals of the curriculum. Looking first at the way in which the curriculum is presented, we have suggested in the preceding section that an educator should select programming that covers the curriculum goals, omits undesired content of any type, focuses on reality rather than fantasy, avoids irrelevant, distracting information, repeats curriculum content exactly and with variations, elicits rehearsal of the content, provides feedback on the correctness of what is rehearsal, shows positive outcomes for acquisition or use of the content, produces moderate arousal in viewers, and presents information in a manner that is easily encoded by the viewers.

Some of these evaluations cannot be made without a clear understanding of the characteristics of the individuals who will be viewing the programming. For example, younger children seem to have more trouble than older children in deciding what content is relevant and avoiding irrelevant content. Consequently, the amount of material that should be considered irrelevant and distracting wiil certainly very with the age and expertise of the viewers. Likewise, decisions about the amount of repetition, appropriate ways to elicit practice, what will produce moderate arousal, and what makes a presentation easily encodable must all be made with the target audience firmly in mind.

The social characteristics and experience of the intended audience should also be considered in evaluating programming. If it is generally true that individuals learn more or accept more information from people more like themselves or remember more of what happens in familiar environments, then curriculum—of whatever type—presented by people with whom viewers can identify, in places and events familiar to them, is more likely to be remembered than is curriculum that is unfamiliar. Thus, the inner-city child profits from numbers, latters, and shapes presented in a ghetto environment by blacks, whites, and hispanics who might live there, but the Navajo child profits more from the same material presented by Navajos and a few western whites and chicanos in a desert environment dotted with hogans.

As stated in the preceding section, certain production techniques are not reliably associated with greater learning. Thus, on the surface, it seems that an educator need pay little attention to the way in which the programme was made. For a number of reasons, such a conclusion may be fallacious. First, since there is reason to believe that "production techniques" can influence information-processing skills, an educator should choose programming that will encourage appropriate information-processing skills. Second, there are indications that different cultural groups within the United States have different behaviours and rhythms in social encounters, may have different learning styles, and do produce qualitatively different television and film programmes. Hence, an educator must relate audience characteristics to such production variables as the pace at which material is presented, the ways in which the camera is used, the editing, and the sequencing of material. Finally, since at least a modicum of attention must be directed at a presentation if it is to be learned, production techniques that make a programme more attractive decrease the need for a teacher to encourage attention to the programme.

With the advent of "Sesame Street" has come increased knowledge about what makes a programme appealing, at least to a preschoolage viewer. Researchers have used attention ratings of children watching "Sesame Street" in small groups in a naturalistic setting and of children watching in a laboratory with a slide show distractor, From these ratings, the research staff has concluded that young American children are attracted by other children, animals, short and self-contained segments, catch-and-get-caught rhythms, change, slapstick humour, the familiar, animation, and pixilation. They do not like adults, talking, abstract argumentation, nonsense or ambiguity, and low key material.

Our knowledge of the preferences of older children, adolecents, and adults is limited to programme characteristics such as action, humour, characters with whom they can identify, and moderate familiarity. We may not need as much information about these older viewers, since it is much easier for adults to predict what they will like than it is to predict what young children will like.

Educators can obtain sufficient information to begin to make some reasonable choices about programming appropriate for the students for whom they are responsible. One additional step is highly advisable: trying out material with a representative target audience. There is no substitute for the information obtainable from watching children watch a programme and talking to them afterwards. This procedure has been followed recently by groups responsible for the production of "Sesame Street," "The Electric Company," "Carroscolendas," "Fat Albert," "Cezmics," and a few other commercial, public, and instructional programmes. In all cases it has led to some beneficial revisions of material. Of course, teachers, network and station executives, and parents also attend on a more informal basis to the opinions of the students, audiences, or children they wish to influence. Still, such tryout is worth recommending explicitly, since the information that can be gained from such a procedure can help educators adapt their programme choices so that they better fit the interests and needs of their students.

UTILITY OF TELEVISION AND FILM TEACHING

As has already been demonstrated, television and film can successfully teach a variety of content and skills, and students from preschool through college can find television an acceptable and attractive teacher. Therefore an evaluation of the utility of television and film as teaching devices must be based on criteria such as the expertise with which they can present a particular curriculum area, ease of delivery, and cost per pupil. The ease with which these media can be transported to a wide variety of educational environments and the economies of cost that may result from broadcasting television, but not film, programmes to a large audience no doubt account for the fact that television and film are most often considered to be effective tools for teaching large groups of students.

Television and film are often thought of as replacements for more traditional classroom teaching. The comparisons of the effectiveness of live and television or film teaching in the second section above, reflect just such a view. They overlook, however, the fact that each teaching method has particular advantages and is peculiarly able to communicate certain information of skills. Television and film can (a) capture the uncommon or hard to duplicate and make it available to everyone; (b) present static and moving visual information easily; (c) alter visual, auditory, and temporal characteristics of material and phenomena; (d) resort to animation; (e) reach a very large audience; and (f) be repeated endlessly. On the other hand, television and film cannot as easily (a) respond to students as they are learning the lesson; (b) foster practice of reading, writing, and speaking skills; (c) oversee students learning through their own activity; and (d) take the idiosyncrasies of each student into account.

Thus the question "Which medium is better?" is probably better rephrased as "Which medium is better for what?" Separate decisions must be made for each educational goal.

At another level, the choice of teaching medium must be based on decisions about the feasibility and cost of delivery by that medium. This is the point at which television and film become more nearly uniquely appropriate for large groups. Both television and film programmes are educational packages that are easily transportable *in toto* to a wide range of students and locales. In this way they differ significantly from more traditional teaching methods. A curriculum or a master teacher can go wherever there is equipment for showing a film or receiving a television programme. While this mobility has the advantage of making more unusual experiences available to a wide range of students, it has the disadvantages of requiring relatively expensive equipment for broadcasting and of tying students and educational systems into relatively inflexible times for receiving a television broadcast or viewing a film. For this reason, many classroom teachers find television and film considerably less desirable than they would if these media could be viewed at times chosen to match individual classroom schedules.

The costs of television and film vary considerably depending upon the type of production and reception hardware, the type and quality of programmes produced, the delivery system, and the audience size. Production costs for both media are relatively high and cannot be reduced without significant reductions in the quality of the programme. In those situations where programmes are viewed by highly motivated or well-supervised students, simple productions made with a low budget may be perfectly adequate, but in situations where programmes must complete for viewers (for example, "Sesame Street"), high quality programmes and the attendant higher costs are essential. Thus, reductions in per pupil costs most often come from economies in the delivery system and increases in the audience size.

In the last decade at least four separate studies have been made of the costs of various means of instruction and the factors that most influence these costs. Each of them indicates the extreme variation in per pupil costs that may result from differences in production equipment and quality, delivery system instructional use of the medium, and audience size. For example, a poll of educational television stations across the country found that estimates of per student costs for inschool programmes during the 1970-1971 season varied from $0.006 to $7.00 per week, with the average for thirty-three stations being $0.43 per student per week. In 1969 Miller estimated that the cost of live closed-circuit or broadcast instructional television ranged from $0.02 to $10.00 per user-hour, while the cost of taped closed-circuit or broadcast instructional television ranged from $0.01 to $5.00 per user-hour. As a comparison, Miller estimated that the cost of classroom lectures ranged from $0.15 to $3.00 per user-hour, and the cost of small discussion groups ranged from $0.50 to $15.00 per user-hour. Neither of these studies provided estimates of the cost of using films.

In 1968 the General Learning Corporation published a major summary of the costs of instructional media. Estimates were based on 1,000 hours of production per year per school system, which would represent heavy reliance on instructional media. The study concludes that instructional television broadcast only locally (about 15,000 students) would cost between $30 and $40 per student per year. When the broadcasting was to a city or metropolitan area (at least 150,000 students) costs fell to approximately $10 per student per year. On the other hand "Sesame Street," with an estimated audience of about seven million, cost approximately $0.65 per viewer for its first season. Instructional films cost about $50 per student per year regardless of the size of the student propulation utilizing them. Greater economy cannot be achieved with film because of currect duplication and distribution systems. Thus, while television and film have been viewed as equivalent educational systems throughout most of this chapter, they are very unequivalent systems when cost is considered.

All of this ignores the fact that most intstructional television is viewed by students in a traditional classroom with a teacher present. The teacher must still be paid and so his or her costs must be added to those for the television programme. This does not mean that television teaching is always costly or that it is always necessary to have a live teacher present for television to be an effective teacher. "Sesame Street" is a prime example of the benefits obtainable from unsupervised viewing of educational programming, and many other examples are avilable at the college and adult education level. Thus, television may profitably substitute for a traditional classroom teacher. It is also useful as a suppelment to traditional classroom teaching, because it can provide a different learning experience and relatively unusual materials.

INTEGRATING TELEVISION AND FILM TEACHING WITH CLASSROOM TEACHING

Teacher Facilitation of Television and Film Teaching

We have some knowledge about ways in which classroom teachers can facilitate learning from television or film presentations. These are perhaps most easily divided into activities prior to, during and after viewing. Each strategy asks teachers to help students learn better from televised or filmed material. The alternatives of asking television and film to help students learn better from live teachers and of combining teaching modes to produce maximum learning have not to my knowledge been explored, although they seem equally legitimate goals. We need to know how to use each teaching medium to facilitate the work of the others and how to put them all together to bring about the maximum learning of which each student is capable.

Prior to viewing a television or film programme, a teacher can either motive students to at learn the content that will be presented or provide them with structures for assimilating that content. Either of these activities should increase the likelihood of learning from the presentation. A teacher may motivate students by promising a monetary reward for learning, praising or criticizing their learning, or promising a related activity subsequent to viewing. All three of these strategies have been shown to increase learning of television or film content by military recruits and junior high school, high school, and college students. High school students who are intrinsically more interested in the content, and therefore self-motivate, will also learn more than students who are not. Providing introductions for students prior to viewing has been recommended by Chu and Schramm in their extensive review of learning from television and by Chen in his exploration of ways to increase active participation by viewers of "The

Electric Company." Neither or these recommendations is supported by strong research evidence, but it is reasonable to assume that introductions would increase learning by increasing codability of material, providing a little learning prior to viewing, and increasing the availability of structures within which to assimilate the information.

During viewing, a teacher may increase learning by insuring attention to the programme, eliciting rehearsal of the content, providing feedback on the correctness of the rehearsal, and commenting positively on those aspects of the programme the teacher would like remembered or performed. We have clear evidence for the utility of rehearsal and feedback from a number of studies of junior high school students. For example, Michael and Maccoby found that stopping a film and asking students to rehearse what they had just seen increased learning over that which occurred when students watched the film straight through. Feedback on the correctness of what was rehearsed also improved learning; Michael and Maccoby concluded that this activity improved learning more than any of the other three variables they studied (participation, overt and covert practice, and extrinsic motivation).

There is also evidence that adult commentary on the social acceptability of material, while, it is being viewed, influences children's later performance of what they have seen. For example, if children see an aggressive performance and an adult expresses approval of it, the children are much more likely to be aggressive in subsequent test situations than are children who have heard an adult disapprove of the action. Interestingly, the impact of such comments apparently varies with the age of the child. Preschoolers will show the influence of an adult's commentary only in test situations where that adult is present, while seven-year-olds will show that influence whether or not the adult is present in the test situation.

Subsequent to viewing a programme, a teacher may facilitate learning and performance of the content by providing practice and feedback, by differential reinforcement, and by integrating the content into other material and activities in the class. The utility of practice and feedback has been amply demonstrated throughout this chapter, but it is perhaps worth noting that music, jingles, slogans, doggerel, and the like from a programme are particularly easy for students to practice—and something they enjoy practising. This fact is most often applied to teaching young children and to teaching foreign languages, but it applies equally well to older students and other subject matter. Reinforcement effects have been demonstrated for learning and performance of all kinds of intellectual and social information and behaviours. Thus it is no surprise that reinforcement can affect retention and performance of what has been seen on television. There is scant evidence for the utility of integrating television or film content into other material, although it is a common suggestion to teachers. In fact, many programmes put out teacher guides that contain a plethora of suggestions about how to integrate ideas from the programme (or series) into other classroom activities. This piece of folk wisdom would undoubtedly be borne out in more refined experimental tests of its utility, but we now have little experimental support for it.

Most of these strategies for increasing learning from television and film are familiar to classroom teachers and utilized by them. Reviewing them only serves to emphasize the benefits that may be derived from a teacher's acceptance of television or film teaching and integration of it into the entire educational experience of the student. Teachers who are most comfortable with television and film often depart from these more usual teacher-directed uses of television and film and use the media in more individualized, innovative ways.

Uncommon Uses of Television and Film

Some teachers have capitalized on children's extensive attraction to television and film by piggybacking other learning onto involvement with television programmes or film production. Most of these activities are enthusiastically received, but their usefulness has not often been evaluated. Teachers in Philadelphia who used scripts from television programme to teach reading report imporved reading scores and much more interest in reading. Television scripts were even stolen from a classroom—the first known theft of reading material in that school. Borton has added a second audio track to popular childeren's television programmes and demonstrated that children who listen on an FM station while they view the programme learn the vocabulary and concepts it presents. Others have used film making as a vehicle for practising reading and writing, as well as planning, skills. Still others have asked students to view particular programmes at home because they present information relevant to class curriculum. There is every indication that learning results from home viewing of such programmes by pre-schoolers, elementary school students, high school students, and adults. Finally, some teachers have used entertainment programmes as material for discussions about social issues, for concept formation, and for teaching the ordering of events in time.

Relatively inexpensive videotape equipment has been used to teach performance and role-taking skills, again with little or no formal evaluation of its utility. Videotape records provide excellent feedback to a student. For example, programmes in such areas as speech, dramatics, and athletics have used videotaped records of students to give them more feedback on their performance. Others have used videotape to document social interactions so that participants can analyze their roles without the distortions that arise when one attempts to remember such interactions. Finally, videotape has been used to foster role-taking skills by providing students with an opportunity to act out a variety of roles and to receive feedback on their performance. One such experimental programme with adolescent delinquent boys resulted in increased role-taking skill as measured experimentally and in decreased arrests over a one-year period. Of course, the boys may simply have learned enough role-taking skills to avoid being caught rather than learning to empathize with their victims. The experimental evaluation was not fine-grained enough to rule out this possibility.

The last-mentioned uses of television and film are appropriate for small groups of students, but not for large. Each of them demands supervision by a classroom teacher. In them television and film become useful tools for arousing interest in the actual curriculum area or for providing feedback to students. Thus, one can begin to think of television and film not as simple substitutes for a lecture, but also as instruments for increasing interest, for eliciting practice of particular skills, and for providing elaborate, realistic feedback on a learner's performance.

CONCLUSION

Television and film can certainly be used to teach cognitive, social, and emotional content and information-processing skills to students who range in age from preschoolers to adults. In doing so television—but not film—can be cost-effective when the student population it serves is relatively large. Thus an educator need not worry about whether or not to use television or film; rather the teacher must decide when to use them, how to produce or evaluate a programme, and how best to integrate them into an entire educational experience.

Television and film are most likely to be successful teachers when educators participate in careful planning of the material, select material that conforms to our present knowledge about the more successful ways of presenting curriculum content, and actively work of integrate television or film material into the entire educational experience of the student. The most useful strategies for increasing learning, either within a programme or through classroom activities, are active participation by students, feedback of student responses, and repetition. As with all education, these strategies must be evaluated within the context of student characteristics. It is up to the educator and the producer, with little help from existing research, to find the correct blend of curriculum content, of effective means of presenting it on television and film, and of consideration for the unique characteristics of the target audience—no mean job for any of us.

7

EDUCATIONAL TELEVISION

To most Americans, television simply means entertainment and, to a lesser degree, news and information. But to industry and science it is, among other things, a versatile electronic tool, carrying out diversified tasks ranging from the surveillance of shop-lifeters to relaying spectographic impressions of distant stars. Above all, television is the most powerful communication medium ever devised. Quite conceivably, it could revolutionize the entire educational process. Thus far, the American educational system has tapped a mere fraction of television's vast potential. Even so, teaching-by-television has caught on as has no previous innovation in American education, a field where—in a familiar estimate—a new idea commonly takes fifty years to gain wide acceptance.

The military services pioneered in the use of television for direct instruction. Early in the 1950's, in the infancy of commercial television, a few educators envisaged television as an integral part of the instructional programme. Slowly at first, private and public institutions began adapting it to the classroom. Now, less than a decade and a half later, some ten million students in the United States are receiving at least part of their instruction through television. Today practically every course in the school and college curriculum, from first-grade arithmetic to college zoology, is being taught somewhere over television.

Highlights in the brief history of instructional television suggest the momentum behind its development. One of the first and most dramatic experiments began in Hagerstown, Maryland, in 1956, linking dozens of schools to receive televised lessons. In 1957 an ambitious venture known as the National Programme in the Use of Television in the Schools was initiated by Dr. Alexander J. Stoddard and financed by the Fund for the Advancement of Education of the Ford Foundation. Participating in this project were some fifteen major cities, thirteen states, and hundreds of thousands of elementary and secondary-school students.

In the spring of 1961, the six-state Midwest Programme on Air-borne Television Instruction, with headquarters at Purdue University began broadcasting lessons to schools and colleges from high-flying airplanes, covering some three to four hundred square miles within a perimeter that includes Milwaukee, Detroit, Cincinnati, and Louisville. The broadcast service has been particularly helpful to small towns and rural schools. Potentially, the Airborne experiment could transmit simultaneously, over six channels, a total of seventy-two lessons a day to schools and colleges enrolling about five million students. At present the two transmitters available in each aircraft (broadcasting on standard-brand UHF channels) carry courses ranging from elementary-school level through college, six hours a day, four days a week, during the academic year. In its second year of operation, many problems still remained: programmes varied from excellent to poor, and reception was unpredictable. By 1964 Airborne was attempting to expand from two to six UHF channels and, with improved aircraft and technical equipment as well as superior courses, to attract enough schools to become financially self-sustaining.

What Airborne does for thousands of schools by stratovi sion, Hagerstown does by coaxial cable for the public-school students of Washington Country, Maryland. Almost one hundred miles of cable, with a potential of six programme channels connect forty-three schools. Each student in these schools reserves at least one period of televised instruction daily, and the system offers a total of 125 lessons weekly in all major subjects to all twelve grades. Programmes originate from headquarters that include five well-equipped studios and separate offices for about twenty-five television teachers.

Hagerstown has led to other closed-circuit or wired-television installations such as the South Carolina state network, which links up widely scattered high schools. Beginning with one high school in 1958, a statewide multichannel, closed-circuit system covering 167 schools has rapidly evolved. This huge installation, leased from Southern Bell and independent telephone companies, reaches out to all of the state's forty-six countries, embracing major population centers as well as rural districts. Responsible to the legislature for the operation of the system is a seven-man Educational Television Commission, which is seeking to allevaite South Carolina's acute shortage of qualified teachers. Recently the commission has expanded into industrial, vocational, and medical education; it has also built several educational television stations.

Closed-circuit television is currently being used at all levels of American education, but particularly in higher education. In 1963 there were closed-circuit systems in 310 educational institutions, plus 60 in armed-forces training centers. Except where television is used merely as a demonstration magnifier in a large college auditorium, most closed-circuit experiments have been attempts to multiply the services of one teacher in order to serve students in a number of classrooms. Universities hope thereby to lower the costs of instruction, as well as to improve courses by allowing a teacher more time for preparation. University closed-circuit installations usually link lecture origination points with classrooms on a single campus, although they sometimes serve students on other campuses by coaxial cable or microwave relays. Classrooms accommodating from fifty to one hundred students and larger auditoriums are often equipped with a number of viewing monitors. In many cases "talk back" arrangements make it possible for students to relay questions to the lecturer at predetermined points in the presentation. Similar but usually less elaborate facilities are to be found in many high schools throughout the nation.

An outstanding early example of closed-circuit instruction is the television experiment at Pennsylvania State University, which has produced such varied courses as chemistry, psychology, music, speech, and German. Operating on the campus are three separate closed-circuit systems valued at $50,000 each and costing about $40 an hour to operate. The estimated saving to the university in classroom space alone is some $100,000 annually. In 1961, the University of Texas initiated the nation's first closed-circuit television network to link several college campuses by microwave. This network now includes eight other colleges and universities in the state. The Texas programme includes basic courses in chemistry, German, history, mathematics, music, psychology, and science, either presented live or video-taped by outstanding authorities. Ohio State provides a good example of the impact of television on university instruction. In 1958 the university experimented with using its UHF educational television station to teach some 575 accredited students; by 1962 the pressures of scheduling, space, and staff had increased the total number of students to 75,000. Ohio State is now operating an elaborate campus-wide closed-circuit system in addition to their broadcast station.

Although it is certain that in the coming decade other school systems will follow the example of Hagerstown and South Carolina, up till now most school administrators have opted for open-circuit broadcasts rather than closed-circuit presentation transmitted by cable or microwave directly to their intended viewers. The reason is economic rather than administrative or technical, since open-circuit is often cheaper on a per-pupil basis. Moreover open-circuit broadcasting allows a university or school system to reach the general public as well. Some idea of the scope of open-circuit telecasting is provided by a 1960 report which indicated that 569 school districts across the nation were making regular use of television instruction and that credit for television courses was offered by 117 colleges and universities (a development often referrred to as "The University of the Air").

In the United States the first extensive open-circuit effort was the "Chicago Junior College of the Air," broadcasting credit courses over WTTW, the educational station in Chicago. The Fund for the Advancement of Education originally allocated $475,000 to the project, and the Chicago Board of Education, which supplied an original $600,000, is continuing to subsidize it. The junior college offers from four to twelve televised courses each semester in accounting, astronomy, biology, business, English, humanities, literature, mathematics, music, political science, psychology, Russian, social science, Spanish, and speech. Registration ranges from 94 to 801 students per course. About two-thirds of those enrolled complete the courses, and some qualify for the Associate in Arts degree, a two-year certificate given by Chicago City College. In recent years more than one hundred colleges and universities have put their professors before studio cameras, although few have tried programmes as ambitious as Chicago's.

Certain procedures have now become standard throughout the nation in developing extension courses of this type. Basic planning is the joint responsibility of specialists in subject matter, curriculum, and production. Student viewers receive special study guides. Registration for credit is limited to students meeting regular admission requirements; in many cases periodic conferences of teachers and viewers are arranged: and only those students receive credit who pass carefully administered examinations. College lectures televised by the national commercial networks have enrolled the largest numbers of students. "Continental Classroom" and "Sunrise Semester," for instance, have had as many as seven or eight thousand students enrolled for credit.

Generally speaking, television for schools has taken one of three distinct courses. The first is "direct instruction." The second is loosely referred to as "enrichment," for lack of a better word. A third variant, known as "total teaching," is generally confined to the higher levels of education. Here television assumes almost the entire obligation for the instruction of the student, who does not attend classes but views the programmes and pursues his studies at home. College extension courses (such as the "Chicago Junior College of the Air") use this format, as do certain high schools for students with advanced standing.

In direct instruction, television provides the bulk of the instructional content; the classroom teacher serves primarily as monitor and discussion leader, and administers examinations and grades papers. This pattern is most frequent in subject areas where there is an acute shortage of trained teachers. It also appears in elementary schools for the more complex subjects beyond the scope of many teachers. Science, foreign languages, social studies, music, and art are relevant examples. The teaching of foreign languages in the elementary schools constitute the most controversial use of direct instruction. Excellent nationally syndicated language programmes exist in Spanish and French, such as "Parlons Francais," which offers not only direct language instruction but also records, tapes, and relevant cultural material. But many administrators prefer to produce their own lessons locally; because most elementary school teachers are so unconversant with foreign languages that they cannot utilize packaged courses effectively.

For instructional television lessons to be of value, the school staff must integrate them as thoroughly into the educational programme as the prescribed textbook. Direct instruction is in essence a form of team teaching which can be no better than the participating teachers, whether televised or "live." The point was perceptively set forth by Fred Hechinger of the New York *Times* in testimony before the Television Advisory Panel of the U.S. Office of Education:

> Bad teaching is magnified many times over on TV. By the same token, good teaching is not only magnified by TV, but

becomes contagious. In spite of the difficulties and problems faced in the Washington County, Maryland, TV system, there is a beneficial effect of TV, not only on the carefully trained TV teachers, but through the effect of these teachers on the other teachers. This doesn't merely mean that the TV teachers are the superior teachers, but it means that we have broken the confinement that has forced teachers to become locked up in their classrooms (after they finish their practice teaching) with no criticism of their work. This criticism is something TV is offering us now by opening an avenue of comparison.

When the number of television lessons in a given subject amounts to one a week or fewer, televison is little more than enrichment. Ideally such telecasts can supplement the work of the regular teacher and illuminate aspects of the curriculum uniquely suited for the medium. They can bring unusual experiences into the classroom at modest cost. Such programming has proved most effective in elementary schools throughout the country, particularly rural and underprivileged schools. The best of these programmes show the influence of overseas school broadcasters such as BBC, CBC, Radio Television Francais, and Radio Japan. Instructional television in these countries, which is heavily subsidized, is primarily restricted to enrichment broadcasts of high quality. Since enrichment programmes are supplementary, it is often difficult to persuade administrators and teachers to use them effectively. There is, however, an encouraging current trend toward combining the best features of enrichment and direct instruction to produce more versatile and better integrated programmes.

No facet of the curriculum from kindergarten through college has withstood the phenomenal growth of instructional television. The most recent edition of *Telecourses for Credit*, published by Michigan State University in September, 1963, contains 250 pages listing thousands of courses ranging from art to zoology. Educators have become sufficiently adroit in their control of the medium to assign it a multitude of highly specialized functions. Many medical and dental schools use closed-circuit television so that large numbers of students can observe the filling of a tooth or surgical procedures, sometimes in colour, (an extension of the work formerly done on film). Television now permits students in law, education, psychology, and other subjects to observe without intruding upon the practitioners. Most significant in view of the continuing debate, over teacher training is the use of television to enable student teachers to observe new teaching techniques or to provide various kinds of specialized in-service training. A major use of in-service telecasts is to acquaint the teacher with a new curriculum and, incidentally, clues and pointers in the art of teaching.

The prime reason for the rapid spread of school television was the educational emergency of the fifties, plus the impetus supplied by massive foundation support. Most school administrators accept television mainly as a means of coping with classroom and teacher shortages and only secondarily as a means of improving the quality of teaching and extending the reach of the superior teacher. Most of them hoped to reach large numbers of students at a relatively low per-pupil cost. And, indeed, by keeping construction of facilities and programming costs to the minimum, some of the larger school systems realized impressive economies. Dade County, Florida, for example, claimed a saving of three million dollars in school construction alone during the first three years it used televised instruction (total project savings are now estimated to exceed ten million dollars).

The rush to exploit the advantages of television (and foundation subsidies) produced quantities of material, but in the process it highlighted the problems of instructional television. Programmes were put together quickly, cheaply, often with inadequate plant and by limited personnel. Even so, television proved a powerful adjunct to the teaching of large classes and showed its capacity to improve the quality of instruction without increased cost. As Wilbur Schramm, director of the Institute for Communication Research at Stanford University, wrote in 1961, summarizing the extant research findings on television teaching:

> There can no longer be any doubt that students learn efficiently from instructional television. The fact has been demonstrated now in hundreds of schools, by thousands of students, in every part of the United States and in several other countries....
>
> Instructional television is at least as effective as ordinary classroom instruction, when the results are measured by the usual final examinations or by standardized tests....[And] employing the usual tests that schools use to measure the progress of their students, we can say with considerable confidence that in 65 per cent of a very large number of comparisons between televised and classroom teaching, there is no significant difference. In 21 per cent, students learned significantly *more*, in 14 per cent, they learned significantly *less*, from television.

There is evidence, however, to suggest that the results might have been even more impressive had the television lessons themselves been better. Perhaps the sheer size and pell-mell expansion of instructional television have constituted the major obstacles to quality.

The mass of material required by instructional television continues to pose a major problem. Hechinger has said:

> Even if we had enough money, we do not have enough talent to keep TV stocked with superior performance, educational or otherwise. TV should be cut up into smaller segments so that an expensive production would not be a one-time show. This would be one way out of the cost dilemma of ETV. In terms of in-school TV, one of the greatest hopes of the future is the prospect of relatively inexpensive video-tape equipment so that schools could shoot and bank some of their own better TV performances. This could lead to an exchange of talent.

Indeed there has been a tremendous duplication, of courses throughout the country, because until recently it has been cheaper to produce a course "live" each year locally than to record and store, or exchange, film or video tape.

Technological developments are steadily reducing costs to the point where it is practical to record lessons in advance for later broadcasts and/or possible exchange. Lessons, which the teacher can record in the studio at his convenience, can be shown repeatedly on one or more stations and ameliorate the problems of scheduling. These lessons could also be nationally syndicated, reused in subsequent semesters, and revised as necessary.

An encouraging development is the growth of state and regional networks, as well as regional libraries of television courses on video tape and film. Extensive libraries are maintained by the Midwest Programme on Airborne Television Instruction and the Instructional Library Project. The latter comprises the National Instructional Television Libraries in New York City, San Francisco, Lincoln, Nebraska, and Cambridge, Massachusetts. They currently handle 324 recorded telecourses at all levels. This project was established in 1962 by the U.S. Office of Education as a pilot library system. Collective ventures like the recording and networking of instructional materials, promising as they are, must make their way against the bias of American education for local autonomy.

Instructional television has already demonstrated that it can offer unique advantages as a medium of instruction: it can vastly extend the reach of the nation's best teachers, and it can bring to students educational experiences beyond the potential of conventional means of instruction. Present-day instructional television, its form molded by the experience of the late fifties, is unquestionably a remarkable teaching tool.

There is, however, increasing evidence that the high hopes once held for instructional television have not been fully realized. One reason is that school systems allocate only a minute portion of their budget for basic research in the development of new instructional materials, It has always been the practice of administrators to delegate development to the publisher or producer in the marketplace, and they have carried this restful custom over into instructional television and other recent innovations. The few courses which exploit the unique aspects of the television medium have been produced by commercial publishing and film companies for national syndication on a royalty basis. Most school administrators appear content with their own local production, however inadequate, and are reluctant to apportion the time, money, and staff required to produce instructional material of substance and quality.

It is obvious, moreover, that more money and more attention to the format of television lessons are only initial steps. Perhaps the greatest difficulty is that educators, from administrators to teachers, are not only unfamiliar with the television medium but lack familiarity with the basic psychology of visual perception and the nature of visual communication. They are incapable of conceiving subject matter in terms of moving images, and consequently the visual component of most instructional television is woefully inadequate. The average lesson places its emphasis primarily on the words of the on-camera teachers. There is no denying the usefulness of an electronic record of superior teaching to many classroom teachers for whom it provides valuable on-the-job training. The efficacy of the "talking face" as a teacher training device, however, is no rationalization for short-changing children by giving them old-fashioned, mediocre instruction via an up-to-the-minute medium.

Programmes have been unduly influenced by the requisite "hardware"...perhaps inevitably in so mechanized a society as ours. It is may view that the time has come for educators to focus their attention on the lessons which the transmitters and cables send out. Indeed, radically new material is at hand. The recent development of an inexpensive 8 mm. cartridge projector which makes short single-concept films readily accessible appears to be an ideal way for rapidly increasing the visual component of instructional television. The activities of Dr. Louis Forsdale's Project in Educational Communications at Teachers College, Columbia University, and of Educational Services, Inc., and the National Film Board of Canada suggest that an extensive library of such cartridges could be imaginatively and inexpensively produced.

The rushed experimentation of the late fifties inevitably developed a cult of amateurism within the instructional television movement that is responsible for the televising of teachers rather than the televising of instruction. Although there are magnificent exceptions and much competent instruction, pressure and precedent have too often resulted in a dispiriting norm. Yet the able teacher, possessed of a sense of the medium, has demonstrated that intelligence, experience and ingenuity can exceed all the expertise of the well-equipped studie. If it is to be anything other than televised mediocrity, school broadcasting requires the highest standards of academic, creative, and technical competence.

8

COMPUTER ASSISTED INSTRUCTION

In this chapter programmed instruction (PI) and computer-assisted instruction (CAI), viewed in their primary roles as methods of teaching one person at a time, are defined and reviewed. Neither PI nor CAI is seen to be a subset of the other, for the first is defined as a systematic development process rather than a product form, and the second is still too complex to be characterized as a kind of instructional medium. A synthesis is possible, however, around the idea of a "design science of instruction."

A CHARACTERIZATION OF PI AND CAI

Programmed Instruction: A Process Definition

In the early 1960s, definitions of programmed instruction focused on easily recognized features of format (small frames, requirements for responses, and the like). Susan Markle wisely pointed out that such definitions unnecessarily restrict the class of instructional materials that can be called "programmes." Instead, she proposed a definition that focussed on the characteristics of the process of development rather than the characteristics of the product of that development. She defined an instructional programme as a "reproducible sequence of instructional events designed to produce a measurable and consistent effects on the behaviour of each and every acceptable student." This definition and very similar statements have received widespread acceptance, and the term "programmed instruction" has in many circles become synonymous with the term "validated instruction."

It has been shown, however, that even validated instruction can be worthless. A programme may teach irrelevant objectives extremely well, thus meeting external criteria of validation as set forth in Markle's definition, while being of little value in terms of accomplishing worthwhile educational goals. Geis has suggested that the term "validated instruction" should be reserved for instruction that (a) is the result of an empirical development process that guarantees that it meets its stated objectives, (b) is directed at objectives that reflect meaningful real-world performances, and (c) includes technically accurate instructional content.

Whatever definition one chooses, obvious problems arise when one attempts to define instruction that encompasses a variety of media, from striped pages and interactive lectures to tape-slide and television productions, and employs a myriad of techniques derived from different psychological theories and a number of clever rules of thumb. Yet there seems to be some agreement. It is the process of developing instructional programmes that determines whether experts in the field will accept a given piece of instruction as being "programmed." And this process must include an empirical validation step in which student performance after instruction is compared to stated programme adjectives. The definition can be extended if we make some inferences based on the term "validated instruction." The definitions of Markle and Geis both include references to the comparison of postprogramme student performance with programme objectives. This kind of definition allows us to infer two phases of the process of programme development —one in which evaluation of student performance on objectives takes place and one in which the programme objectives are developed. Certainly this kind of definition indicates that there must be a phase during which instructional objectives are used to direct the development of the instructional programmes.

This reasoning leads to an even fuller description of a three-step process required to produce validated instruction. The process involves (a) some form of problem analysis that focuses on desirable real-world performances and results in specific statements of instructional objectives the achievement of which is measurable; (b) a design and development process that insures instructional materials (displays, frames) directed at fostering achievement of the stated objectives, using the most efficient and effective instructional strategies or techniques; and (c) an evaluation-validation phase. During this third step, students representative of the intended target population use the programme and then are evaluated as to their achievement of the stated objectives, changes are made in the programme wherever the students do not achieve the objectives, and the evaluation-revision process is continued until the programme demonstrates that it does indeed have a measurable and consistent effect on the behaviour of students who meet entry-level requirements.

Thus, programmed instruction is instruction that results from a systematic development process in which the developer assumes the responsibility for student learning.

Computer-Assisted Instruction: A Delivery System Definition

The early literature on computer-assisted, computer-aided, computer-based, and computer-managed instruction is filled with a variety of not too enlightening attempts to define and distinguish the three-letter acronyms beginning with "C" and ending with "I." Computers and specialized terminal devices can be engineered and programmed to perform work needed in any of the processes of instructional management, delivery to an individual or to a group, design and development, and evaluation, research, and administration. The more generic term, "computer uses in education" (CUE), does not limit the use of computers prematurely to models and applications that have gained early prominence.

In this chapter, "CAI" is used as a primitive term, not an acronym, to refer to that class of situations wherein a student may, for educational purposes, interact with an electromechanical device that (a) can display information in one or more forms, such as printed graphic, audio, and tectual displays or mechanical movements, and (b) can receive responses from the student in one or more forms, such as keyboard responses, pointing responses, movements of mechanical objects, vocal responses, or recorded changes in physiological measures. The educational purposes at which this interaction is aimed may encompass cognitive, affective, or psycho-motor objectives and also exploration, creative problem solving, design, testing, diagnosis, and prescription within an individualized multimedia instructional environment. In short, CAI is defined as an interaction between a student, a computer controlled display, and a response-entry device for the purpose of achieving educational outcomes.

This definition excludes batch jobs (slow turn-around programmes submitted by students) submitted without benefit of an interactive terminal, but not a computer-managed instructional interaction wherein the student gets a test scored and receives a diagnosis and prescription within five minutes or less. It excludes data collection for management or research purposes, which may also be accomplished through recording due from the above-defined cybernetic interaction between student and artifact. It excludes the interactions between teacher, proctor, and operator that may occur at the same student terminal or at a special terminal used to assist in the monitoring and management of groups and of single students. It excludes the interactions that may occur at a terminal among in instructional designers, authors and media packagers to promote the development and revision of instructional materials. All these are important aspects of the more general term "computer uses in education."

This definition focuses on the operational constraints on display and response, and on the control and measurement, that can be applied to the contingent relationships between subsequent displays and response. CAI limits display types and formats to what can be shown on a particular device. Some examples are teletypes (upper-case alphanumeric characters), a television or plasma display (alphanumeric characters and graphics), movies, audio, a Braille typewriter, or a "Turtle." For the purposes of interpreting alternatives and controlling contingent actions, CAI limits responses to a sequence of key depressions on a keyboard, a pointing response with a finger or light-pen, or other more esoteric methods of entering data into a computer. It should be noted that instructional designers do not always limit themselves to response that can be received by the device and used to direct contingent actions.

There is no conceivable limit to the variety of algorithms that can be implemented. These algorithms control the content and sequence of displays and feedback messages. The algorithms can be made contingent upon student responses, historical data about students, temporal variables, and models of the student and of the learning process. The hardware of display and response serves to limit and bring under control the events of display and response. Similarly, the algorithms programmed into the computer make explicit, limit, and control the sequential and contingent processes occurring in an episode of instructional interaction.

CAI thus offers itself as instrumentation and, through its explicit algorithms, as notation for a new science and technology of instructions. Its potential has barely been tapped. It is the epitome of instructional technology. Performance objectives introduced the limiting of instruction to a display specification, a response specification, and a performance standard. In so doing, they evoked the often valid complaints of humanist that the tacit components of person-to-person instruction were being lost. CAI limits display and response no more than does programmed instructions, for a computer can control—or reference —any kind of media. CAI brings the *process* under greater control, however, and thus invades the domain of human teachers in a more threatening and potent way.

CAI will bring a new science and technology of instruction and can further strip away certain valued tacit components of learning. Or, if it is used wisely in concert with organized patterns of human interaction (student-to-student and student-to-teacher), it can effects a resurgence of the human aspects of learning and teaching. It can help both by highlighting what is *not* essentially human and by freeing teachers from those tasks.

The Three Technologies of CAI

The three technologies of hardware, software, and courseware elaborate CAI's essential features of explicit and limited display, response, and contingent processing. The designers of CAI systems must span, in one person or as a team, many specialities. Expertise in hardware must include a knowledge of (a) a variety of display and response devices, (b) techniques and trader's in data communication, (c) varieties of information storage devices, (d) the capabilities of various new micro-circuits, and (e) kinds of memory storage devices and ways to organize them hierarchically to achieve design objectives. Special hardware technologies for audio and video storage and reproduction, as well as for computer graphics, are evolving rapidly. Creation of the architecture of the various hardware elements that make up a CAI system may be as deceptively simple as adapting an existing intelligent terminal with a built-in microcomputer, or as complex and responsive to different purposes and philosophies as the architecture of PLATO and TICCIT, which are discussed later in this chapter.

Software is distinguished from courseware in CAI parlance because the "software" of systems analysis and programming is distinctly different from the "software" of instructional materials development, although their relationship is full of provocative analogies. Systems programming gives authors, teachers, and students access, by means of command language statements and a hierarchy of levels of control, to the hardware features of the terminal and the central computing and storage devices. Operating systems, structured file-access systems, and languages for entering, editing, and revising any course materials must be provided. Artificial intelligence promises to make this software more sophisticated and general.

The courseware itself is seen as consisting of special purpose programmes and data files, which require for their implementation the general purpose software provided by the systems programmers. Courseware also includes instructional materials coordinated with the computer programmes, but not provided through the computer, such as workbooks, videotapes slides and audio-tapes. The nature of the emerging science and technology underlying courseware design and development has been elaborated in previous yearbooks of the National Society for the Study of Education and is discussed further in the next major section of this chapter.

An Intellectual Bifurcation in CAI

A bifurcation exists between the computer science perspective and the instructional science perspective. Persons proficient in the hardware and software technologies underlying CAI (primarily electrical engineering and computer science) have a different perspective than those proficient in the courseware technologies (instructional psychology and media).

The former group sees the intellectual history of CAI in terms of (a) the development of time-sharing capability, which has afforded mass access to computer terminals and computer power, (b) issues in man-machine interaction, programming, computer simulation, and artificial intelligence, and (c) fundamental computer science concepts, such as data structures, alternative representational schemes, and alternative algorithms. To them the computer is of profound, intellectual interest in and of itself, not just as a possible new method of mediating old subject matter in old ways. It is itself a message and a metaphor. Learning to use formal languages, create models, and implement them in a computer is seen as worthwhile in its own right. More than that, it is seen as an indispensable part of the creative professionals' future problem-solving and design activities. For the teacher in any field, the notions of data structure and formal model may generate new ways of conceiving the very structure and organization of a portion of one's subject matter. The use of computer graphics, computational power, and information retrieval power suggests alternate ways of presenting the subject matter to students. Computer applications in research and instruction in one field serve as metaphors to prompt restructuring and invention in other fields. The *Proceedings* of six national conferences on Computers in the Undergraduate Curriculum have documented a diverse array of computer applications to instruction in a wide variety of undergraduate disciplines. These efforts by creative faculty members are for the most part notably untouched by much knowledge of programmed instruction as defined above. Yet the great majority of instructional activities on computers that fit our definition of CAI fall into this category.

The courseware technologists see a different intellectual history behind the use of CAI. Fitting CAI into a framework of systematic design and evaluation makes it a medium of instruction. Its capabilities for dynamic branching, storing large files of data, score keeping, dynamic graphic display, and the like, might be implied by a set of performance objectives and a list of implementation constraints. Like any good medium, it will then be designed into a total individualized instructional environment where it can meet certain requirements uniquely well, or better than any other medium, and still keep costs within bounds. This "mainline" use of the computer as a part of a total instructional system stands in contrast to the adjunctive approach that emanates from the "computer qua computer" perspective.

It may be possible in the near future for a synthesis to occur, based perhaps on the analytic PI approach described below. The result, a more mature science and technology of instruction, could encompass the unique aspects of both PI and CAI within a coherent intellectual framework. In the meantime, faculty members at all levels of education and in almost all disciplines are trying their hands at CAI without benefit of PI's hard-won knowledge of how to specify, design, and validate good instruction.

CAI's Economic and Intellectual Potential

CAI could well be likened to the invention of printing, which brought another technology, the book, into wide use. CAI represents a potential breakthrough of similar social and intellectual significance. Economically it is a breakthrough in the capability of performing the work involved in teaching one person at a time and managing the learning environment required. Individualized instruction often founders on the problem of work, which expands enormously in the initial production of materials, the updating and revision of materials, the management of individual paths to learning, and the provision of detailed practice with feedback.

CAI as defined here does not itself reduce the work involved in the authoring and updating of materials. Even as the algorithms for student instruction are made explicit and operational, however, the processes involved in authoring are being made explicit. Generative CAI is one result. At the Ontario Institute for Studies in Education, an extensive system of remedial mathematics modules has been developed. Only one prototype problem for each exercise format and test item format is provided, and random numbers are generated according to parameters to create an infinitely large problem file. Using state-of-the-art PI techniques outlined in this chapter, the TICCIT project introduced an authoring approach, described below, that has simplified the process of developing large volumes of courseware. The rapid editing and updating capabilities of computers, coupled with data collection routines that can summarize student data to pinpoint revision needs, provides powerful assistance in the work involved in updating and revision.

The problem of managing individual paths to learning is easily handled by CAI systems, which can maintain a representation of the complete set of individualized instructional modules, along with a record of which ones any student has completed, still needs, or is working on. Using this information, the system can provide reports to teachers or instructional managers on the status of students, alone or in groups, summarizing exceptions for action.

It is difficult to find a teacher willing and patient enough to work with individual students to provide detailed practice on problems or exercises in such areas as basic mathematical and language skills. Tutoring bureaus at colleges attest to the need for such services. CAI provides this high volume of detailed, tedious (to a human) work for many students at once. The established success of drill-and-practice CAI in elementary schools is a notable example of the work breakthrough at the level of repetitive practice.

While there is increasing understanding of how to use computers to perform instructional work, the prices of computer equipment are still dropping rapidly, even during these inflationary times. CAI was oversold during the middle sixties, and overoptimistic claims have deserved much of the criticism they received. Past errors of overselling CAI should not be repeated. But so long as intensive individualization is a valid educational goal, the work potential of CAI, its increasing availability, and its decreasing costs make its expanded use likely.

PI: THE STATE OF THE ART

The programmed instruction movement hit the fields of education and training like a whirlwind in the early 1960s. Educators were told that here at last was a guaranteed method of teaching, and trainers seized on PI as a cost-effective method for increasing the performance capabilities of their charges. Striped textbooks and small steps became the order of the day and literally thousands of "programmes" began to flood the market. Small companies of programmers sprang up and almost anyone who had "taken" a programme began to write one. Guidance for the novice programmer was limited with only a few texts providing much help (for example, Markle's *Good Frames and Bad*).

The claims of programmers generally far outreached their skill, and the shelves began to fill with unused programmes that provided mute testimony to the fallacy that small steps and overt responding ensure effective instruction. The product definition of programmed instruction contributed to a rapid demise of the field. The easily recognized and reproduced features of format that were used as defining characteristics of programmed instruction deluded many into thinking they could be programmers. These same features deluded publishers into thinking that a book with "frames" is a programme. The calls for validation were often looked upon as little more than signs of weakness or lack of confidence on the part of overly systematic psychologists.

By the late 1960s and early 1970s, the realization that effective programmed instruction had to be the result of a systematic, and empirical development process had been added to the earlier experiences to instill a new maturity into the field. Publishers had seriously retrenched, with most of them leaving the programmed text business. The output of programmed materials had slowed to a trickle.

The military and industrial training communities had come through the 1960s with a relatively healthy respect for programmed instruction. This was due mainly to their contact with several professional groups (for example, the American Society for Training and Development, the National Society for Performance and Instruction, and the Association for Educational Communications and Technology), to their commitment to internal training departments, and to regulations or policies that outlined procedures and made "systems approaches" to training mandatory. Today the military and industrial communities continue to support a modern brand of programmed (validated) instruction. Many millions of dollars were expended in 1975 on programmed materials for the Training Extension Courses (TEC) of the U.S. Army alone. The TEC programme continues to flourish with an even greater expenditure expected in 1976.

Three Approaches to One Process

The process of developing instructional programmes

described earlier in this chapter is diagrammed in figure 8.1. Phase I of this process yields a complete list or hierarchy of objectives. Phase II results in the completed instructional materials, and Phase III yields a specification for revision that may result in a refinement of the objectives or a revision of the materials or both. There is considerable agreement concerning the need for an instructional development process which involves these phases. An analysis of current trends, however, reveals a plethora of specific methodologies, techniques, and models for implementing such an approach.

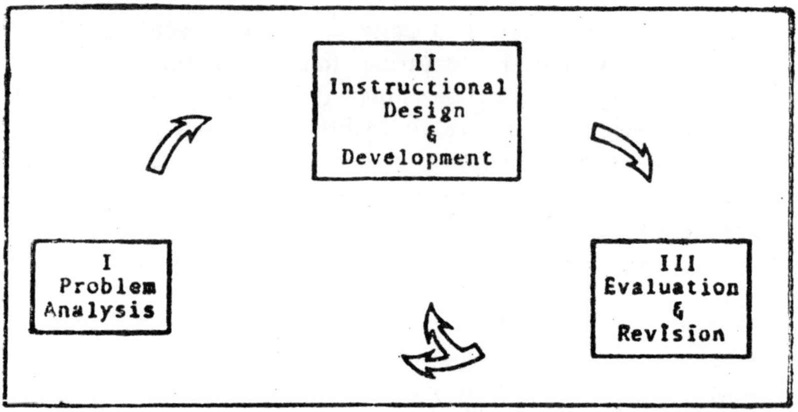

Fig. 8.1: Three basic phases in a systematic approach to instructional development.

Although some procedures for Phases I and III of the instructional development process differ, an analysis of most systematic models reveals considerable agreement. The major differences in technique and in attitudes toward instructional development are found in the activities of the design and development efforts of Phase II.

Three basic approaches or philosophies can be used to bring some order to the variation in the design and development phase of the systematic models that have been proposed. Models seem to focus on either empirical, artistic, or analytical approaches to the development of instructional materials.

The Empirical Approach

The empirical approach is probably the longest-lived and most written about. It is a product of the basic psychology laboratories that spawned programmed instruction in the late 1950s and 1960s. The Skinnerian (operant conditioning) model of observing student behaviour and of reinforcing successively closer approximations of desired performances has its analogue among programme developers. The developer produces frames, presents them to students, and observes reactions. Frames that do not produce desired behaviour are changed, and gradually the programme is "shaped" by the close interaction of developer and trial student. Gilbert describes the programming procedure as one in which you "take your first crude effort to the student." He describes a trial and error procedure in which "the important thing to remember is to keep varying your behaviour until you are successful." This procedure is repeated with several students until the programme is reaching desired levels of effectiveness. Gilbert predicts that "after fewer than ten tries you will have a programme which will teach 98 per cent of the students."

This much reliance on an empirical approach can have several problems, not the least of which are the inefficiencies in development and learning times that can result. The empirical approach provides little guidance as to the design (sequence, strategy, and the like) of the initial sequence of frames. Therefore, the initial sequence could be extremely ineffective and provide little that can eventually be used to teach students. Inefficiencies can also be a problem on the learner's side of the table. The initial programme may not contain all that is needed for learning; or it may contain considerably more explanation, practice, or other verbiage than the student will need. The problem is that the empirical approach provides limited data concerning such inefficiencies. Lean programming and related techniques have been developed in order to produce programmes that present just enough material to teach, and no more. The advice to programmers is to start with only a few frames and add frames only where they are needed.

In general, the small-group tryout and reliance on individual and small-group data advocated by those using empirical approaches are not only reasonable but are also extremely important components of other approaches. Nonetheless, reliance on these techniques during the design and development phases places considerable strain on the talents of the programmer. He must be extremely observant, must establish excellent rapport with trial students, and must be able to make both content and strategy decisions based on individual data. History indicates that few good programmers can use this model effectively.

The Artistic Approach

The artistic approach arises from a totally different intellectual base. It involves heavy reliance on communications concepts and technology. This approach assumes that subject matter experts or teachers know what to teach and how to teach, but that they need assistance in delivering their instruction to the learner. The emphasis, therefore, is on the design and development of effective delivery systems or instructional media. The techniques and procedures used either are intuitive or stem from the literature concerning the medium being used (for example, television, film, graphics). The products of this approach are generally judged on the basis of their aesthetic appeal.

The artistic approach is by far the most widely used approach to instructional development. Publishers, film makers, and educational television studios are generally staffed by persons who come from the editing, layout, film production, or educational and broad-cast television communities. These persons tend to assume an artistic model when confronted with instructional development projects. Materials developed through an artistic approach are usually not systematic in the sense of being directed at specific objectives and evaluated with measures of student performance. Certainly much instruction is developed in an unsystematic manner. The users of artistic approaches, however, are the most likely to abandon the three-step process outlined above in favour of less systematic procedures.

For the true artist, the medium is the message and evaluation and validation based upon student performance are of little importance. In most cases, validation can be extremely expensive for those who use the artistic approach. Since the bulk of the dollar investment in instructional development goes into the production of "hard copy" media, even small changes can double or triple the cost.

Whenever major emphasis is placed on hardware technology or its design and development, the artistic approach is easily adopted. This has been true in the field of CAI. Institutions or organizations that have focused on the development of interactive graphics, simulations, and gaming have tended to ignore principles of systematic instructional development and to focus on the affective and aesthetic qualities of their product.

The Analytic Approach

The analytic approach is based on the belief that instructional science has developed to the point where prescriptive rules can be derived and used to develop effective instructional materials that have a high probability of first-trial success. This approach assumes that the subject matter expert may know what there is to teach but needs help in determining exactly what, how much, and how to teach. The approach emphasizes systematic anylysis of instructional outcomes and content, and the design of effective instructional strategies. The procedures used are based on prescriptive propositions developed through basic and applied research on human learning and the instructional process. Products of this approach are judged on the degree to which they work to help students achieve prescribed objectives. But the goal is to predict probable effectiveness of particular instructional programmes in advance of extensive tryout and revision.

The analytic approach can be likened to the approach taken by the architect. The architect knows that carpenters and bricklayers may subtly modify his plans, but he still uses a host of conventions and prescriptive rules (eighteen-inch centers, stress models, and the like) to develop a blueprint that, when followed exactly, has a very high probability of resulting in a house of the desired quality, durability, and aesthetic appeal. Similarily, the instructional developer using an analytic approach applies the output of instructional science to develop an instructional blueprint that, if followed, has a high probability of meeting his goals in terms of affect and instructional effectiveness.

Generally speaking, we see the analytic approach offering the greatest hope of providing specific guidance to the instructional developer on the specific rules to apply in order to go from instructional objectives to effective instructional materials. This approach is the newest and least developed, yet its rate of progress and ultimate promise justify considerable excitement.

Proponents of the analytic approach have directed their efforts at solving problems in three major areas of concern: the selection and sequencing of content, the development of instructional strategies, and the selection or design of instructional delivery systems. To provide a basis for the attack on these problem areas, taxonomies of terms and concepts that could be used to describe instructional phenomena had to be developed. The taxonomies provide a basis for the analysis of instructional phenomena, the identification of instructional variables, and the precise communication of research results. Once developed, the taxonomies can be evaluated through research on relationships between instructional phenomena and instructional outcomes. These relationships, when stated in the form of propositions, become the prescriptive rules that can be used for developing instructional materials.

Attempts at developing systems (taxonomies) to describe instructional phenomena first concentrated on descriptions of classes or levels of learning outcomes. The pioneering effort by Bloom resulted in a taxonomy of educational objectives that, while historically important, was difficult to apply in the area of prescriptive rules for instructional design. Later taxonomies of instructional outcomes have been simpler and easier to use and have provided a basis for research and development on prescriptive rules. It is from these prescriptive rules that analytic instructional development models have been developed.

The propositions used in analytic approaches fall into two basic categories: those allowing diagnosis or prescriptions concerning content structures or sequences and those useful in diagnosing and prescribing instructional strategies and tactics.

Content analysis procedures. A variety of procedures have been developed for analyzing instructional outcomes or contents. These procedures are variously designed to aid the instructional developer in (a) selecting those objectives that should be taught from the myriad that could be taught, (b) determining the most effective instructional sequence, and (c) presenting instruction in such a way that it will be easily remembered and used by students.

Gagne's hierarchical task analysis focuses on the coordinate and subordinate relationships between tasks, or between terminal and enabling objectives. It provides the developer with a task structure that indicates what students should be able to do after instruction (terminal tasks or objectives) and what must be learned (enabling tasks or objectives) in order for the student to be able to perform satisfactorily. It also provides a hierarchy of tasks or objectives—a hierarchy that indicates prerequisite learning relationships usable in instructional sequencing. The entailment structure method of Pask, as well as the content analysis method proposed by Merrill, considers the structure of content and the desired behaviour of students separately in arriving at aids for the instructional developer.

Strategy analysis procedure. Methods for analyzing and prescribing instructional strategies fall into two basic categories —those derived from operant models of learning and those derived from cognitive or information processing models of the learning process. Proponents of an operant approach have developed methods that require analysis of the behavioural chains and the stimuli that signal the beginning and end points of those chains.

Merrill and his associates, Markle and Tiemann, Gagne and Briggs, and Gerlach and Ely have attempted to develop a set of principles that can be applied in the design and development of instructional materials. Each position begins with some classification scheme by which objectives can be classified and appropriate instructional strategies selected.

One of the most complete systems to date is that represented by the Instructional Strategy Diagnostic Profile (ISDP) developed by Merrill and Wood. The ISDP is based on a detailed system for classifying objectives and an extensive taxonomy of instructional variables. The ISDP is both diagnostic and prescriptive. It consists of five separate sets of evaluative statements that can be used to rate instructional strategies. The five sets of statements were generated from five analogous sets of prescriptive rules for the effective teaching of concepts and rules (principles). Each set of statements and rules is related to a hypothesis concerning instruction. The hypotheses deal with the role of consistency, learner control of strategy, the selection of instances for use in instructional sequences, the representation form (for example, object, symbol, picture) of instructional components, and the presentation of mathemagenic (comprehension-facilitating) information (for example, algorithms, heuristics, prompts, and the like). The profile has been used to predict the effectiveness of several sets of intructional materials, as measured by student performance on criterion tests. Early results, although limited because of restriction in the sample materials evaluated (that is, all had been developed systematically and were rated relatively effective) have shown high correlations (r=.80 to .90) between strategy ratings and programme effectiveness. The descrptive rules from which the profile was developed have also been used in a prescriptive manner to develop design and authoring guides for instructional developers, and these guides have been shown to be effective in streamlining the design and development process.

Systematic Delivery System Selection

The design and selection of instructional methods and

media have long been influenced by technological innovations, salesmanship, and political and economic constraints. Many attempts at classifying methods and media by capabilities have been made to provide some systematization of the process. But the categorization schemes have been all too general, have usually been of value only to the novice developer, and have been proven wrong-time and again by the creative developer who can mix methods and media to increase overall capability. For example, the statement that television cannot be interactive, allow for student practice or provide feedback is generally true until the energetic developer uses videotape players to present a variety of situations, stops the tape has, students respond, and then presents feedback to their responses.

As the analytic models have been developed and their associated taxonomies and rules have been refined, a broad base has been established from which more sophisticated media-selection algorithms can be developed. The most promising of such algorithms consider basic learning requirements, rules for selecting an effective strategy, and the level of learning to be achieved, as well as the more common considerations of display capabilities (for example, dynamics, graphics, audio). One such model was developed by a team of psychologists for the Navy's S-3A Air Crew Training Programme.

The model was developed after careful consideration of resource constraints, basic learning requirements, and the capabilities of specified instructional methods and media. The first step in the process was to analyze budget, facilities, and other constraints to determine a variety of delivery systems (for example, film, CAI, workbook, and the like) that could possibly be used on the project. Then an analysis of the basic instructional reqiurements for learning different types of objectives was completed, following the procedures of Merrill and Wood. This analysis was used in prescribing the components to instruction for various instructional strategies (again keyed to objective types) that could be built into the methods and media available for the project. Detailed specifications for methods and media were then developed. For example, a lecture method was designed that incorporates important components for concept and principle learning objectives (for example, sets of examples, opportunities for student practice, instructor feedback on practice, and the like). The methods and media, specified in this way, provide an instructional capability considerably greater than "traditional" use of these same delivery systems. In all, ten "high capability" methods were specified for this project. These were then analyzed as to their display capability appropriateness for use with different objective types and a method/media decision model was developed.

The model is presented as a flow chart by Hymes et al. to guide the decisions of the designer. It can be used to select from among the specified methods and media those that are most appropriate for teaching a particular kind of objective. The developer, therefore, must have his objectives specified and classified before using the model.

This model, although it has some generality, is valid only as long as the specifications for the methods and media are followed. It does not apply to the usual "artistic" conventions for using these same media. Further, the model does not concern itself with costs except before the fact (for example, in selecting media that will be used as possible end points for the selection algorithms). The design of complete media selection models continues, and there is much work to be done. Models like the one discussed above, however, are a definite step in the right direction in that they focus on learning and teaching requirements of specific learning situations as major factors in method and media selection.

CAI: THE STATE OF THE ART

Historical Notes

The literature on CAI is voluminous. It emanates from a variety of disciplines and from many perspectives within and across these disciplines. During the 1960s, much of it was found primarily in technical reports, informal newsletters, and the like, rather than in referenced journals or books. This situation is slowly changing as studies involving CAI become more professional and editorial policies become more accepting.

Four Pioneers

This chapter is not the place for a history of CAI. Other sources may be consulted to piece together this short history. For the purposes of this chaper, only four centers where early work (prior to 1965) established trends will be mentioned: Dartmouth College, the University of Illinois, Stanford University, and the IBM Corporation.

Dartmouth College. The BASIC language and time-sharing system, developed at Dartmouth College, made computing easy to learn and more readily available to students and teachers. Software and applications that have led to sales of minicomputers and microcomputers to schools today trace their history to this development. The adjunctive use of CAI in many disciplines from elementary school through graduate school represents by far the heaviest use of CAI as defined here. All of the better established computer companies have a version of BASIC available. Some of them, notably Digital Equipment Corporation and Hewlett-Packard, also have catalogs describing libraries of adjunctive curriculum packages consisting of printed manuals and interactive computer programmes, primarily written in BASIC.

University of Illinois. In 1959, Donald Bitzer conceived PLATO I and undertook to implement it on a 1954 vintage Illiac I computer. PLATO is an acronym for Programmed Logic for Automated Teaching Operations. Since 1959, PLATO has gone through four versions. The present version, PLATO IV, is a computer-assisted instruction network utilizing a large-scale computer (CDC 6500) with 900 graphics terminals attached. Most of the terminals are in Illinois, but some are as far away as San Diego and Boston. They are located in universities, junior clloges, elementary schools, military training bases, and employee training centers.

Much has been written about PLATO and need not be repeated here. Early publications and models from the PLATO project influenced the field indirectly, and the network of 900 terminals now connected to the Illinois computer brings a rich interactive graphics capability to many users who, because PLATO is a network. can share ideas and materials, conduct research, and train the next generation of CAI developers and users.

Also at the University of Illinois, Lawrence Stolurow developed an ealy CAI system called SOCRATES. Because of his familiarity with training research and programmed instruction, his early research and writing influence the develoment of the instructional science view of CAI. SOCRATES did not survive as a viable hardware alternative. But PLATO did, and is discussed in more detail below.

Stanford University. The Institute for mathematical Studies in the Social Sciences, headed by Patrick Suppes and Richard Atkinson, provided early leadership that continues today. Two early contributions were the design, in cooperation with IBM, of the IBM 1500 CAI system, and the development, demonstration, and propagation of drill-and-practice systems in elementary mathematics and reading. This early work is well documented. The drill-and-practice concept has been validated by others. Vinsonhaler and Bass report the results of ten studies using Stanford's drill-and-practice programmes. These data show that ten to twenty minutes of drill per day at a teletype or at a simple cathode ray tube terminal will produce significant gains in the mathematical skills of elementary school children. Such programmes are also successful with deaf and disadvantaged students. While drill-and-practice programmes have been implemented widely, the largest CAI network for school children is in Chicago, where 1,000 terminals serve over sixty elementary schools. The justification is effectiveness. Disadvantaged children who are slipping behind each month (averaging .74 months gain on standardized tests for each month of work) strat to catch up (averaging

1.1 months gain per month) when given a few minutes a day on the terminal.

International Business Machine (IBM). There is no wish here to imply that the products of one computer company are superior to the products of others because of the influence of early contributions. Even a brief review of early influences on the field, however, must include IMB's development of the Coursewriter language and the 1500 system.

Seeing a potential market of vast size and social significance, IBM committed a substantial investment of capital and human talent to the task of realizing CAI. This investment has not yet yielded the expected return, but unlike smaller companies that made similar premature investments, IBM was large enough to absorb the losses and consolidate gains. In the mid 1960s, IBM entered into joint relationships with several universities—Pennsylvania State University, Florida State University, and the University of Texas. These agreements involved research on early typewriter-terminal systems using IBM's Coursewriter language. With Stanford University, IBM had meanwhile developed the 1500 system, with sophisticated displays providing cathode ray tubes with both limited graphics and textual display, computer-controlled random access image projection, and audio. Light-pen and keyboard response entry were available. About twenty-five of the IBM 1500 systems were placed in schools, colleges, military training centers, and industrial training centers. Good maintenance and training support was given to the users.

By 1970, IBM management had withdrawn the research and development, marketing, and production support from the 1500 system and has since allowed the systems in the field to dwindle almost to extinction. Nevertheless, a great deal of knowledge was generated by the intense research and development activity around these systems, and many people were trained in CAI as a result. The Association for Development of Computer-based Instructional Systems, a professional society that now publishes its own journal, was originally an

IBM 1500 users group. The designers of the TICCIT instructional model described below were influenced by five years of research and development using the IBM 1500 in a learning resource center environment.

IBM users of System 360 and 370 Coursewriter still constitute the largest single group of users of tutorial CAI. The Coursewriter author language has influenced a host of newer CAI author languages. Yet, because of the narrow conception instruction and learning strategies inherent in the primitive commands and intrinsic branching in Coursewriter, this influence has probably passed the peak of its usefulness.

Boom and Decline

The year 1965 marked the beginning of a boom in CAI. Great expectations for profits filled the minds of industrial leaders. Computer companies were merging with publishing companies, in anticipation of a new educational market. Under the regime of President Johnson, federal aid for research and development in instruction flowed freely, and many projects were started in schools, colleges, universities, and industrial laboratories. Seven years later, however, the federal funding had begun to dry up, the hope for a new educational market had not materialized, and the computer companies had either retrenched or gone out of business. By 1975, all of the publishing companies that had invested heavily in CAI had either withdrawn from the field or had sharply curtailed their activities.

CAI had been oversold, and the complexity of mastering its three technologies greatly underestimated. The problems inherent in the sociology of change in educational institutions had not been anticipated and were not well understood.

The PLATO and TICCIT Projects

In 1971 the National Science Foundation (NSF) funded two major demonstration projects. The PLATO project was funded to stimulate the completion of the PLATO IV hardware and software, and to develop courseware for community colleges, elementary schools, and universities in order to demonstrate and test PLATO. The TICCIT (Time-shared Interactive Computer-Controlled Information Television) project was funded at the same time to develop, test, and demonstrate a minicomputer-based CAI system supporting 128 colour television display terminals and delivering courses in freshman and remedial mathematics and English composition in two community colleges. The Educational Testing Service was given an independent contract to evaluate the effectiveness, technology, and costs of the two systems. Having observed the limited progress on many of the federally funded CAI projects undertaken during the middle and late 1960s, NSF provided more substantial funding for a longer period of time. Both projects were given five years to deliver and demonstrate their alternative hardware, software, and courseware systems, and to be evaluated by the Educational Testing Service.

PLATO. The main emphasis of the PLATO project has not been to develop a computer-based curriculum but rather to develop a comprehensive set of hardware devices and the requisite software to operate them. Perhaps the most significant hardware development has been the invention of the PLATO IV terminal. Unlike the familiar television tube, which must be refreshed sixty times per second to maintain a visible image, the PLATO IV plasma display panel remembers information displayed on it and requires no refreshing. The terminal contains a 22-centimeter square plasma panel consisting of 512×512 display positions, each of which may be turned bright orange by passing a current through neon gas trapped beneath each point. The display has high resolution, and the hardware and software developed to drive the display allows for flexible graphics capabilities, including selective erase, creation of special characters, animations, and alternative symbolic alphabets (for example, Russian or Chinese).

The TUTOR language, developed at the University of Illinois to assist the authoring of courseware, has graphics command that allow for large-sized writing, figure rotation, and an extensive set of graph-generating commands. TUTOR also has extensive calculational, branching, and response-handling capabilities, and is considered by CAI experts to be a versatile programming language for generating interesting interactions on a graphics terminal.

In addition to the graphics capabilities of the plasma panel, each PLATO terminal may be equipped with a pneumatically driven random access microfiche projector. This retrieves one of 256 colour images within a quarter of a second and projects it on the back of the translucent plasma panel. The terminals may also be equipped with a touch panel, which has been used to teach reading to elementary school children. A magnetic disc that provides random access to twenty-two minutes of audio messages has also been developed, but has not seen wide use. Because of the availability of PLATO terminals over telephone lines, the PLATO network now has a large number of users. These users have developed CAI programmes in a variety of disciplines, at all educational levels, and in military and industrial training. Because of the flexibility and reliability of the PLATO hardware and software, and because it is a network that can reach many users throughout this and other countries, PLATO's influence will probably increase during the late 1970s. Bitzer has plans for adding another large computer for managing 1,000 more users after the first 950 terminals are installed on the present system. In the 1980s, a communications network servicing one million or more users and communicating by satellite is envisioned.

TICCIT. The TICCIT system was conceived by the MITRE Corporation in 1969 as a stand-alone minicomputer-based configuration of primarily off-the-shelf hardware elements. Plans at that time were to utilize 128 television terminals with digital graphics capability for computer-managed elementary school instruction. In the late 1970s emphasis shifted to providing support for mathematics and English instruction at community colleges. The user interface specified required an "authoring system" with both hardware and software elements and a "learner control command language" to facilitate student interactions and promote self-directed, enjoyable learning. MITRE selected hardware that was low in cost in 1971. The costs have continued to decrease. The terminal is a twelve-inch Sony colour television set modified to be refreshed by a solid state device located centrally. Characters can be modified "on the fly" to produce any character set or to compose any graphic, whether describable easily by an elementary function or as a digitized version of free-form artwork. A modified television camera and graphics entry system scans and digitizes the artwork, which is then stored centrally. The graphics editor permits authors to plot any elementary or parametric function and to edit these and the digitized artwork at will. Displays are composed on a grey background in seven brilliant colours. The crisp digital colour displays are a hallmark of TICCIT.

Authoring systems have taken a variety of forms. The graphics camera and editor is only one part of the user interface designed to make the TICCIT computers easy for authors to use. The authoring system is more than an "authoring language" such as TUTOR or Coursewriter. Such languages are written to control the basic hardware and logical capabilities of a given CAI system. They do not include in their semantics the fundamental concepts of systematic instructional development, such as those described above as the analytic approach. An authoring system is an integrated set of computer programmes, formatted manuscripts, and management procedures designed to facilitate the various steps in the instructional development process.

MITRE developed the operating systems, compilers, and related software for use by authors and students. Brigham Young University developed software to permit data entry and editing, graphics entry and editing, report generation for teachers and authors, and other user utility programmes. Manuscript formats were developed for use by authors in producing "maps," tests, objectives, rules, examples, practice problems, and helps and the same formats were embodied in the authoring software. Similar manuscript formats and on line embodiments for coders were developed to provide for display specifications. file creation, and answer analysis coding.

This authoring system resulted in the production of a large body of courseware at Brigham Young University. Starting with a review of arithmetic, the mathematics materials extended from a review of fractions through elementary and intermediate algebra and elementary functions (except trigonometry). The English materials provide two catalog courses, a remedial grammar and mechanics course and a freshman composition course, in which the teacher's role is vital in generating ideas and grading writing assignments, but not in teaching structure or editing skills. Regardless of the success of the TICCIT community college courseware, the authoring system approach first implemented on TICCIT appears to be proliferating. A commercial company (courseware, Inc., of Orem, Utah) has taught this approach to a number of customers in the military services, industry, and colleges. The training has resulted in the production of tens of thousands of segments (objectives) of instruction, some on CAI and some in workbook or mediated forms.

It is useful to consider TICCIT's learner-control language in the context of historical developments in the field of computer-assisted instruction. Most early work in CAI can be divided into four programme categories: drill-and-practice, tutorial programmes, simulations and games, and use of computer terminals in problem solving. Three of these categories—drill-and practice, simulation, and problem solving —are adjunctive applications in which the computer is a supplement to the main instruction, provided by teachers. Tutorial programmes could also be used in an adjunctive mode; they were designed, however, to handle a heavier burden of instruction, usually involving concepts and rules. Concepts and rules characterize most instruction above the junior high school level. By contrast, the objectives of drill-and-practice instructions focus on memorization skills. Simulations and games focus on the application of concepts, rules, and information rather than the initial acquisition of them. The early research revealed that considerable motivation accompanied work with simulation, games, and problem solving. By contrast, students caught in the network of preprogrammed branches that comprised a tutorial programme expressed less motivation and enjoyment.

At the University of Texas considerable work was done on earner control in an effort to capture some of the motivation inherent in the use of problem-solving languages and simulations. Simultaneously, work was being done at Brigham Young University by Merrill and his coworkers on synthesizing the literature on concept and rule learning to provide a taxonomy of theorems for teaching concepts and rules. The cybernetics models developed at Texas and the instructional psychology ,theorems daveloped at Brigham Young University ultimately came together in the TICCIT learner-control language.

The British cyberneticist, Gordon Pask, provided basic concepts for the design of the TICCIT learner-control language, Pask's work, reviewed in more detail below, led to the concept of three levels of discourse a concept liberally adapted by the designers of TICCIT, so that the resemblance between TICCIT and Pask's conception is now slight. However conceived, the concept of three levels of discourse affords a powerful model for designing man-machine dialogues, and others have used the concept as well. For the purposes of TICCIT, it was useful to think of three levels of discourse between student and machine: Level 0, Level 1 and Level 2. At each level is a language: L0, L1, or L2. L1 and L2 are metalanguages for discourse about the next lower level language. At Level 0 in any computer-assisted instruction system there exist commands that students can use for responding to questions and to the solicited decision requests intrinsic to any preprogrammed network, such as a tutorial programme. Student control is limited by the author's sequence strategy.

L1 is a metalanguage for talking about the strategies that the author may have used at Level 0. In learner control, L1 gives the student control over sequence strategy. A stretegy consists of at least four phases: a survey phase, a learning tactics phase, an evaluation tactics phase, and a reviewed phase. TICCIT provides general commands to control all aspects of strategy. Most of these are implemented as special keys on a learner control panel.

At Level 2 we can conceive of a metalanguage for talking about L1 strategies in general. A Level 2 language would allow student-machine dialogue concerning general aspects of strategy and tactics that are independent of content. How well is a student strategy working? What other strategies are available to the student? In the TICCIT system, an advisor programme collects data on student performance. It uses colour coding on structural representations (called MAPS) of the course, unit, and lesson hierarchies to indicate which segments, lessons, and units the student has passed (green), which ones he has failed (red), and which ones are in progress (yellow). The student may solicit status information at any time by pressing the MAP key and observing the colours, and by pressing the ADVICE key for more specific status information. General sugestions concerning the sequence the student might take through lesson and unit MAPS and concerning evaluation and learning tactics are also available from the advisor. The advisor also interjects unsolicited advice on strategy and tactics.

It is important to recognize that all the major CAI systems developed over the past twelve years, with the exception of TICCIT, have worked primarily at Level 0. The drill and tutorial programmes written in existing CAI languages have only occasional instances of Level 1 and Level 2 functions. This description applies to all the major CAI languages, including Coursewriter and TUTOR (the PLATO language). The description does not apply to the use of APL (IBM's array-oriented language based on a powerful rotation for applied mathematics), BASIC (the most widely used language for student programming) and other languages used for solving student problems. Here the student has complete control over the programmes that he himself writes. These problem-solving applications, however, are not appropriate for mainline instruction in concepts and rules, nor do they provide Level 2 support to help students develop better strategies.

Development of a set of student commands, especially in the areas of survey tactics and learning tactics, required the application of research and theorems from instructional psychology related to the acquisition of concepts and rules. The taxonomy developed by Merrill served as the basis for the design of student commands. It was desired that student commands should manipulate important instructional variables. A further constraint was that the student would not be given a control command in an area where he had no information to guide his choice. The commands were implemented as buttons on a special learner-control keyboard, and as choice points on MAP displays on the Sony television terminal.

PLATO and TICCIT differ substantially in terms of all three technologies (hardware, software, and courseware), in total concept, and in philosophy. The major hardware difference comes in the mode of solving the data communications problem. PLATO is a network and distributes terminals to users at any location by means of telephone lines. TICCIT, like the old IBM 1500, is designed to centralize terminals in a learning resource center. Since centralized terminals can share hardware (for example, graphics, charcter, generation, audio) instead of duplicating it at each terminal, TICCIT terminals are considerably less expensive than PLATO terminals, but lack the dynamic graphics (except on videotape), large computer power, and network advantages of PLATO.

The authoring models of PLATO and TICCIT provided a sharp contrast initially, although each project has begun to adopt the strengths of the others in the authoring area. The TICCIT project evolved an analytic PI process and used differentiated terms of authors. These concepts, and learner control, were designed into the very hardware and software of TICCIT. The TUTOR language ignores the semantics of any particular instructional model, and of the PI process, and leaves the authors free to generate any strategy using a powerful and versatile computer language. This freedom typically results in the artistics approach, exploiting the dynamic graphics and calculation power of PLATO as message rather than medium.

Alternative Theoretical Positions

Design Science and Technology of Instruction

Hilgard has provided a synthesizing framework for alternate theories of learning and instruction. He showed a continuum ranging from basic laberatory learning studies, having no immediate relevance to instruction, through field applications in the classroom having immediate relevance. He placed the programmed instruction approach centrally, under technological research and development instead of under pure research, referring to the empirical and artistic approaches to programmed instruction that predominated at that time. The programmed instruction process using an analytical approach, as outlined earlier in this chapter, encompasses four of the six stages of Hilgard's continuum, from the use of data from human verbal learning and concept formation through tryout in a normal classroom.

Because of its scope of application, its use of research data, its "falsifiability," and the possibility of its being framed in a coherent alternative philosophy of instructional science that breaks down the dichotomy between basic research and educational practice, the programmed instruction process using an analytic approach represents a distinct theoretical alternative. This alternate philosophy would view learning and instruction as a design science instead of a natural science. Simon has dwelt on the possibilities of artificial sciences and has urged that the concepts of this artificial science of design should be a part of the liberal education of all professionals.

Simon's distinction between a natural science and an artificial science is provocative. The term "design science" will be used in this chapter despite the precedence of Simon's terms. A natural science deals with natural objects and phenomena while a design science deals with artificial or man-made objects and phenomena. The principal distinction, however, is that a natural science deals with efficient causes and material causes while a design science deals with goals and values (final causes) and the plans (formal causes) that motivate the shape of a design. The distinction is clarified by Aristotle's four-fold classification of cause. A natural science deals with the material cause (that is, the composition of the materials in a natural object) and the efficient cause (that is, the sequence of mechanistically describable actions and the causal relationships among these actions). Adapting Aristotle's concept of formal cause to instructional design, we identify the pattern or blueprint (course, unit, and lesson specifications). His final cause corresponds to the training goals and the related and overarching set of values that motivate and shape the design.

A further distinction is that natural sciences are descriptive, whereas design sciences are prescriptive. That is, given the needs, goals, and operational design objectives, what prescriptive statements will allow us to achieve these design objectives under constraints of cost and time? Prescription can occur through the use of the analytic model described above, through the use of simulators to preassess alternatives, and through the use of optimization methods and other quantitative analytic techniques, such as Atkinson's, discussed below. Instead of repeating the term "design science and technology of instruction" to characterize this approach, we shall use the term "designtech."

A Decision-Theoretic Analysis of Instruction

Atkinson has articulated an approach to the derivation of optimal instructional strategies that utilizes decision-theoretic analysis. The approach is applicable to a variety of instructional decision situations, but in particular to the derivation of sequencing strategies in CAI. There are four criteria that must be satisfied in Atkinson's approach to a theory of instruction: (a) a model of the learning process must exist; (b) admissible instructional actions must be specified; (c) instructional objectives must be specified; and (d) a measurement scale must exist that permits costs to be assigned to each of the instructional actions, and values or payoffs to the achievement of each overall objective.

When a precise definition can be given for each of these four elements, then it is generally possible to derive an optimal instructional strategy, using powerful analytic tools recently developed. A model or theory of instruction defined in this manner proves to be a special case of what has come to be known as *optimal control theory* in the mathematical and engineering literature. The solution of instructional decision problems defined within this framework leads to the selection of the instructional policy or strategy (from several specified alternatives) that will yield positive gains and reduce possible costs in an optimal or near-optimal manner.

The TICCIT learner control model, a reflection of the "designtech" approach, is a distinct alternative to the optimization model of Atkinson, and to other approaches that are primarily programme controlled rather than student controlled. The TICCIT approach posits that important gains can be achieved in learning strategies and in attitudes of approach and responsibility. These objectives are at least as important as the objectives of efficiency, effectiveness, and the minimization of costs sought by the optimization approach. Giving the student the choices inherent in a learner-control command language may be a necessary prerequisite to the achievement of these other educational goals, and need not sacrifice mastery and efficiency. The contrast is this; Programme control may be shown ultimately to be applicable to complex cognitive learning, such as that involved in the mathematics and English courseware on the TICCIT system. Even so, those who espouse the learner-control and the "designtech" alternative would be loath to adopt programme control insofar as it precludes the opportunity for student growth in areas of personality separate from the acquisition of specific content objectives.

For teaching vocabulary lists and other paired associate skills, however, it may be inadvisable to give students a choice over the detailed and precise sequences of individual items. In this application there would appear to be no conflict between learner-control approaches and optimization approaches. Learner control could be used for survey tactics, evaluation tactics, and for learning tactics related to the learning of concepts and rules, and programme control for the sequencing of individual items in long lists. Optimization procedures could also be used at the general levels of the system for the scheduling of students to alternate media, as Atkinson has demonstrated elsewhere.

Artificial Intelligence

The general goal of artificial intelligence (AI) research has been to emulate with computerized systems the intelligence exhibited by humans and to create machine extensions of human processes deemed to be intelligent. AI research and theory has affected CAI in at least two ways. One way is by metaphor to the kind of thought processes exemplified by AI; the other is by mechanism—the production of intelligent computerized teaching systems.

The metaphorical application of AI. The TURTLE project at MIT, directed by Papert, is beginning to affect many CAI projects because of its philosophy. This philosophy is consonant with some of the basic propositions that have emerged from artificial intelligence research. Some of these basic propositions: are (a) to exhibit intelligence, a computer programme must have a formal representation of the problem domain; (b) the computer programme must have a set of heuristics that can guide trial and error; (c) it must have a way of detecting errors in its tentative attempts to solve a problem, and it must have a way of correcting those errors; and (d) it must also have a way of incorporating the knowledge gained through experience with the class of problems and of using this knowledge to shorten the solution process in new problems. Why should students not have the same opportunities and characteristics shown to enhance the performance of supposedly intelligent computer programmes? Papert thinks they should. He feels that students should be given the opportunity to build models, both in a formal language and in their heads, of various kinds of information processing sequences. Students should be given formal languages to enable them to represent these models, as well as tools to help them "debug" their own models and procedures. They should learn good debugging techniques, such as how to formulate simple but critical test cases. A student should be able to feel that, even though he may not have an adequate model at one point, he can make a better model through intelligent effort and the application of trial and error debugging procedures. This approach provides a strong contrast to the helplessness engendered by the prevalent notions in our culture about aptitudes and gifts related to mathematics and other forms of learning. Instead of this helplessness, the student should, through being given creative experiences with formal systems he can manipulate, develop confidence in his own ability to model processes of interest.

Papert has attempted to achieve some of these general goals by teaching children a version of computational geometry called "Turtle geometry." Students are taught to use a programmable robot called a Turtle, which maneuvers about on paper with its pen up or down, to draw geometric figures. By controlling the movements of the Turtle and the figures that it draws, students gain a feeling of control over the processes of constructing geometric patterns and figures. They come to understand the computation underlying the processes, for they must programme each algorithm for producing the Turtle's movements, using the simple language called LOGO. When the Turtle does not do as the student intends, the student is able to debug the programme and improve the model. Minsky has commented on the absence of such techniques as mental modeling and debugging in the curriuclum of schools: "This is not because educators have ignored the possibility of mental models' but because they simply had no effective way before the beginning of work on simulation of thought processes to describe, construct, and test such ideas.

Artificially Intelligent Tutors. Early attempts to build intelligence into CAI tutors were more interesting for their promise than for their achievement. Even the influential paper by Carbonell illustrated the promise of this technique with an instructional paradigm of little efficacy (asking questions and getting answers about specific geographical facts related to South American geography). What Carbonell did demonstrate was a question-answering system that permitted mixed initiative dialogues; that is, the dialogue exchanges can be initiated either by the student or by the computer. What information is presented by the computer depends on the model of the subject matter and on the depth of information already covered by the student. Carbonell's original system to teach geography is now being extended to embody various tutorial strategies.

The most impressive artificial intelligence-based CAI system now developed is the system called SOPHIE (Sophisticated Instructional Environment). This system was designed to provide a simulated electronic trouble shooting trainning laboratory interaction. The SOPHIE programme makes possible a mixed initiative CAI interchange but, unlike earlier versions, SOPHIE uses several representations of subject matter and has inferencing procedures designed for each of these representations. The system contains an English language processor, a semantic interpreter, an electronic circuit simulator, and a semantic network. SOPHIE can randomly generate an easy or hard fault in a simulated circuit. The student then can ask in English for measurements at any test point in the circuit. The student may ask his questions in rather informal English, of the sort that can occur in a casual conversation between people working on devices in an electronics repair shop. The language interpreter uses previous information from the student to "disambiguate" his casual comments. The computer can provide the student with the simulated measurements he asks for in this informal version of English. It can also query him about his hypotheses and check whether they are consistent with the information previously given. All in all, the reading of a protocol of dialogue between a student and the SOPHIE programme gives one the eeric feeling that a rather sophisticated and knowledgeable tutor is at work with the student.

SOPHIE is promising but requires much more extensive testing with students. The modeling procedures and natural language procedures used in SOPHIE also have implications for simplifying and upgrading the authoring of mixed initiative instructional dialogues in CAI.

Cybernetic Theory and Methodology

The last alternative theoretical position to be discussed bears some resemblance to AI modeling procedures. Unlike these procedures, that worked out by Goldon Pask in England is based on a comprehensive cybernetic theory, whereas the applications of AI to CAI in the United States have primarily had the purpose of engineering AI into specific applications to training. Pask's work is not well understood in this country, perhaps because of the extreme novelty of his concepts. In addition, it has been difficult to obtain a sufficiently complete set of his papers. This latter problem should be alleviated with the recent publication of two books summarizing Pask's experimental and theoretical work over the past decade. Additional volumes are promised.

Pask attacks the natural science model that is at the foundation of psychological experimentation. In the standard psychological experiment, there is a clear distinction between observer and organism (or subject). The observer pretends to be objective and not influence the outcomes. The variables are usually changed singly, and the effects are noted. This paradigm runs into trouble when the variables are strongly related and when the organism changes or adapts while the experiment is in progress. Obviously this is what happens in an episode in which the student learns anything substantial.

Pask redefines a psychological experiment as a conversation between two or more participants on a series of topics that form a conversational domain. One participant is the subject; the other may be a machine or a person acting as the experimenter's agent. An experiment seen as a conversation fits what Pask calls a "normative" paradigm. In this paradigm, the experimenter negotiates an experimental contract in a meta-language. This is an observational language for talking about experiments, describing the system in which the experiment will be conducted, prescribing actions to be taken to pose and test hypotheses, and negotiating the contract for the experiment.

The participant must agree to speak an object language throughout the course of the experiment. This object language is to be used inside a cybernetic learning environment. Because of the complexity of this environment, it usually involves some kind of complex electronic equipment. The object language has certain of the qualities of natural language. For example, it allows commands and questions of a certain form. Unlike natural language, it is formally stratified into an upper level and a lower level. The upper level is used for commands to the student to learn and requests for explanation by the student and the lower level is used for commands and questions about the building of models within the cybernetic system. The construction of models amounts to a practical explanation of what the student has learned. (Compare the model-building activities of the TURTLE project discussed earlier). Given the contract between subject and experimenter to speak in precise languages, the knowledge and understanding of the experimenter and the student can be brought into the public arena. This conversational procedure for exhibiting learning and problem-solving strategies as observable behaviours is called Cooperative Externalization Technique. For Pask, then, an experiment is seen as a conversation between two or more participants within a well-defined conversational domain, with cooperative agreements to make aspects of the conversation explicit and measurable.

The conversational domain in which an experiment or learning episode takes place is specified by a large grid showing subject matter topics and their relationships. It is similar in some ways to Gagne's learning hierarchies and the maps of the TICCIT system. Pask calls this grid an entailment structure. The procedure for developing the entailment structure, however, is much more formal and systematic than procedures for developing learning hierarchies. It involves six steps, starting with a discussion with the subject matter expert, going through a series of manipulations based on graph theory, and ending in the entailment structure, the final product with which the student interacts. Using a large representation of an entailment structure developed for teaching elementary probability (called CASTE), Pask and his colleagues have conducted research to test his theory. Using this large grid, the student can specify goals—that is, the topics and the related performance capabilities he wishes to achieve. The nodes on the entailment structure convey status information as the student works. Signal lights indicate whether the node is a member of the set of topics the student is currently engaged in learning and whether the node is understood.

Understanding is demonstrated by both verbal and non-verbal procedures. The verbal procedure involves a verbal conversation between the student and the experimenter in which the student "teaches back" by explaining the subject to the experimenter. This externalizes concept reproduction and allows the experimenter and student to compare their explanations. The student also demonstrates his knowledge by creating a model. In the system built to teach probability a "Stat lab" is provided as a formal modeling facility for a strict conversation about probability. The student demonstrates topic relations by model-building activities that simulate real world statistical experiments.

Because of the breadth and novelty of the theory, Pask's approach is not strictly comparable to the other three theoretical positions (that is, designtech, optimization, and artificial intelligence) discussed above. Some comparative comments can be made, however. There are many superficial similarities between Pask's CASTE system and the TICCIT system, which is an embodiment of the designtech position. The map structures and their corresponding externalization of survey tactics and review tactics bear a definite resemblance to Pask's entailment structures. The maps, however, are developed by a rather pragmatic analysis of component behaviours, not by Pask's rigorous use of logic and graph theory. Pragmatically, it remains to be seen whether students may not learn about as well using maps developed by this less formal procedure. Theoretically, however, it makes a great difference, since an entailment structure is related to a model of the student himself. In Pask's system the entailment structure involves a set of relations between topics that can be expressed by some ordered combination of relational operators. The entailment structure, then, is a model of the same transformations as the cognitive operations that a student (or more generally, the "psychological individual") is assumed to have in his mental repertoire, but the transformations are not assumed to be identical with these cognitive operations. The TICCIT maps do not have this depth of theory underlying them. They are seen as pragmatic representations of what the student must accomplish—representations which enable him through survey tactics to plan an attack, and through the advisor to see what he has accomplished and where he is weak. The maps have a pragmatic utility for the author in that they structure the authoring process and allow this process to be monitored and managed.

TICCIT's evaluation procedures (tests available from the maps and items in the practice files) are also much more pragmatic and less theory-oriented than Pask's evaluation procedures. The combination of Pask's teach-back and modeling facility appears to be more powerful (but much more costly) than the sequential testing procedures used in TICCIT tests, or the simple mastery tests used in most CAI courseware in this country, except in the AI community.

Pask's system does not lay heavy stress on the careful design of instructional sequences or interactions to teach a particular topic represented in an entailment structure. The printed materials that the student may read in connection with mastering a given node are witness to this. In this area, the "designtech" approach seems to have some advantages. The analytic approach described in Section II has been cross-validated in the production of a large number of instructional materials in CAI, workbooks, slides, tapes, and lectures. The

Instructional Strategies Diagnostic Profile is provocative of additional research and more elaborate theory building in the second phase of the PI process.

There are not as many points of contact between Pask's approach and the optimization procedure developed by Atkinson. The philosophies of science underlying Pask's approach and much of Atkinson's research appear radically different. Nevertheless, optimization is theoretically neutral and appears powerful as a technique for developing instructional sequences at the microscopic level—that is, within a node on Pask's entailment structure, or as a technique for optimizing the use of instructional resources in the institutional environment which houses a CAI system.

It would appear that the Pask theory of strict conversations might provide an overall theoretical framework for the mixed initiative dialogues now being implemented by the AI community. The AI community could also be of great service in providing a wide variety of modelling facilities analogous to Pask's statistical laboratory in which nonverbal understanding could be demonstrated.

The Pask theory may have considerable influence on future theories of learning and instruction and on the design of products based on these theories. But its implications could be even broader, with relevance to the epistomology of subject matter organization, and to the philosophy of science.

CONCLUDING REMARKS

Space does not permit a detailed prognosis of the future of PI and CAI. This future, however, promises to be exciting. The computer represents a breakthrough in man's ability to get done the work associated with instructional research, development, and delivery. Until the advent of the computer, we were unable to manage the work associated with tracking the diversity of student paths through individualized systems, providing detailed practice with feedback, and collecting precise data for the revision and improvement of courseware. If the work potential of the computer can be harnessed through the application of instructional science, a quantum leap in our capability to deliver effective instruction to individuals will result. This advance will occur especially in areas that require self-pacing and extensive practice, and in areas where materials must be developed, evaluated, and improved. In the past ten years the cost of computer components has dropped dramatically each year, and projections are that it will continue to drop for another ten years. As solid state technology has made calculators feasible for every teacher and most school children, so the microcomputer revolution (associated with such developments as the videodisc) should in the next five to ten years make CAI terminals widely available. Such low-cost terminals will have many of the capabilities of PLATO and TICCIT and be available in offices, proprietary education centers, homes. and schools.

The task of hammering this raw computer power into educational plowshares will fall to instructional science, which in the next five or ten years to likely to provide a rich base from which increasingly sophisticated analytic approaches to instructional design, development, and delivery will evolve. Manufacturers tend to design products for mass markets such as entertainment or business. The failure of the earlier boom in CAI has made them cautious. Yet if instructional technology is to have high impact, CAI systems must incorporate sophisticated instructional models to mediate the interactions (or conversations) between the student and the machine. As was noted in the previous section, some promising beginnings have been made toward the development of such models.

Another problem impeding the promised impact of computers is that of producing cost-effective and instructionally effective courseware. This problem is presently sharpened by the lack of generally available, tested, and prescriptive analytic models for development of such courseware. In addition, there is a lack of sophisticated programmes for training authors to use these prescriptive models, and it is difficult to make this courseware technology usable with available hardware and software systems. The problems of training authors can be solved once the analytic models are developed, and progress is being made in this direction. To build design and development models for courseware into the hardware and software of computers will require the development of authoring systems, but not, however, merely the authoring languages that have been the stock in trade of computer-oriented CAI developers during the past fifteen years. Authoring systems will reflect and facilitate a systematic approach to instructional development. They will provide guides and editing tools for the author in the thinking stages of content and strategy analysis, in the design of intermediate products, and in the management of day-to-day production of intermediate and final design products. The computer can be engineered and programmed to facilitate the data-gathering, decision-making, and prompting stages that an author needs in order to go through each of the intermediate steps of the systematic design process. A computer for use by authors should not require them to learn computer programming, which, as now practised, takes authors into a complex and demanding area essentially unrelated to the analysis of content, behaviour, and strategy.

In addition to the need for authoring systems for tomorrow's low-priced and widely available computers, the problems of human factors have not been met. Teachers as a group are uneasy about the introduction of computers into the instructional process. Both because of the mystique of the computer as something difficult to understand, and because of the threat that automation will restructure or even replace jobs, teachers are often such to seek out CAI. The teacher's role in relation to new instructional and computer technology is too broad a subject to be treated here. Suffice it to say that the teacher's role is radically changed—though not necessarily for the worse—when computers are introduced in a substantial manner into the instructional process. They become managers, helpers, provokers to creativity, instructional developers, and serve less as a kind of delivery system.

It is not only the knowledge of how to use computers, but the new knowledge brought by instructional science that challenges the existing education profession. The field of education has changed slowly in the past. It is probable that CAI and PI will be adopted more rapidly in military and industrial training, in proprietary educational institutions, and even in homes than in the schools.

Both PI and CAI have passed their infancy. Both have been oversold and have settled down to the sober and difficult task of building firm theoretical and empirical foundations, and of establishing traditions and technologies that will serve educational needs. The symptoms of this increased maturity are apparent in the field of PI and promising beginnings have been made in CAI. The synthesis of the two in the form of authoring systems, teacher oriented management systems, and student-oriented learning environments could have profound implications for education.

COMPUTERS IN EDUCATION

Increasing numbers of school districts and higher learning institutions are installing electronic data processing systems (EDP systems) for the management of educational data. This development, coupled with the already extensive use of electronic accounting machines, i.e., card punching and sorting equipment (designated EAM), in the pupil-personnel, registrar, and business offices, seems to portend even further automation in our schools and universities. There is good evidence, too, that this automation will gradually extend into the classroom itself. This evidence lies in the research in new computer technology described in the subsequent pages of this report. For if the developments of automatic translating machines, computer-based teaching devices, rapid document retrieval systems, computerized models of school system operations, and other similar applications of computer technology come to fruition, the digital computer and its peripheral equipment will support most of the subsystems in the total school system complex.

This expansion of automation in educational processe has been attributed to the growing crisis in education. With greater numbers of students to educate and re-educate in increasingly complex subject matter, and with proportionately fewer teachers to teach them, further automation in education seems almost imperative. The problem has not been "should we automate?" but how to avoid a piece-meal approach to implementation. The EDP or even the EAM system which grows like Topsy without adequate systems planning generally results in procedures that are unnecessarily complicated and often redundant in nature. Even more serious is the inability to take subsequent advantage of new developments or applications as they emerge from the laboratory. These later applications can be introduced only if the educational planners have built a modular data system can be expanded

It would certainly seem self-evident that a total systems concept in planning the EDP operations of a school district or university would benefit education. As an example of the lack of an adequate systems approach to new EDP installations, we can point to the banking industry. After the installation of new EDP systems, many banks began to recognize that the theory of accounting was the same for different banking jobs; that it was possible, for instance, to perform all of the necessary posting jobs in a single, continuous computer operation, and also to store all records for a customer in one place on magnetic tape. With total retrieval capabilities, the customer could be furnished, in his one statement, with a record of his checking account, current balance in savings account, unpaid balance on instalment loan and current balance on his mortgage. Unfortunately, some of the necessary prerequisites in equipment and methodology for centralized record-keeping had not been anticipated in the initial planning of in-house EAM or EDP systems. Any bank that wanted to take advantage of these money-saving procedures had to spend an inordinate amount of money because of this lack of foresight.

In an educational system, one integrated data center might serve the needs of the administrator, teacher, counselor, curriculum developer, and student. For instance, in the school system laboratory model at the System Development Corporation, described below, students carrying on independent study with programmed materials leave a detailed record of their learning experience by making multiple-choice answers to frequent diagnostic questions on materials displayed in teaching machines. These records are stored in a Philco 2000 computer on magnetic tape. The information thus stored is of interest to the counselor, for it reveals each student's individual learning problems. The curriculum developer has summary data covering the learning experiences of many students for specific curriculum evaluation and modification. Teachers have an up-to-the-minute account of each student's level of understanding of the subject matter and the extent of his progress. The school librarian can update the student's information-need profile and guide the teacher in selecting special materials intended to resolve some of the student's learning needs. Rate of progress of the individual learner is of interest to the administrator who may need to monitor and schedule individual study programmes in the individualized, nongraded school system environment that the laboratory represents.

This example of the total systems concept in the storing and retrieving of educational data and information serves to make the point. Even though present applications of EDP systems in education are limited in scope, if the results of current research are applied to the future configuration of school system, and if centralized data processing continues to expand, educators are in for a major technological change in their profession.

The Computer-Based Teaching Machine

Certain principles of learning, developed in psychological laboratories and validated in educational practice, have currently been applied with considerable success to the development of new self-instructional textbooks and teaching machines. These principles have been identified with the educational process called programmed learning.

Programmed learning is a method of self-instruction, carried out by the individual student working with a special teaching device. The teaching device displays educational material to the student. The material has been broken down into its conceptual elements, with each concept taking from twenty to forty teaching machine items for exposition. An item is simply a frame or a slide of information of one or two sentences in length, usually followed by a question.

As each student proceeds through the instructional material, which is carefully prepared (or programmed) in small easy-to-take steps, he is required to respond actively at each step by filling in a missing word or selecting a multiple-choice answer designed to test his understanding of the information in that step. As the student writes down his answer to each step, the answer is recorded. This provides a basis for revising the educational programme so that it will teach better and more efficiently. The data left by students also provides a powerful tool for learning about human learning.

The student's response sets up a means for reinforcing or rewarding the student as he learns. The machine immediately indicates to the student whether he is right or wrong, informs him of the correct answer, and keeps a record of this and subsequent responses.

Much of contemporary teaching machine programming has been derived from the systematic position advanced by Skinner, who holds that the teaching sequence should be organized to maximize successes and minimize failures. The teaching sequence for a given body of material will then necessitate a lengthy series of teaching items to be seen sequentially by all students. Every student will traverse the same sequence regardless of his previous educational experience and aptitude.

Another position on teaching machine programming is that the machine should be flexible enough to adjust itself to every student's unique abilities for learning a subject. Such a programme utilizes a varying number of items and varying sequences of items. Each student will go through a teaching-session seeing a sequence that best fits his ability. The student will see additional items when his errors indicate his inability to grasp a point or a concept. He then will be shown easier items on the same concept, which are intended to help him over the hurdle he has just met. A student who meets no hurdles will skip redundant items.

What was developed in this system was a form of "machine responsiveness" or adaptive control based upon individual student learning needs. The machine does not impose a behaviour pattern on the student but seeks a compromise with the learner. First it challenges the student with moderately difficult material and cooperates with him when he needs help by presenting easier questions with more prompts. The machine adjusts the difficulty level and selects a variety of approaches to a given conceptual goal on the basis of needs of the particular student.

Machine Responsiveness to Student Learning Behaviour

The potential of the computer for handling individual student differences in learning rate, background, and aptitude is of primary interest to most researchers working with computer-controlled automated teaching systems. Machine responsiveness to student learning behaviour can be achieved by branching the student forward, laterally, or backward through subject materials primarily on the basis of his response to content questions seeded throughout the instructional programme.

Multiple criteria for branching is a goal in research with computer-based teaching, machines, but generally the current teaching machine will only branch for the following reasons:

1. Characteristics of student response—the promptness and/or definitiveness of his reply.
2. Nature of response—was it right or wrong, what specific errors were committed by the student.
3. History of student learning behaviour—his previous response pattern, problem areas, and reading rate.
4. Relevant student personal data—his IQ, sex, personality, aptitudes.

5. Nature of subject matter.
6. Degree of student motivation.
7. Student-generated requests for re-routing.

The term "flexibility" has two applications in connection with the computer-based teaching system. First, the machine is capable of modifying its own mode of instruction during the course of a training session. Item sequence, knowledge of results, and other such variables depend on the factors cited above as well as on the instructions programmed in the machine. It is this type of responsive self-modification which significantly distinguishes this flexible machine from the many non-computer-based teaching devices commercially available. Conceivably, this unique characteristic may lead to a major improvement over other conventional and automated instructional techniques in terms of teaching effectiveness.

A second type of flexibility, of great importance to any teaching machine intended as a research tool, pertains to the ease with which the machine's operation can be altered between training sessions. Such alterations are necessary to permit the investigation of different training procedures or machine characteristics.

The "responsive" experimental teaching machine demands a considerable degree of complexity in the machine control unit. The only type of control unit which provides the necessary flexibility is the digital computer, because the computer is the only instrument capable of determining the item sequence and knowledge of results to be presented to the student as well as carrying out the bookkeeping activities upon which such determinations will be based.

Inputs from the student are usually introduced by means of a typewriter keyboard connected to the computer control unit. These inputs consist of the student's responses to instructional items, or, in some cases, of requests for further information from the computer.

Two general types of stimulus material are usually presented by the computer-controlled machine to the student. The first type, consisting of the actual instructional items, can be displayed by a slide projector or TV display acting under the direction of the computer control unit. Signals from the computer control the sequence of items to be presented.

The second type of computer-based teaching machine output consists of evaluative information concerning the student's performance on the instructional items. This information is often printed out on the page printer of the same typewriter used for student inputs.

This brief description of the essential elements of an automated teaching system controlled by the digital computer does not, of course, hold for the specific configurations of components used in research.... It should also be stressed that the tools of this research are of less significance than the purpose for which the tools have been devised, a point sometimes overshadowed by the luster of the computer.

Information Retrieval Systems and Education

An information retrieval (IR) system can be defined as a man-machine system combining human intelligence and electronic and photocopying equipment for the purpose of gathering, classifying, and storing factual and textual material, and for retrieving and disseminating this information upon demand. Only such a broadly defined IR system would adequately serve the information needs of the educator and the student, for the integrated IR system will eventually supply all elements in the secondary school or university with information organized appropriately to the users' individual needs. It would be an error to think of IR applications in education as limited to automating the library or placing record files on microfilm. The computer-based IR system will improve the performance and efficiency of the administrator, counselor, teacher, student, and certainly the librarian by automating the organization and display of *current* educational data needed to carry out their special tasks. Unfortunately, such a system does not presently exist, even in the design of extremely expensive hardware systems developed for military or governmental agencies. However, the research now underway in the related areas of automatic abstraction, coding, and dissemination of information can lead to a major breakthrough in educational technology.

The Complete IR System in Education

Extrapolating from the present trends in IR, it is possible to envision some of the characteristics of advanced educational systems in the 1970's. Describing futuristic school sytems in this manner will serve to point up ongoing research and developments in the IR field.

1. *The Specialized Information Center for Local School Systems.* Future universities and secondary schools will be linked by data transmission lines to regional information centers. These centers translate and select items of information for automatic indexing, abstracting, and coding into magnetic tape files for subsequent feeding to remote school systems. These central archives will gather information from high-utility sources such as reports of experimental and test results, technical publications, patents, doctoral dissertations, government reports, etc. Archives will employ subject matter specialists for locating and weighing the importance of incoming documental materials in specific subject areas. These specialists monitor the input to the computer-based IR systems which are optically scanning the contents of the documents selected and converting them to tape. Once converted, the material is translated, abstracted, indexed, and coded for efficient retrieval. Files are constantly updated and purged, with the most significant information in a particular field kept immediately accessible.

Such information centers will prove efficient and economical by preventing costly duplication in processing of information and purchase of hardware at each and every school system. They will put the major catalogs of the world at the command of the local school library. In addition, they will supply information of interest to the school superintendent and local administration such as data on economic and population trends, predictions on the outcome of projected bond issues based on past voting behaviour of property owners in local school districts, etc.

The evidence for these projections lies in the current trend toward such information centers as ASTIA, the Armed Services Technical Information Agency, and the Scientific and Technical Information Facility dealing exclusively in the space and aeronautical sciences. Regional Technical Report Centers in twelve universities across the country have recently been designated to process, annotate, and convert to machincable form all of the research reports sponsored through government contracts. Language translations are now capable of being performed by machine. The IR systems established by the National Science Foundation and the Atomic Energy Commission have been disseminating translations of Russian research papers for the past few years. Considerable material from these and other information retrieval centers, such as Western Reserve and Georgetown University, is already on magnetic tape and currently available to the regional information center.

2. *Machine Readers Automatically Analyzing and Coding Documentary and Factual Material.* In the school system of the 1970's, students and educators will have access to vast stores of information from IR centers primarily because optical scanners coupled to digital computers will be examining the printed and handwritten texts, notes, and statistical computations of scientists and educators from around the country. Reading machines will reduce groups of words to simpler vocabulary when appropriate for a particular grade level, and automatically abstract original, unedited text. Statistical, syntactic, and semantic analyses of scanned material will permit factual or content retrieval of information to an extent impossible in today's libraries. Card catalogs will be a thing of the past, with up to date listing by author, concepts, or key words available to the library customer in books periodically printed by a highspeed printer controlled from the remote computer center.

3. ***Dynamic IR Systems for Self-instruction and for Educational Management.*** The school or university of the 1970's will have a dynamic system of information retrieval serving the entire school system. Instead of a passive cumulative record file and libraries waiting for customer requests, the IR system of the future school will direct information to a person "who has not yet asked a question but who does have a need for the answer." As an example, the dynamic IR system would index the content of a new document and mathematically select customers whose interest or information-need profiles indicate the content would be of some relevance to them. Automatic dissemination would then result. Feedback from the customer, i.e., the student or the educator, would continually update the store of profiles of potential users. Student learning performance would also cause changes in these profiles, for as students progress through new subject material, both interests and information needs evolve.

The use of the school's information retrieval system by both the educated and the educator will frequently involve the same information. Some predictions for IR system applications of stored information can now be made:

(*a*) *The student*

Computer-based independent study cubicles will line the halls of the advanced school system in the early, 70's. These study areas will combine information retrieval and automated teaching equipment to give the individual student aid in compiling bibliographies and recovering facts for the preparation of essays' and assistance in reading text material by supplying outlines, or arranging content in graded levels of difficulty. For learning purposes, the IR teaching machine would be arranging graded sequences of computer-constructed items occasionally seeding in a diagnostic test item to test the student's understanding. This teaching machine system would have the potential for handling individual student differences in learning rate, background, and aptitude. Sequences of educational material would be retrieved and organized on the basis of the student's response to the diagnostic questions as he is learning and on the specific student's learning abilities and aptitudes.

Recognizing that most students come to their studies in different states of ignorance, the IR teaching machine would help a student redefine his area of concern. The student might write a short essay detailing what he thinks is descriptive of the information he wants. The essay would then be handled in the fashion of an automated abstract and the words selected from the essay would be compared with words similarly selected from the documents or facts stored. The teaching machine would encourage the student to explore new but related areas of knowledge, browse through updated information, and search for alternate solutions to problems. Once the student was generally oriented to the subject under study, he might explore the area with a subject-matter expert via a two-way TV hookup.

(*b*) *The Teacher, Researcher, and Counselor*

The same equipment used by the student for self-instruction can be utilized by the teacher for research purposes or for updating himself in subject matter. Rapid changes in academic subjects can cause considerable information lag in the resource books used by the teacher. The computer-based IR system will help the teacher in assembling programmed instructional material and serve as a source of current information and necessary data for upgrading an outdated curriculum.

For classroom management purposes, the teacher will have displayed, in the classroom, certain diagnostic information in an interpreted form helping him to individualize his instruction. To deal with early-in-the-semester classroom grouping problems, the teacher can retrieve student information with suggested groupings of students along many different dimensions.

The counselor in this advanced school system will use IR storage and retrieval capabilities for doing a more efficient job of counseling. Using IR files for counselling purposes involves the storage of all student personnel records on magnetic tape. If these records include aptitude test scores, family background information, or student's past grade record, as well as his current record of progress, the counselor will have at his disposal all the appropriate information he needs. As the stored information is continually updated by the daily progress of each student through the course material, the counselor will have the capability of monitoring the progress of any one student and of applying preventive measures *before* a student has developed a serious educational problem.

Computer-Based Simulation

Simulation has been a part of the arsenal of instructional techniques in education for many years. The school store in which elementary children learn how to make change and purchase goods and the mock UN Assembly in which college students learn parliamentary procedures are two familiar examples in education. Simulation has been used for learning new attitudes (creative dramatics), understanding the problems of leading group discussions (role-playing), increasing motor skill proficiencies (mock-ups), solving written case problems (paper and pencil simulation). More complex machines such as the flight trainer, the automobile-driver trainer, and the "slowed down" computer have only recently come into general use in secondary and higher educational institutions.

The extent of simulation can be identified, along a continuum, from a high fidelity replication of reality (the Link Flight Trainer) to a complete abstraction of it (mathematical equations reprèsenting business operations). The purpose in simulating may be (1) to effect the analysis of an ongoing situation; (2) to aid in the development and evaluation of a new design, system, or organization; and (3) to train humans in new and old skills. These three functions of analysis, development, and training can be carried on independently or concurrently. They are made possible by according the experimenter or instructor control over a portion of simulated reality, permitting him to manipulate relevant variables and to study the effects of this treatment under observable conditions.

Some Simulation Applications in Education

Some new and interesting techniques have been recently developed for the training and selection of new teachers and administrators. Dr. Bert Kersh at the Center for Teaching Research at the Oregon State System of Higher Education has reported on a classroom simulation for training student teachers. The student teacher is seated at a desk facing a large rear-projection screen upon which a life-size image is projected. Short film clips present a variety of classroom situations to which the student may react.

On the basis of the "acting out" of the student teacher to the filmed stimulus situation, the supervisor of training will select from three projectors a sequence of film which may (1) show the classroom disintegrating as the result of lack of forceful direction on the part of the student teacher, (2) have the students going to their seats but erupting in new problems if the teacher is not vigilant, or (3) result in an effectively managed classroom if the teacher trainee performs adequately. The limitation of this method is, of course, determined by the variety of feedback films that are available for matching the responses of the student teacher. However, a computer-sequenced bank of film cartridges would improve the realism and appropriateness of feedback.

Simulation studies for training and evaluating administrators have been carried out under the sponsorship of the University Council for Educational Administration. Several universities have used films, film strips, tapes, and printed materials developed by Drs. Hemphill, Griffiths, and Frederickson for simulating situational tests for researching certain patterns of school administrative behaviour.

By using in-basket techniques, increasing amounts of stress are applied to administrators operating in the simulated environment. Those who exprienced the simulated situations felt the simulated materials held promise for evaluating and selecting new school administrators.

The use of simulation for evaluation and analysis purposes is also not entirely new to education. Research laboratories in the universities, supported by government and private foundation grants, have long used this technique for controlled and careful observation.

For advanced planning and analysis purposes an example of mathematical modelling of educational systems operations can be found in the work of Drs. Kershaw and McKean at the RAND Corporation.

Kershaw and McKean did an exploratory study for the Ford Foundation to assess the possibilities of making quantitative comparisons of elementary and secondary school systems. They conclude that data collected from a large simple of schools can result in a meaningful comparison of the effect of different input variables on educational achievement. Innovations, such as educational television; changes in a school system, for example, increasing teacher salaries; and differences between schools, i.e., pupil-teacher ratios—all of these can be costed and related to output measures like standard test scores. Kershaw and McKean propose that this kind of statistical analysis will be of the sort "that can help administrators and others choose improved educational systems."

In the new systems simulation laboratory at the System Development Corporation, preliminary studies are underway for the modelling and simulation of an advanced, individualized, secondary school. Problems of allocation and numbers of individual study carrels, materials, and personnel will be explored. As immediate and accurate information is provided by the computer on the state of academic knowledge of individual students, and as students proceed through instructional material at their own rate, implications for changing study schedules on a daily basis, for student advancement requirements, and for homogeneous class groupings can also be explored. The role of teachers, principals, and other school personnel can be clarified and re-stated in terms of changed pupil progress and system needs.

The system simulation studies at SDC will eventually lead to modifications and improvements in the design of prototypes of future schools.

Dr. Alvin Grossman, Director of the California Department of Education's new Center for Research and Development in Educational Data Processing located in Sacramento, California, has received a grant from the U.S. Office of Education to conduct and support simulation studies in areas of educational data processing, such as scheduling, guidance, validation of counselling procedures, and curriculum changes. Computer models developed in the new center will permit educators to experiment with techniques of solution before expending funds on untried programmes of services. The center will experiment with methods of stimulating and aiding in decision-making with the RCA 301 Computer supplying feedback on the consequences of decisions.

The Automated Classroom

A new facility for the research and development of a complete educational system that would provide optimal learning conditions has recently been completed at SDC. This facility, designated CLASS (for Computer-based Laboratory for Automated School Systems) is a part of the large, general-purpose Systems Simulation Research Laboratory using a Philco S-2000 computer as the central control mechanism.

CLASS permits simultaneous automated instruction of 20 students, each of whom receives an individualized sequence of instructional materials adapted to his particular needs, or learns in a group mode of instruction mediated by the teacher or computer. Application of modern data processing technology to other functions normally associated with a school district can also be explored in CLASS.

...Each student has a manually operated film viewer containing 2,000 frames of instructional material. In addition, he has a response device, Linked to the Philco computer, which indicates the sequence of slides to be seen by the student, enables the student to respond to questions, and presents knowledge of results to the student in the form of coded lights. These lights add a kind of pinball effect for the motivation of the student.

The Philco computer maintains performance records for all students and makes these records available to the teacher, counselor, or administrator.

Provision is made for two teachers in CLASS. Each teacher has console facilities which make it possible for her to call up computer-generated displays showing the current progress of any student or group of students. Automatic alarm lights will alert the teacher to students who are performing unsuccessfully in their lesson.

CLASS will be more than a multichannel teaching machine. It will permit instruction through different media including television, films and slides, as well as conventional lecture and textbook methods. Moreover, it will be used to study the application of modern data processing methods in many school functions. Special areas will be available in CLASS for administrative and counselling activities. Computer programmes will store and prepare student attendance, curriculum and grade records; perform statistical analyses for summary and predictive purposes; and provide simulteneous student scheduling and registration.

Simulation Techniques

Simulation techniques will be used extensively for administrator and counselor training since the restricted classroom and counselling facilities in CLASS do not provide adequate "live" stimuli for the decision-making activities normally conducted in the typical school district. A series of simulated messages which require policy and administrative decisions can be presented, and the probable consequences of decisions made in response can be fed back from the computer.

Ignoring the administrative and counselling functions to be explored in CLASS, and the use of the computer for development of flexible scheduling and data processing programmes, we will discuss the application of computer technology to increasing teacher efficiency and effectiveness in the classroom. This application will be one of the primary concerns over the next few years for research in the new computer-assisted CLASS facility.

One of the paramount problems in classroom instruction is to coordinate learning activities among a group of students who have heterogeneous abilities and educational backgrounds. If we look closely at the good instructor practicing his art, we find him individually tutoring students, helping to resolve their individual learning problems. We find him making expedient use of the social and motivational benefits of group instruction. Finally, we find him adapting curriculum materials appropriately for both the individual and the group modes of learning.

The computer-based classroom fitted with automated teaching devices provides individual tutoring—a luxurious arrangement which the conventional classroom, with teachers thoroughly outnumbered, fails to provide.

Students who miss school because of illness can catch up by working individually, while the teacher monitors their progress or difficulties by checking the analyses based on their performance. The bright student, whose interest wanes under conventional classroom conditions while he waits for the less gifted to set the learning pace can now move ahead at his own speed.

With the advantage of immediate analysis of student performance which the computer provides, the teacher can promptly diagnose student weakness and redirect his instruction or bring up new media for approaching the same conceptual goals.

Student Record

One of the most important aspects of automated teaching is the record which the student leaves of his learning experience. As students are required to respond activily at frequent intervals by filling in a missing word or selecting a multiple-choice answer, they leave accurate and detailed records which provide a basis for revising the educational programme so that it might teach batter and more efficiently.

As already stated, these records of student learning will be of interest to an entire school system. For counselors they will reveal individual student learning problems. Curriculum developers will have an effective tool for curriculum modification and evaluation. Instructors can get an up-to-the-minute account of each student's level of understanding on subject matter, the particular learner's skill levels and difficulties, and the group spread of response.

Liberated from most record keeping, paper-grading tasks, and the basic necessity of packing students with factual material, the teacher can concentrate on the extension of student understanding on stimulating student creativity, on challenging student imagination, and on providing individual help and counsel.

Group Instruction

Another approach to classroom instruction is, of course, the group lecture or discussion method, sometimes with the use of audiovisual materials. In CLASS, the instructor has the convenience of a remotely controlled central projection system which displays short film clips or brief sequences of slides through the closed circuit TV monitor. There is no darkening of the room required, no projector to thread. For a fully automated mode of group instruction the random-access projector can be put under computer control and sequences of material ordered by some group response norm. Individual feedback can still be given by means of the lights on the individual student response devices. Thus this group instructional programme would have some of the properties identified with individual teaching machines such as correction feedback, controlled sequencing, and prior programming.

The instructor in the computer-assisted classroom can evaluate his teaching or lecturing ability by seeding his lecture with diagnostic questions and receiving immediate analyses of the group response through his digital display. He may then elect to branch to simpler materials or to alter his approach.

Teacher Freed of Clerical Work

The teacher can be expected to be relieved of certain non-instructional functions in the computer-assisted classroom of the future. Much of the clerical work in the classroom can be abolished.

According to some educators, the teacher spends at least a third of his time not teaching. He acts as host, clerk, librarian, counselor, housekeeper, decorator, ticket seller, attendance taker, data processor, analyzer, and policeman. In tomorrow's classroom, many of these activities can be automated. Attendance taking in CLASS is accomplished by the teacher's punching in the student key on his instructional console. Data processing and analyses are performed by the digital computer. As students take action on their response devices, these data are collected in real time (as they happen) and stored on magnetic tape by student and item number. These data include answer selected, time taken to respond, feedback message student receives, and whether he was right or wrong. From these data, the computer makes a tabular listing in a prespecified format: (1) summing all actions for a given student by a particular lesson; (2) summing student responses for a particular item; or (3) ordering response data by concept. From such baseline data various statistics can be requested by the teacher. Furthermore, reports can be prepared on off-line printers. Clerical tasks such as lunch money accounting, home cards that need addressing, and homework assignments can be performed automatically.

Teacher Training

It cannot be assumed that because teachers are liberated from paper shuffling tasks or have access to meaningful learning data they are automatically going to use such data. Many teachers will need to be trained in the effective use of more free time. Some sophistication in variance and factor analysis, some experience in data processing methods and their potential, an understanding of tutoring methods—all of these will be needed by the teacher in the computer-assisted school system.

Training of teachers will be one of the primary functions in the new laboratory. Plans have been laid for bringing school children and experienced teachers into the CLASS facility. For an extended period of time, observation of learning activities will help to generate meaningful hypotheses for experimentation. Hopefully this research will have immediate application in real school situations.

COMPUTER-DIRECTED INSTRUCTIONAL GAMES

A combined course in economic theory and social studies may sound as though it belongs in a college curriculum, but sixth graders have taken just such a course in the form of a computer-assisted instructional game. Sitting at typewriter-like computer terminals, the students entered a simulated environment where each became the ruler of a city-state in the ancient land of Sumer. Cast in a dramatic story role, the student "rulers" sought to feed their people in the face of catastrophes like floods, through technological advances like fertilizer, and the introduction of foreign trade.

The experiment was carried on under the direction of Richard L. Wing of the Northern Westchester (New York) Board of Cooperative Educational Services, with the participation of the Advanced Systems Development Division of International Business Machines Corporation. The original idea for such a game-playing use of computers was suggested by Bruse Moncrieff who coined the term *simulated environment* used in much the same sense as the more popular term *game*. The Sumerian Game was written by Mrs. Mabel Addis, a teacher at the Katonah Elementary School, Katonah, New York.

A similar game based on the economy of modern-day Sierra Leone was tested at the same time. Here, the student's role was that of an American economic advisor to a newly emerging nation. (A modified IBM 7090 computing system was used. It has since been dismantled. Parts of the games were reprogrammed for other systems and have been used experimentally and in demonstrations since 1966.)

Students play the games by interacting via the typewriter terminal. Messages from the computer are printed on the typewriter, and students use the terminal keyboard to make responses. The keyboard is normally locked, and is unlocked only following a message requesting the student to respond. At that point, a green "proceed" light flashes on and the computer-programmed game waits for the response. When the student completes his response, by striking a special end-of-message key, the game continues. A prerequisite, of course, is that the student know how to use the typewriter-like keyboard and be able to understand the messages sent to him. In actual operation, the terminals are brought to a ready-to-play state by the teacher-monitor.

A preliminary lecture, delivered via a conventional tape recorder driving a slide projector, introduces the subject matter and suggests the learning method. This takes about 20 minutes. The student is then seated at a terminal keyboard and told to begin the programmed play.

The first messages introduce the proper use of the terminal and acquaint the player with his game objectives. After this, the student receives a first seasonal population and harvest report (Fig. 8.1), providing facts about population, acres of land for planting grain, number of farm workers, grain recently

Initial Economic Report Made to the New Ruler of Lagash by his Humble Steward:

Total population now	500
Total farm land under cultivation, acres	600
Total grain in inventory, bushels	900
one season old	900
two seasons old	0
three seasons old	0
Total grain just harvested, bushels	13000
Total resources, harvest and inventory	22000

You must now decide how to use your resources.

How many bushels of grain do you wish to feed your people?

————

How many bushels of grain do you want planted for the next crop?

————

This means that————bushels must be placed in storage. Is this all right? Do you wish to (1) let your decisions stand, or (2) revise them?

————

Resulting inventory ————

The steward will execute the royal commands and return in 6 months.

Fig. 8.1: The Initial Seasonal Report

harvested, and grain remaining in inventory from previous harvests. The last part of the report asks the student to allocate his resources (grain harvested plus grain in inventory) to meet three requirements: food for the people, seed for next season's planting, and inventory for future needs. Such seasonal reports (a sample is shown in Fig. 8.2) with their related allocation decisions comprise the basis of play of the entire game.

The passage of time is signified by successive reportings. Good play is identified by an increase in population and harvests, poor play by a decrease.

Economic report of the ruler's steward for the fall season in the year 14 of Luduga 1.

Population at previous report	514
Change in population	12
Total population now	528

The quantity of food the people received last season was satisfactory.

Harvest last season	15829
Harvest this season	15829
Previous inventory	2620
Change in inventory	—456
Present inventory	2164
Total resources, harvest+inventory	17993

You must now decide how to use your resources.

How many bushels of grain do you wish to feed your people?
9500

How many bushels of grain do you want planted for the next crop?
4500

This means that 1829 bushels must be placed in storage. Is this all right?
Do you wish to (1) let your decisions stand, or (2) revise them?

1

Resulting inventory 3993

The steward will execute the royal commands and return in 6 months.

Fig. 8.2: A Typical Seasonal Report

The method of computing a change in population from one report to the next is illustrated in Fig. 8.3, which shows that the best amount of grain to use for food is 18 bushels per person. The formulas used to compute the harvest (Table 8.1) do not show the effects of disasters or other temporary variations in harvest. Also, the numbers in the formulas do not remain fixed through a complete play of the game; for example, the formula for the harvest, H=4S (Item 1), becomes H=5S after the use of fertilizer is introduced.

TABLE 8.1

Formulas Relating Harvest to Seed Planted, Land Cultivated and Number of Farmers

---

Symbol Definition

Let H=the number of bushels in the harvest
S=the number of bushels of seed planted
L=the number of acres of land cultivated
W=the number of workers on the farm lands

Formulas

1. If too much seed has not been planted

$$S \leqslant 6\,L$$

and if there are enough farmers

$$W \geqslant L/4$$

then

$$H = 4S$$

2. If too much seed has not been planted

$$S \leqslant 6L$$

but there are too few farmers

$$W < L/4$$

then

$$H = (4\,W/L)\,4S$$

3. If too much seed has been planted

$$S > 6\,L$$

and if there are enough farmers

$$W \geqslant L/4$$

then

$$H = 24\,L$$

4. If too much seed has been planted

$$S > 6\,L$$

and there are too few farmers

$$W < L/4$$

then

$$H = 96\,W$$

Let P=the population

$\triangle$P=the change in population over one season

F=the number of bushels of grain set aside as food for one season

X=food per person in one season

then X=F/P

and the ratio $\triangle$P/P is given in the graph below:

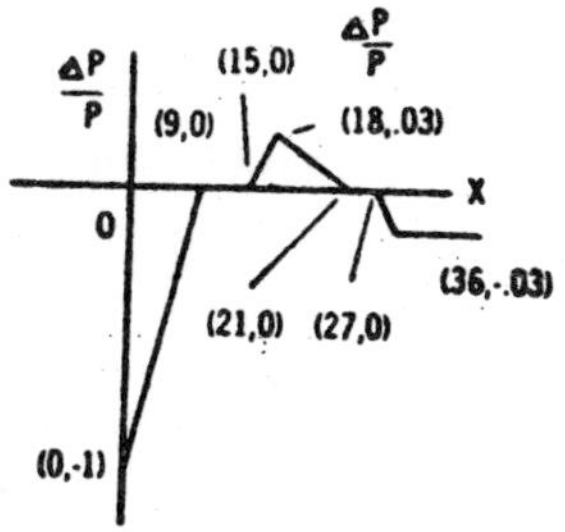

Example: If P=600 and F=10,200

then X=17, $\triangle$P/P=.02

and$\triangle$P=12

The next population figure would then by 612.

Fig. 8.3: Graph Relating Population Change to Food Consumption

In the text of a typical seasonal report, the comment, "The quantity of food the people received last season was—," is modified to read "far too little," "too little," "satisfactory," "too much," or "far too much." The rules for insertion of the ratings are shown in Table 8.2.

Occasionally, brief reports of events that alter conditions in the city-state follow the season report. The most persistent happenings are natural disasters—floods and fires that kill people and ruin the harvests. These natural disasters point up the need for maintaining a well-stocked inventory. Both the occassion and severity of the disasters are determined by a pseudo random computation procedure known as the Monte Carlo Method.

TABLE 8.2

Message Inserts

Let the comment "The quantity of food the people received last season was . . . ." have a variable insertion, to be specified below:

Let X=food per persons in one season (see Fig. 8.1); then

If $X=<9$ the insert is "far too little."

If $9 \leqslant X \leqslant 15$ the insert is "too little."

If $15 < X < 21$ the insert is "satisfactory."

If $21 \leqslant X \lhd 27$ the insert is "too much."

If $27 \leqslant X$ the insert is "far too much."

Another frequent report concerns the rotting of grain left in inventory. The comment, "Sir, I am sorry to report that—— bushels of grain have rotted or been eaten by rats this past season," is given if the amount of rotted grain is not zero. The calculation of the amounts is given in Table 8.3.

TABLE 8.3

The Grain Rotting Computations

Let l_0=grain put into inventory this past season

l_1=grain put into inventory one season back

l_2=grain put into inventory two seasons back

l_3=grain put into inventory three seasons back

$\triangle l$=the change in inventory due to rotting

There are four rates of rotting. The applicable rate is determined by other factors e.g., the extent of the use of clay pots, rather than baskets, for the storage of grain.

1. $\triangle l = .1\ l_0 + .25l_1 + .25l_2 + .75 + l_3$
2. $\triangle l = .75l_2 + l_3$
3. $\triangle l = l_3$
4. $\triangle l = .5l_3$

The economic condition of the city-state may improve in two ways: through good management of the basic grain allocation and by accepting with some good judgement a sequence of innovations presented in special end-of-season reports. Improvements of the seeond kind show themeselves dramatically—a harvest productivity parameter is increased by 25 per cent, the rate of rotting is cut by 50 per cent, or perhaps the number of farmers required per acre of land is reduced by 50 per cent. Progress through the game can be measured in terms of the number of special reports reviewed by the students. These reports normally follow a strict sequence in which no report can be given before a specific predecessor. Some of the reports are not offered until the student has exhibted some "good" judgement, e.g., has fed his people satisfactorily for two consecutive seasons. The student is often required to respond to questions during the reporting and any of the state-of-the-nation variables may have its value altered in the process. Such alterations invariably show themselves in subsequent propulation and harvest reports.

All of the state-of-the-nation variables used in the Sumerian Game are described in Table 8.4. For one group of variables, values are maintained over four seasonal report times. This "brief history" provides information for judging the "goodness" of play. Another group of variables is for current playtime only.

The Sumerian Game is played in three successive parts corresponding to the reigns of three rulers, Luduga I, II, and III. In addition to contributing to the story line of the game, this organization of the game makes plausible the resulting of the state-of-the-nation variables. That is, no matter how a student has directed the city-state through his reign as Luduga I or Luduga II (he may, for example, have increased his population by 20 per cent or decreased it by 30 per cent), he would start his play in the role of Luduga II or III with a standard set of values, for the state-of-the-nation variables. The story line explanation is that a period of time elapses between the completion of one part and the start of the next.

TABLE 8.4

State-of-the-Nation Variables

Four Time Periods

The first group of variables have values maintained as of 4 distinct points in time (simulated play time). They are the current seasonal report, seasonal report time 1 season ago, seasonal report time 2 seasons ago and seasonal report time 3 seasons ago.

P=the population

F=the amount of grain allocated for food

H=the amout of the harvest

S=the amount of seed planted

L=the number of acres of land under cultivation

W=the number of workers in farming

I_0=the amount of grain in inventory zero seasons old

I_1=the amount of grain in inventory one season old

I_2=the amount of grain in inventory two seasons old

I_3=the amount of grain in inventory three seasons old

Current Play Time Only

Values of the following group of variables are maintained only for the current-play time.

R_0=the normal rate of return—harvest to seed planted

R_1=the maximum ratio of seed planned to land cultivated for normal harvests

R_3=the minimum ratio of farm workers to land cultivated for normal harvests

R_4=the ratio of farm workers to total population

Y=the number of seasons played

SOME DESIGN CONSIDERATIONS

Some of the techniques used in the design of the Sumerian Game are independent of the subject matter and, perhaps, usable in a broad context.

To enable rapid differentiation between student and computer information, the following design rule was selected: computer type-outs (the larger volume of material) will appear in black; student type-ins in red.

The design of a student response syntax is a more involved problem. In responding to questions printed by the computer, the student must express himself in a from anticipated by the game designers. In specific sections of the games, responses might be acceptable if, for example, they are only single-digit or single-word type-ins. This kind of constraint is determined by the game authors depending upon the context of the response. A more basic set of syntactical rules applicable to *all* responses is listed below:

A response is made up of a sequence of typewriter keystrokes, the last, a special one signaling an end-of-message.

Words and numbers may be constructed using a special alphabet; the normal alphabet a to z, the digits 0 to 9, and the special characters @#$,.+—and/.

The distinction beween upper and lower case letters is ignored.

Either space or tab keystroke indicates a separation between words or numbers.

A backspace keystroke in a response indicates that the preceding non-backspace keystroke is to be deleted.

Other keystrokes not explicitly mentioned above are simply ignored.

A sequence of characters staring with a digit, a decimal point, a plus or minus sign, and extending to a non-digital character other than a period or comma, will be treated as a number. Acceptable forms are:

1234	1,234,000	1.234
.0034	+4.5	−67.8

The Sumerian Game also demonstrated the technical feasibility of incorporating an evaluation of student response and a printout of a report card. A general report-card form (Fig. 8.4) was established to accept a recording of a grade (A, B, C, or D) in each of four categories of questions: impossible, hard, easy, other. The format also includes recordings of time-of-response in the same four categories. The instructor may request a report at any time, but normally it is printed at the terminal immediately after a student has finished a section of his play. The report card data in Fig. 8.4 shows that a total of 40 questions were put to the student, the average time of response was 11.4 seconds, 2 answers earned a grade of D, 9 a C, 8 a B, and 21 a grade of A. The overall grade was 88 based on weighting the secores: 50 for a D, 70 for a C, 85 for a B, and 100 for an A. In the experiment the report card was not used to measure a student's play except in scattered instances for demonstration.

Category	N	T-Ave.	D	C	B	A	GRADE
Hard	10	10.65	0	3	1	6	89
Easy	5	9.69	0	1	0	4	94
Other	23	12.78	2	4	7	10	86
All	40	11.40	2	9	8	21	88

Fig. 8.4 Report Card

Procedures were designed to handle two exceptional conditions that might be detected by the camputing syetem. If, during the time the green "proceed" light is no, no key is struck within a period of approximately 30 seconds, the keyboard is locked and the light is turned off. The procedure for handling this is to return the carriage, advance the paper, and reinitiate the ready by turning the green "proceed" light on again. If during a transmission of information to or from the terminal a bit of information is either lost or picked up from some noise source, the transmission is terminated and the normal sequence interrupted. If this condition is encountered while sending a message to the terminal, the carriage is returned, "Machine Error" is printed in red, and the carriage is returned again and the last printed unit of information is reprinted. If the condition is encountered while composing a message at the terminal, the carriage is returned, "Please retype reply" is printed, the carriage returns again, and the "proceed" light turns on.

A complete play of the game spanned a number of days. Picking up a play of a game was very simply done by selecting from a system memory device a copy of the previsious day's programme. This "saved" programme contained records identifying the student, his play in the play of the game, and a summary of the effects of his past decisions.

While some design problems are technical ones, not especially related to methods of teaching, the simulated environment mode does require a unique organization of the subject matter.

Many aspects must be planned in the development of such games: the script the rules which control the sequencing through the script, the model governning the computations of report content, and the overall programming problems of making the computer "understand" the above specifications.

A team for developing a computer-controlled game might include: a subject matter specialist or teacher to interpret the overall educational objectives and write the script; a human-factors specialist to advise on the best manner of interaction between student and terminals; a mathematical model builder to create computational schemes which embody the desired theoretical behaviours; and a computer programming specialist to translate the specifications into computer programmes. This last specially may become unnecessary in view of the present trend among computer manufacturers to make application-oriented programming languages available to equipment users.

The principal output of an instructional game development project would be the computer programmes and perhaps other media such as recorded sound passages, recorded TV picture sequences, photographic film images, and print materials. The computer programmes would contain both the conversational control procedure (*what* message is shown to the student *when*) and the conversational material to be printed (the script). Also desirable is a comprehensive description of the game, with the complete script, a list of other informational units such as pictures, and a description of the control mechanisms. Control can best be described by charts showing lines of flow of control and branch points at which a description of the conditions for branching is included. The parts of the script corresponding to unbroken conversational phrases should be uniquely labeled and referred to at the appropriate places on the flow chart. Similarly, the other informational units should be labelled and referenced.

In designing the Sumerian game, a most crucial design decision was the degree of freedom to allow a student in constructing responses. The student's role always seems too passive in that he is always strictly led by the programme. A more positive role could be assumed if the student had some sort of command laguage available to him in which he could type, for example, "stop the play. What was the ratio of grain harvested to grain planted for the past three seasons?"

Why not a command language then? On the one hand, to attempt to translate student commands expressed in natural language is foolhardy on two accounts: the domain of conversational interest in a game is, and should be immensely restricted compared to the domain of possible conversation; and the problems of machine translation of natural language are so great that present eforts in this direction have only limited objectives.

The possibility of inventing artifical language exists, but here, the other side of the need for the problem enters—the student to know the language. One sensible approach is to introduce the student to the game playing material by way of a course in understanding and expressing ideas in a man-machine communication language. The more such an artifical language could be made standard across many computer-controlled courses, the greater the usefulness of the language.

Characteristic of the makeup of a game is the simulated situation—the dramatization of a changing situation which embodies the knoweldge to be taught. It is not a presentation of abstract theories followed by examples illustrating the value of the theories. Rather it is the creation of an exemplary situation that exposes the student to an experience in which he can be involved and from which he can extract the underlying theory.

Also characteristic of this approach is the necessity of repetition. Multiple exposures are more or less needed by the players depending upon the abstractness of the theories relative to the situations embodying them.

The Sumerian Game is an interesting new use of modern technology in education. The novelty of the educational ideas embodied in the game (other than simply using EDP equipment) lies in the degree to which they are now being employed. Game-like situations have been used in the past to present knowledge in an especially palatable form. The notion, too, of displaying knowledge in unrefined form with a natural amount of "noise" surrounding it is not in itself new. What is new is the technology which gives a new freedom to employing the instructional games methods.

COMPUTER-ASSISTED INSTRUCTION—WHERE ARE WE?

More than ever before, we are concerned with the nature of the educational process, with the goals of education, with the impact of change—and,...with the techniques and devices that can be used in improving the educational enterprise....Indeed, to the outside observer it must seem as if we were preparing to embark upon a permanent revolution in education.

Jerome Bruner made the above observations in 1962. There can be little doubt that we are now writing the early chapters of this "permanent revolution" in education. To date, we are not sufficiently experienced to be able to define adequately its nature and scope, but one fact stands out clearly: Technology will play a major role.

Robert Hutchins, writing in 1967, sees the possibility that changes brought by technology "... may go so far as to dissolve the institutions we have known, or make them largely unrecognizable." The real danger, however, warns Hutchins, is that the technology of education may come to determine the methods and aims of education itself.

Perhaps these issues are nowhere more evident than in the current research and discussions on the use of the computer in the instructional process, most frequently referred to as computer-assisted instruction (CAI) or computer-based learning.

Since the early sixties research money appropriated for the development of CAI and documents probing the boundaries of this technology have swelled enormously. Educational institutions and business corporations have begun or are making plans to begin extensive CAI projects. And in the midst of all this activity we are continually being reminded that CAI will bring about dramatic and far-reaching changes at every level of education.

To many on the sidelines, this must present a confusing, if not a bewildering situation. Where in fact do we stand with CAI? What do we know? What are the advantages? Where lie the dangers? On what timetable are we to prepare for the changes this technology will bring? These and many more questions are being asked today in both professional and lay circles.

Unfortunately, there are few references that deal with these questions in a comprehensive and constructive manner. Most assuredly, CAI technology must be given time to grow and mature, but in the meanwhile there is urgent need for continuing professional assessment and evaluation.

In the following pages, an attempt will be made to take a look at CAI from several vantage poinst. First, what results are being reported about CAI research? Second, what is being said about the kinds of research needed? Third, what generalizations can be made about CAI research reported to date? Fourth, what trends in CAI seem to be evolving at this time? And fifth, what overall conclusions can be drawn about CAI based on our current understanding of this technology?

The information presented for the first three objectives derives from some recent work during which a large number of documents dealing with CAI were analyzed and evaluated. Objectives four and five will be primarily personal value judgments, although they are based in part on discussions with teachers and researchers currently involved with CAI.

For additional background information about CAI and for some different points of view, a number of sources are available.

RESULTS FROM CAI RESEARCH

Summarized below are research conclusions concerning CAI as reported in a fairly broad sampling of journals and institutional reports. Actually, only a relatively small number of research reports were found to be readily available. This is understandable, however, for as Hansen points out: "The vast majority of CAI projects have expended tremendous energy in the development of curriculum materials; consequently, this development phase has limited the availability of research findings.

The references cited refer either to research reports or to sources where the investigators have commented on research they or others have conducted. It was not possible in every instance to separate carefully controlled research from anecdotal accounts or general observations.

The conclusions listed would probably be considered tentative by most of the researchers and lack broad generalization at this time. In any event, taken as a whole, they would seem to represent a reasonable picture of the current state of the art of CAI as reflected in the literature.

1. Students seem to learn at least as well with CAI as with conventional classroom instruction. Most of the researchers report this conclusion for various short courses. Some researchers indicate that greater learning and retention can occur with CAI. In addition, Coulson has reported an example of raising the performance of lower aptitude students to that of higher aptitude students.

2. CAI can provide learning and retention at least equivalent to conventional techniques in the same amount of time. Some report significant reduction in time required.

3. The computer learning programme can make logical decisions and adjust to individual student differences with regard to learning sequence, depth and mode of material, and rate of progress.

4. The computer can record and manipulate a wide variety of learning data about the student during instruction. For example, sequence of learning steps, response time, number of errors, cumulative performance, etc. All researchers report this conclusion as being will within the capability of the present technology. However, in view of the quantity of information that can be collected, it is difficult to select only that information which can be permanently recorded.

5. The computer can reduce certain kinds of tedious work usually required of the student. For example, in mathematical logic.

6. The computer programme can integrate and control a wide variety of audio-visual aids in the learning programme, for enrichment and motivation. The computer can also provide dynamic real time displays of mathematical and physical relationships, and relieve the students of a large number of routine calculations. However, computer-controlled slide presentations are not necessarily better than visual materials presented in booklet form.

7. Time sharing (a number of students using the same computer simultaneously, and perhaps at remote distances from the computer) is within the capabilities of present technology.

8. A broad range of courses can be programmed for CAI. No known limits have been reported as yet to the kinds of subject matter or conceptual level that can be programmed. Well-structured subjects can, in particular, be easily handled by CAI tutorial systems.

9. Students are generally interested in and like the CAI form of instruction.

Student attitude toward CAI generally relates directly to personal performance.

Appropriate pacing of materials presented and time-out limits can keep the concentration of even very young children at a relatively high level in a CAI system.

However, students often feel the need for shorter sessions with more discussion and teacher interaction.

10. Learning time and learning effectiveness with CAI depend on a number of factors.

With respect to learning time:

The major determinant of time to complete the computer programme is the number of student responses required to meet internal course criteria established by the author-teacher.

Employment of optional delays in the learning programme, plus the opportunity for review and remedial work, would provide help for some students.

There is great variability in how long children will work at the computer instructional terminal when free to decide. Deterioration in learning performance has been noted in grade school children when sessions run longer than 20-30 minutes.

With respect to learning effectiveness, we need to examine the factors of learning style, instructional sequencing, and learning performance:

The cognitive style of a student appears to be related to his ability and his approach to and utilization of the computer system.

Visual learners respond more favourably to sequences of graphically or pictorially laid-out instructional items, and have been brought to a level of superior performance on achievement tests.

Student errors during instruction and responses to self-evaluation questions provide effective criteria for branching the student to different instructional sequences.

Branching methods can provide more efficient instruction than fixed-sequence presentations.

Allowing students to determine their own sequence of instruction does not work as well with younger children as with older children.

Having too many "help" sequences available could encourage students to rely on this as the easier and faster way of getting an answer.

A sophisticated latency criterion of performance can be easily applied in a computer-based laboratory.

When poor typists are permitted to score their own implicit responses rather than type them out, their performance is markedly better.

Auto-instruction can be effective in helping mentally retarded young children to read.

Student responses entered in wrong form (where only one form of an answer is permitted) tend to interfere seriously with student learning.

Some students get flustered by the machinery and need, therefore, a good orientation to this form of instruction.

Students become confused in a time-sharing system, if the computer does not respond immediately to their commands.

A large proportion of the teacher's current responsibility for imparting facts, basic skills, and concepts, as well as his responsibility for providing routine drill, can be handled more efficiently and effectively by the machine.

11. Already existing curriculum materials can be readily used in development of computer courses.

12. The computer has been shown to provide an excellent opportunity for an experimental research lab to study learning.

13. Computer-simulated laboratories can be helpful for:

teaching lab procedures;

exposing students to a variety of analytical problems and physical processes in considerably less time than actual lab analysis;

providing an excellent adjunct to conventional instruction;

reducing student stress in learning by allowing freedom to manipulate objects normally not permitted e.g., in clinical nursing.

14. The beginnings of a versatile computer programming logic has been developed that permits:

easy changes from one subject matter to another;

a syntax for the student to use in communicating with the computer;

some ease and flexibility in preparing programmes;

substantial possibilities for constructed student responses.

15. Time for qualified personnel to write, de-bug, and validate one hour of CAI instruction may be from 75 to 150 man-hours. Total cost, including machine time, may be several thousand dollars. (These are private guesses based on conversations with people involved in programmed instruction and CAI. Actually, there are so many variables involved, such as quality of instructional materials, level of instruction, and extent of validation, that rules of thumb such as the above are not very helpful. The literature is almost completely silent on cost-benefit analysis.)

Most of the above findings have resulted from very short courses conducted with small numbers of students. Long-term CAI data involving sizeable numbers of students have not yet been collected.

RECOMMENDED RESEARCH AREAS

Many searching questions have been raised about CAI in the literature. It is difficult to categorize these questions neatly because they probe far-ranging pedagogical and technological issues. However, the following will perhaps give a brief picture of those questions considered most important and most frequently recommended for further research:

First, there are some strictly pedagogical issues. Questions related to the *effectiveness* of CAI have drawn a great deal of attention. How effective can CAI be in providing individualized learning opportunities, separate from or integrated with conventional forms of instruction? What is the best way to divide a student's involvement with CAI among remedial, review, drill and practice, tutorial, and interactive learning experiences? To what extent can creative and original thinking be encouraged in a CAI environment? What kinds of information are important for developing meaningful student learning profiles? How should this mass of information be organized and presented to teachers so that they can further prescribe and work with students on an individual basis?

Underlying these questions, researchers realize, are more basic concerns to which research attention must be given. For example, extensive consideration must be given to modes of presentation; programme structure, and types of learning reinforcement. Ways must be found to desing computer progarmmes which will be able, in a sophisticated way, to analyze and act on student background, ability, and progress. This in itself implies a systematic classification of individual difference variables and their interaction with instructional materials and modes of presentation.

The *effects* of CAI present another area of intriguing questions for further research. For example, what are the psychological and physiological effects on students after long-term or intensive short-term use of CAI? What are the sociological implications? What will be the effect of CAI on the teacher's training and school role? What additional skill roles will be necessary? What effects will CAI have on school systems design, allocation of resources, and administration? In short, what jobs are best handled by machines and what jobs by humans?

A wide variety of questions probing technological issues have also been presented in the literature. Typical examples would be the following:

> What requirements should CAI input-output devices have in order to be easy and natural for the student to use and as little distractive as possible from the learning process? What requirements should CAI languages have to allow teacher-authors not familiar with the operation of the computer to use its full power and capability effetively in developing learning programmes and collecting student data? What are the requirements for the student to be able to use his own natural spoken or written language in carrying on an extended dialogue with the computer learning programme?

While preliminary research efforts have been directed toward some of the above questions, the extent of our knowledge is sketchy and tentative at this time. Many of the questions raised have much broader implications than just CAI, and some will not be researchable for a number of years. In order of importance, the most critical research needs at this time reside in the pedagogical questions raised.

GENERALIZATIONS ABOUT RESEARCH

Several major criticisms (perhaps limitations in the better word) can be made which apply generally to CAI research methodology. Attention has been drawn to some of the factors affecting the validity of the research designs.

Very little effort is made, in most instances, to *consider other pertinent research studies* (not necessarily CAI), and to show how the current research fits into the broader picture. As Krathwohl has pointed out, no research starts *de novo*: it is part of a continuum, and such studies should, over the course of time, deepen and broaden our understanding.

There are *biases of selection*. The methods of selecting students for CAI studies generally prohibit any generalizations of results beyond the subjects themselves in the particular situation they were exposed to, at the time they were exposed to it. A number of replications of the studies, plus the application of random selection techniques, would have to be made before any meaningful generalizations could be derived. (Usually, the researchers themselves express reluctance to extend their conclusions very far from the specific situations tested.)

There are *maturation effects*. It is probable that the student's behaviour is affected by his interaction with the computer during the instruction. For example, being bothered or upset by the machinery can too easily introduce changes which are confused with the effect of the experimental variable. In addition, many of the experiments are short. And with the small populations used, individual influences on the student can become extremely exaggerated, e.g., sickness, time of the year.

Also, there are *reactive arrangements*. Frequently, the artificiality of the experimental setting seems to militate against the external validity of the research design. To take students out of class, to have them meet at special times and places, and to introduce them to a special setting where they will work with the computer inevitably influences the students, particularly over shot periods of time. Is the student pleased because he is getting special treatment? Is he impressed with the equipment? Does he feel he must do better because he is being observed or knows he is a part of an experiment? Thus we must ask, "Are student performance differences really attributable to the experimental variables under study?" In short, reactive arrangements (and similarly, selection biases and maturation effects) confound our understanding of what the real change-producing events are and leave the research results open to question.

A final observation is that there appears to be a feeling or urgency among some researchers to make in-depth comparisons between CAI and other forms of conventional instruction. This is regrettable, in that it tends to force artificial designs on the research and places undue emphasis on proving or disproving CAI as a way of individualizing instruction.

The approach that does seem warranted at this time is to use CAI as a way of *learning about learning.* The powerful data collection and data reduction capabilities of the computer offer immense possibilities for studying and controlling the variables of learning. This, in turn, should lead to the development of thoroughly tested and validated instructional materials and teaching strategies, and ultimately to a theory of instruction itself.

The appropriate question to be asked, therefore, is not "How much better is CAI than the ways we have been trying to teach?" but "How can CAI assist us to understand and control learning itself?"

CURRENT TRENDS IN CAI

Recent history has shown that substantial sums of money are available for CAI development. This trend will undoubtedly continue, perhaps dramatically, during the next several years. The money will come from business corporations, federal and private funding agencies, and the military, and will be directed toward the research and development of curriculum materials and CAI programming languages. The number of educational institutions, manufacturers, and publishing houses announcing or expanding their commitment to CAI development will increase at a similar pace. We can also expect a greater dispersion of research at all levels of education rather than concentration at the elementary and secondary levels. Hopefully, we will also see experts from a variety of disciplines giving their attention to CAI research. Some evidence of this is already apparent.

We should also expect that some institutions will be attracted to CAI for reasons of prestige or misguided enthusiasm. Bushnell, in reviewing Title III proposals for computer technology, shows this is already beginning to occur. Schools which take this approach run a high risk of being quickly disillusioned when they discover the dearth of off-the-shelf CAI programmes available, and the time, personnel, and cost required to develop instructional materials and operate a CAI system. Perhaps education's difficult experience with teaching machines a few years ago will offset this trend.

One of the few centers where significant research with CAI is being conducted is the Stanford-Brentwood Computer-Assisted Instruction Laboratory. In 1964, the U.S. Office of Education granted a contract to the Institute of Mathematical Studies in the Social Sciences at Stanford to set up a computer-based laboratory at a public elementary school. The purpose was to investigate CAI over an extended period of time. Brentwood Elementary School in East Palo Alto, California, was selected as the site for this experiment.

The project is directed by Patrick Suppes and Richard C. Atkinson, senior members of the Institute for Mathematical Studies. Other personnel on the project include about 50 teachers, psychologists, linguists, mathematicians, curriculum and reading experts, writers, artists, and computer programmers.

After two years of planning and preparation, instruction in mathematics and reading was started in September, 1966, with 100 first-grade children at Brentwood. The programme includes both drill and practice and tutorial instruction, and the students are allowed to progress at their own rate. In addition, the sequence of material presented to a student is a function of his prior history of responses. Thus at any particular time each student working with the system can be going through a completely different set of materials from any other student. An extensive history of responses is being collected on all the participants as they proceed through the programmes.

An IBM 1500 system with 16 student terminals is being used as the instructional system. Each terminal includes an audio system, a CRT display with light-pen, a picture projector, and a typewriter keyboard. The system is housed in a special building on the grounds of the elementary school.

This project deserves special mention for several reasons. It is the first project of its kind for bringing about an in-depth integration of CAI into an elementary school curriculum. It is the first project of its kind for collecting an analyzing long-term data with CAI, with a sizeable number of students involved. The project illustrates the kind of effort required to plan, develop, operate, and maintain a live CAI system in an elementary school setting. It also illustrates the costs involved. Direct costs have been estimated to be about one-half million dollars for the hardware and building and one-half million for curriculum development. These figures do not include the costs of previous research and curriculum development.

In time, this type of project can result in thoroughly tested and validated instructional materials which other schools could use at considerably less cost. A great deal of important and useful information should also be forthcoming, particularly with regard to curriculum design, instructional strategies, and basic information related to learning models.

CONCLUSIONS

The following conclusions seem warranted at this time as we survey what we know about CAI.

1. It is important in evaluating CAI to keep clearly in mind the distinction between pedagogical and technological issues. The computer is a powerful tool for gathering and manipulating data, but by itself it tells us nothing about learning or how learning occurs. "The research and curriculum work done thus far as a result of the current interest in teaching machines and programmed instruction show clearly that technology alone is not going to produce any fundamental or long-lasting changes in the curriculum. Only if its applications are guided by appropriate psychological principles and subject-matter insight will such changes be brought about."

2. CAI would appear to offer significant potential in providing individualized instruction. However, we have barely begun the exploration and necessary development. "The problem now is the hard one of finding the critical data that will make such a technological capability truly effective."

3. For some time in the future, then, one of the most critical and important applications for CAI will be as a school laboratory to learn about learning and perhaps ultimately to build a theory of instruction. Education has never had such a unique facility available to perform this task.

4. We can expect for some years to come that CAI will have to be heavily subsidized, because of its high costs and the lack of thoroughly tested and high quality instructional programmes.

5. On of the current dangers is that schools will erroneously attempt an involvement with CAI based only on faddism or a sincere but naive understanding of what is involved.

6. Legitimate research with CAI should be strongly encouraged, but schools should be realistically aware of the kinds of skills required, the kinds of commitment needed from personnel, and the costs that will be incurred.

7. Critical needs exist, therefore, for well-designed and well-executed research extending over long periods of time, coupled with well-planned dissemination of research results. Also vital are periodic professional assessments of the research to maintain a balanced perspective of this emerging teconology.

History may well bear out Suppes' observation that:

> ...it is fair to forecast that in the next 10 years the impact of computer-assisted instruction will be felt in a very large number of school systems in this country. The technology alone is not important. What is important is that by the use of computers we can realize the goals of individualized instruction that have been discussed in American education since the beginning of this century. And we can take another significant step toward realizing the full learning potential of our children.

But in the last analysis, it would seem that we should also heed Hutchins' concern that "...we may come to desire the kind of education that is easiest for the computer to provide. Our final, most difficult decision, therefore, may be whether "The safest course will be to turn over to the machines the task of training and informing, thus relieving teachers for the work of education.

CURRENT PROBLEMS IN CAI

Even the reader who only casually keeps up with developments in the data processing field, or in education and training, is aware that computers are being used in elementary and secondary schools, higher education, business, industry, and government agencies to assist in the process of instruction. There are many different points of view from which these activities can be described—one could list the existing installations, or discuss the different applications, or describe the various hardware systems or languages being used, and so forth.

The aim of this article is to consider the progress in CAI to data, identifying some of the difficulties that have been encountered, and suggesting changes needed if matters are to improve. Accordingly, we will describe CAI developments under the following headings:

1. Ways computers assist instruction—a list and brief description of six different kinds of computer applications in instruction;
2. Issues and problems—a discussion of results of implementing CAI;
3. Suggestions for future developments—a discussion of efforts which are needed to help resolve some of the current issues and problems.

WAYS COMPUTERS ASSIST INSTRUCTION

In this article, we will limit our discussion to those applications in which the computer output produces some readily identifiable effect upon the instructional interaction. Six different categories of such applications are often included in discussions of CAI, and these are shown in Table 8.5.

In the last category—Interactive Instruction—the computer is used as one agent in the instruction interaction itself, and its effect is direct and immediate. In other categories, the effect of the computer's output may take place through an intermediary, or may be delayed in time. For example, where the learner has access to a computer which he uses as a computational aid, the most readily identifiable effect upon the instructional process may be that the teacher can assign work in areas which simply could not be covered otherwise.

TABLE 8.5

Features of Some CAI Applications

Application Category	*Inputs to the System*	*System Function*	*System Output*
1	*2*	*3*	*4*
Computational Aid	Values of variables Data from observations	Solves the formula Carries out the analysis	Solutions to the problem (results of the calculation, statistical analysis, etc.)
Simulation	Responses to instruction or data in the learning environment (decisions in games, procedures for operating on line terminals, tests cases in laboratories, maneuvers in aircraft, space-craft, or naval vessel crew training, etc.)	Uses learner inputs to solve a mathematical model of the process (physical social, organiza-tional, economic, etc.,) being simulated.	Outcomes of the learner's decisions, sometimes expressed as changes in the computer-controlled parts of the learner's environment.
Lesson Material Storage and Retrieval	Information which identifies the learner's area of interest (subject, period, area, etc.,)	Matches identifiers with those of stored lesson or supple-mentary material.	Lesson (or supplementary) material requested by the learner (language exercises,

(Contd.)

1	2	3	4
	or the learner's progress in a particular course of instruction.		classroom or homework assignments, etc.,)
Lesson Prescription	Learner's performance on test administered following last assignment (may be entered by teacher teacher's aide, etc.,)	Matches learner's performance on last test with characteristics of alternative instructional units for next topic.	Assignment of next instructional unit for use in classroom or laboratory, or for homework, outside reading, etc.,
Testing	Answers to drill and review problems	Grades learner's answers (right or wrong); adjusts difficulty level of next problem set; collects data on all students by problem set.	To learner—right or wrong on each problem; per cent for set. To teacher —summaries of learner performance.
Interactive Instruction	Responses to question asked by the system	Analyzes learner's response, and selects next item to be presented to learner.	To learner—for correct answers, indication of correctness, plus next item; for incorrect answers, some dialogue exploring the correct answer. To course designers—error data by item.

By considering only those cases in which the computer affects the instructional process, we will ignore the many computer applications in education and training which affect other processes. For example, we will not consider the uses of computers to assist school administration (such as class scheduling, staff payroll, test grading, or materials inventory), guidance and placement (such as matching job requirements to student characteristics), nor research (such as item analysis for the purpose of test validation).

The purpose of presenting these categories of CAI applications is not to define CAI, but simply to direct attention to those characteristics of CAI which are most fruitful for the discussion which follows.

Of the many issues and problems—foreseen and not—which have resulted from the different attempts to implement CAI in educational, commercial, and governmental environments, I want to discuss three, chosen because their resolution is necessary if CAI is to evolve into a useful tool.

GAPS IN THE INSTRUCTIONAL PROCESS

Perhaps the most widely known applications of computers in education are those which use the drill-and-review materials developed over the last few years at Stanford University. At last count, the system, feeding a PDP-1/PDP-8 combination at the Stanford University Computation Center, included approximately 83 Teletype terminals located in elementary schools in California, Mississippi, and Kentucky. A similar system of 192 terminals, connected to an RCA Spectra 70, is being installed in 16 elementary schools in New York City. These installations deserve careful examination because they involve large numbers of students in widely separted parts of the country, and represent an enormous investment of public research funds. Furthermore, RCA's very active marketing of the drill-and-review approach may pressure other manufacturers into announcing competitive systems.

The problem which such applications raises can best be appreciated by describing how the system is supposed to work. During each meeting of a 7th grade algebra class, for example, each student leaves the classroom in order to spend approximately 5 to 10 minutes at a Teletype terminal. When the student signs on, the computer presents him with approximately 20 drill-and-review questions appropriate to that day's lesson. The exercises are arranged into five tracks according to "level of difficulty," and the computer selects the track from which this student's exercise is taken based upon his performance on the previous exercise. The computer then prepares a daily performance summary for the teacher of each class.

The most important problem raised by this approach is the lack of any direct interaction between the system and those classroom practices which result in learning. In effect, the computer is being used to test the students, and to prepare test performance statistics for the teacher, and that is all. The teacher is given the responsibility both of interpreting the test data, and of altering his classroom practices to compensate for whatever instructional deficiencies are revealed by the test data.

What happens when the computer dumps all the performance data on the teachers? Perhaps we can infer from Suppes' remark "...there are so many questions about performance that can be asked and that the computer can answer that teachers, administrators and supervisors are in danger of being swamped by more summary information than they can possibly digest.". If the teachers cannot possibly digest the information, one wonders how they can use the information to advantage in the classroom.

One researcher on the Stanford project remarked "The only reason the teachers like the system is because it takes attendance for them." But in all fairness, it should be realized that unless the teacher has been specifically trained to do so, he will not know where to start in using the data to improve his classroom practices. Under the circumstances, the teacher may be very well justified in feeling that the computer's only tangible contribution to events in the classroom *is* the taking of attendance.

The current drills-and-review applications, then, point up the difficulties encountered when a computer system is installed to do part of the job, and the responsibilty to do the rest of the job is left up to teachers who are less than adequately prepared to apply the computer's results to their everyday classroom practices. It would be difficult to find a clearer example of the problem Skinner refers to when he describes efforts which concentrate upon "...measuring the results of teaching while neglecting teaching itself."

LIMITATIONS IMPOSED BY SYSTEMS

The characteristics of any CAI system can impose severe limitation upon both the kinds of materials which can be presented to the learner, and the kinds of responses the learner can be required to make. In choosing one CAI system from among those available, and in deciding whether or not to use a given CAI system for a particular instruction task, it is importan for the potential user to ask: "What limitations does this system impose upon the material I need to present, and upon the responses I must elicit?" (Again, because our main concern in this article is the instructional interaction, we will not describe the limitations which a CAI system may impose upon other aspects of education or tranining. CAI system characteristics cannot help but affect the administration of instruction: for example; the system's storage capacity limits the amount of instructional material that can be handled at any one time; the terminals may have to be located within a given number of feet of the central processor, requiring that learners from outlying schools in the district, or offices in the company, would have to be transported to use the system.) Unfortunately, there are few generalizations which are useful in answering this question. It is not useful, for example, to describe the suitability of a CAI system in terms of subject areas because the limitations imposed by any system affect the teaching interaction at the stimulus, response level, and therefore cut across subject areas. To make matters worse, there are no charcteristics common to CAI hardware, nor to CAI software, nor to the kinds of teaching materials used with CAI systems, which can support generalizations about CAI systems with respect to proposed applications.

While a mismatch between system limitations and use requirements cannot be avoided by trusting to generalities, it can be avoided by an analysis which includes a description of the input-output capabilities of the system, and a description of the instructional objectives in terms of the stimuli and responses required.

To show what might be involved in such an analysis, let us consider some representative examples of the kinds of materials we may wish to display to the learner, and of the kinds of responses we may want the learner to make.

1. Kinds of Material to be Displayed to the Learner

(a) Text: in teaching foreign languages, we may wish to display text including special alphabetic characters; in teaching mathematics, chemistry, and logic, we require special symbols, signs subscripts, etc., for displaying equations, formulas and expressions.

(b) Audio: we may want to play back recordings of spoken messages in teaching communication skills, languages or basal reading; and recordings of instruments in teaching music appreciation.

(c) Graphics: we may wish to display maps in teaching history; motion pictures in engineering or science; still photographs in medicine or art; circuit diagrams in electricity; graphs in mathematics or statistics; engineering drawings in blueprint reading; cardiograms in medical diagnosis; and so forth.

At the present time, no operating CAI system (known to this author) is capable of presenting all of the above materials to a learner. Most CAI systems use a typewriter as their interface with the learner, and are not designed to handly *any* of the teaching materials mentioned above. Strum and Ward describe the problems they encountered in using typewriter terminals. The difficulties are even greater, of course, if one wishes to prepare hard copy of any of these materials for use and retention by the learner. The ability to present to the learner each different kind of material usually requires a different kind of presentation device, together with instructions in the computer language to operate the device—in other words, each different kind of display capability may involve its own peculiar hardware and software problems.

2. Kinds of Responses to be Required of the Learner

The terminal behaviour specifications (i.e., the teaching objectives of the course, stated in terms of observable changes in the learner's behaviour) for courses in various subjects might include the following items:

(a) State the expression for the area under the curve.

(b) Translate the above sentence into Russian.

(c) Fill in the missing parts of the following table.

(d) Point to the antibodies in the microphotograph.

(e) Outline the temperate zone on the map.

(f) Complete the circuit diagram.

(g) Describe a relationship

(h) Define a concept.

(i) Explain how something works.

(j) Summarize the speaker's remarks orally.

There are two major sources of difficulty in using a CAI system to teach anything: the system may not have the *hardware* capability to allow the student to make the response, and it may not provide a *language* in which the instructor can specify how to analyze and evaluate the student's response.

Item (a) in the above list requires a keyboard equipped with special mathematical symbols. Item (b) requires a keyboard with a complete Cyrillic alphabet. Item (c) can be handled easily on a system which includes *crt* display, but a system which provides only a typewriter interface requires that the learner reverse line feed until he positions the proper line of typing with the print element. Items (d), (e), and (f) each require special equipment, some of which is now in the prototype stage of development.

Items (g), (h), and (i) pose difficulties of another sort. Using even the simplest available alphabetic keyboard, the student can easily type in his description, definition, explanation, or whatever the question requires him to enter. The problem is that there are no methods for deciding the semantic equivalence of what Spolsky modestly describes as "...a very large number ..." of sentences. As a result, we cannot, at present, tell the computer how to process a learner's input to decide whether or not his response *means the same* as the model answer we have stored for that response. Instead, we force the learner to respond within the constraints of an artifical language, thus allowing no ambiguity. Or, we allow natural language responses, but we restrict the length of the response to that which rules out the most probable sources of ambiguity. At best, we rely upon features of the response other than its meaning (the presence of specified key words, the order in which they appear, etc.) to determine its match to our "answer" (right or wrong). In all such cases, we allow the taill to wag the dog: it is the specification of the learner's terminal behaviour which should determine the characteristics of the response, not our inability to handle problems of meaning, and whenever we modify the requirements for the response in a way that settles for something less than the terminal behaviour specification, to that extent we degrade the quality of the instruction.

In everyday practice, this problem is aggravated by the fact that some of the CAI languages which the instructor must use to specify his requirements for acceptable responses do not allow even the primitive level of analysis represented by such procedures as scanning for key words, editing out punctuation, allowing certain flexibility in spelling, etc.

Item (*j*) presents both hardware and software problems. We do not yet know how to translate spoken words into written words, that is, we cannot speak into one end of a device, and have the text of our spoken words print out at the other end. So we lack this kind of student interface in available CAI systems. But even if such a device were available, we would be just as far from being able to analyze its output as we are from analyzing any other free-form response. Recognition of the meaning of speech therefore involves both a hardware problem which is unique and a software problem which it shares with other kinds of responses.

One revealing question to ask is, "If available CAI systems impose such restrictions as these, how are they being applied to teaching applications?" In other words, how are researchers overcoming the inherent limitations of the CAI systems they are stuck with? Several approaches are being tried, and are worth considering:

(a) Add outside components to perform the functions which the CAI system cannot—for example, if your CAI system cannot present photographs to students, have the photographs reproduced in advance, packaged, and distributed to each student; then at least your course can direct the student's attention to the information, and ask questions based upon the "supplementary" material.

(b) Modify the system—for example, the Slavic linguistics department at Stanford has installed Teletypewriters with Cyrillic keyboards in their introductory Russian course.

(c) Modify your teaching objectives to fit within the capabilities of the system—for example, one of your course objectives may be to teach the student to list the characteristics of something (a chemical compound, a period of a nation's history, a style of poetry, etc.); if your CAI system language will not accept alphabetic inputs, then abandon your original course objective, and substitute another one which can be handled by your computational language—instead of teaching the student to *produce* the list of characteristics, produce each item for him, and ask him to enter numbers which indicate whether or not he *recognizes* that it belongs in the list (your course outline will look the same to anyone who is curious as to what you are teaching).

(d) Conclude that CAI is not a fruitful approach, and continue to teach the way you used to.

None of these approaches is very satisfactory: Adding outside components may pose complicated distribution and inventory problems. Modifying the system can be expensive. Modifying one's teaching objectives to fit the hardware capabilities usually results in a deterioration of the good qualities of the instruction. Concluding that CAI is not a fruitful approach is foolish, unless you have investigated all existing systems, and unless you know that future technological developments will never change the situation.

PRODUCTION OF CAI TEACHING MATERIALS

Since the earliest experiments with CAI systems, it has been recognized that a major obstacle to the successful application of CAI is the lack of quality course materials. As we will see later on, the shortage of qualified people to produce such materials is an important factor here. This lack is not a great problem for industry, business, or government. Each company or agency tends to develop much of its own instructional materials since course content usually concerns facts about products, services, policies, or procedures which are relevant only to a particular organization.

In contrast, the formal educational establishment tends to produce a smaller portion of the instructional materials it consumes, and relies instead for the bulk of its needs upon the textbook publishers, and upon the manufacturers of supplementary materials (audio-visual aids, kits, laboratory equipment, and so forth). As a result, the availability of CAI curriculum materials for use in formal education is a critical matter, and the means employed to meet this need will have far-reaching effects upon the quality of the instruction, and hence upon the acceptability of the concept of CAI itself. The discouraging example of the unimaginative use of educational television should stand as a warning that the availability of hardware with powerful functional characteristics is not enough to result in improvement of education. Today we face the very real danger that the challenge of applying CAI will be avoided, and that this opportunity for educational improvement will be lost. This danger will persist as long as CAI is regarded primarily as a means of extending traditional classroom practices, or as long as educators remain enchanted by visions of using a CAI system because it allows them to "orchestrate" the presentation of multi-media materials. Students do not learn simply because they know they'll be tested, nor because material is presented to them in four colours, nor because they are bombarded with multi-media presentations.

The computer is the most effective tool yet devised for arranging the stimulus-response-reinforcement contingencies which constitute the learning interaction. How CAI course material is designed will determine whether the potential of the computer will be wasted in simulating traditional practices. There is already some evidence of the bad results which can be expected when CAI users systematically disregard even the most general prescriptions of behavioural technology.

From time to time, with emphasis depending on the source, it has been suggested that CAI course materials will be produced by computer manufacturers, school teachers, textbook publishers, and independent companies specializing in curriculum development for CAI. We will briefly examine each of these suggestions.

The suggestions that CAI system manufacturers would produce curriculum materials have died out, mainly because no computer manufacturer (with one exception to be discussed next) has the appropriate resources to attempt the time-consuming and expensive developmental and marketing efforts involved. The one manufacturer having a recognized and respected in-house curriculum development capability is IBM, which bought Science Research Associates, Inc., in 1964. When the IBM 1500 CAI System was announced two years later, the press release stated that course and supplementary materials in nine subject areas were being developed by SRA. Since then, however, SRA has not published any CAI courses, and it is not now clear when, or if, such materials will be available as standard products to educators. In retrospect, then, it has turned out that computer manufacturers have not been an important supplier of curriculum materials.

An alternative suggestion—that teachers produce their own CAI materials—has enjoyed much greater favour. In fact, faced with the current lack of available programmes, there is scarcely any other path open to the would-be CAI user. But there are difficulties in this approach which should be recognized.

First, the time required to produce CAI materials exceeds the time which teachers can reasonably be expected to spend. The accumulated experience in producing programmed instructional materials shows that approximately 100 hours of analysis, programming, and editing effort are required to produce material which occupies the student for one hour.

To this must be added to time required to put the instructional programme into CAI form. Strum and Ward summarize their experience follows. "It has been estimated that the writing of a programmed book absorbs one to two orders of magnitude more effort than is required to write a conventional text on the same subject. The present authors estimate that *another* one or two orders of magnitude separate the computer programme from the programmed text." Reynolds states that "...fairly careful records we have kept in course development in CAI at Texas Christian University (and other sources as well) indicates a minimum of 300 man-hours per hour of instruction..." But even if we assume a conservative 100-to-1 hour ratio, where is the average school teacher or college professor going to get the time to produce CAI material covering any significant portion of a course?

The second difficulty is that there are few people—teachers included—who possess the diverse skills required to prepare self-instructional materials. Such courses are usually produced by a team, combining the skills of:

1. Subject matter experts, who specify content and objectives;
2. Behaviour analysis, who apply learning principles to specified knowledge and skills;
3. Programmers, who convert the behavioural analysis into appropriate instructional interactions; and
4. Programme editors, who revise and refine the instructional sequences in the light of performance data.

In addition, test subjects, typists, draftsmen, and illustrators may be needed from time to time in the production process.

If we consider the teacher or professor developing material for use in a CAI system, we can probably assume that he will be his own subject matter expert. Furthermore, he probably can use his own students as test subjects. And he may be able to use keypunch operators at his institution's *edp* center instead of the typists we have listed. But even with these simplifying assumptions, the central problem remains: few people have the skills required to produce instructional material with predictable performance characteristics. Quality CAI material is not produced by simply using the computer to emulate classroom practice, yet many teachers have little else to guide them when they begin trying to use CAI systems.

THE MANUFACTURERS' CONTRIBUTION

Ironically, the manufacturers of CAI systems have little help to offer. (One example of this deficiency occurred when the Philadelphia City Schools were installing a Philco-Ford 16-terminal CAI system, and had to hire an independent consultant to discuss with teachers the strategies of organizing course material for computer input.) All of the CAI system manuals I have seen assume that the user has already solved the problems of behavioural design and testing, that is, they begin at the point at which the user is ready to express his instructional sequences in a particular CAI language. Even SDC's PLANIT, which guides the programme writer by reminding him of the choices available during his on-line programme construction and entry, actually assumes that all of the important pedagogial decisions have been made before the programme writer makes his entries.

The user's plight is not helped by the style of CAI systems manuals—all of those I have examined start off as if the reader were thoroughly familiar with *edp* concepts, terminology, and procedures. There is no evidence that the authors took into account the background that teachers, curriculum writers, training specialists, and others would bring to the task of using CAI systems.

In summary, then, the lack of available CAI course materials, together with the shortage of people with relevant production skills, have forced many teachers into preparing their own CAI materials. The difficulties they have faced in so doing include their own lack of the specialized skills required to produce self-instructional materials, the restraints on the amount of time they can devote to such work and the lack of any effective help from the CAI systems manufacturers.

A third source of CAI course materials is the textbook publishers. To review some of the developments in this area, we must go back to RCA's entry into the CAI field. At the opening of the RCA Instructional Systems offices in March of

1967, the president of Random House, Inc. (an RCA subsidiary) stated, in discussing the new venture, "Our specific assignment is the provision of the instructional materials themselves." Subsequently, it was revealed that the L.W. Singer Division of Random House is adapting *Spelling-Diagnostic Paragraphs* for CAI. In May of 1967, RCA announced an agreement with Harcourt, Brace and World, Inc., under which the publisher would adapt its *Language and Daily Use* series in grades 4, 5 and 6 for use with RCA computer equipment. Later in 1967, Harper and Row also reached agreement with RCA to produce supplementary material for use with their widely used *Today's Basic Science* series.

THE PUBLISHERS' ACTIVITIES

In a relatively short time, RCA has formed a network of alliances with major textbook publishers which may have far-reaching effects on CAI curriculum development. Such a move is potentially of great benefit to each of the participants. It enables the computer manufacturer to avoid the costly, unfamiliar job of curriculum development, and yet he can assure his potential customers that reputable publishers are busy producing learning materials for use with his system. The publisher also stands to gain: his textbook salesmen have a distinct marketing advantage when dealing with any school which uses (or intends to use) that manufacturer's CAI system. Such schools will be under heavy pressure to show tangible results from their adventures in CAI, and will find it difficult to turn away a textbook salesman who offers a ready-to-go package of computer-based material which supplements an established text series. If the school is already using that textbook series, the argument will be even stronger.

However, the publisher in such an alliance takes a risk to the extent that he invests in developing programmes for a system which may not be well received, or which may become obsolete before he regains his investment. As more different CAI systems are introduced to the market, it will become decreasingly attractive for the publisher to develop materials for any one of them, and increasingly expensive for him to develop materials for all of them. These problems raise the whole issue of a CAI common language, and do so with an urgency which is unique in the development of computer applications. It would not be surprising to find textbook publishers in the vanguard of efforts to establish standards for a common CAI language.

While only secondarily aimed at curriculum material production, several related projects are underway at Mc-Graw-Hill: collaboration with the University of Texas CAI Laboratory in the development of remedial English materials for college freshmen; support of exploratory work at the University of Pittsburgh Learning Research and Development Center relating to innovations in spelling teaching; and collaboration with a major urban school distinct in preparing curriculum packages in areas yet to be specified. The primary aim of these efforts is to help establish the appropriate roles of authors, editors, and consultants in the CAI production process, and to investigate different modes of a publisher's interaction with teachers, CAI programmers, researchers, etc.

The fourth and last possibility we shall consider is that CAI courses will become available from organizations formed for the specific purpose of producing such materials. The largest and apparently most successful of these companies is Computer Curriculum Corp. (formed by Suppes, Atkinson, and Wilson) which started operations in October, 1967. Their major curriculum contract is with Harcourt, Brace and World to produce drill-and-practice materials for use with Harcourt's *Language and Daily Use* text series, but generalized so that they can be used with other language arts texts. Computer Curriculum Corp. employs about 25 writers, editors, and computer programmers, organized into project teams.

It is far too soon to evaluate the impact of these CAI materials production houses. They face the same shortage of qualified people which their competitors do. They have several potential advantages going for them—for example, compared to the efforts of individual teachers, professors, or consultants, they can presumably apply to any given project a greater variety of the skills which are needed to assure the quality of self-instructional materials.

In summary, the CAI material houses are a development worth watching. Their activities are aimed at filling an obvious need, and their activities may have an important impact upon the application of CAI systems.

SUGGESTIONS FOR FUTURE DEVELOPMENTS

In the previous section, we examined three problems which have arisen in connection with the current CAI applications. Several of our suggestions for future developments will, then, deal with the problems we have already mentioned.

1. Some of the funds available to schools for the purchase of the hardware used is drill-and-review systems should be spent instead to study what it takes for the teacher to apply the summarized test data to classroom practice, and to develop a vehicle for appropriate teacher training. The emphasis in drill-and-review systems should be shifted, at least temporarily, from the problem of gathering the data to the problem of understanding and applying the data.

2. Much more work needs to be done aimed at overcoming what Spolsky identifies as "...the present inadequacy or incompleteness of linguistic theory." Ideally, the person writing an instructional programme should be able to state a question to be asked of the learner, provide an answer to the question, and then specify that any response of the learner's which means the same is to be treated in the same way by the programme. Although we may never attain this ideal goal, any approximation to it will have a significant beneficial effect upon CAI applications.

3. In his article in this issue, Zinn points out that the "...benefits unique to computer presentation and

control have not yet been demonstrated ... few lesson designers have made use of capabilities beyond those which can be accomplished with the printed format." One reason this is the case is that most lesson designers are using CAI systems to prepare specific course material, and the exigencies of such work—deadlines, funding arrangements, contract commitments, available time on the system, etc.—preclude the investigation of untried techniques. To correct this situation, projects should be initiated for the primary purpose of making the computer do that which the text—programmed or otherwise—cannot do.

4. While recognizing the dangers of too-hasty standardization, efforts aimed at specifying a common CAI language should continue. This work will be most difficult, since it will require reconciling the conflicting interests of such diverse parties as hardware manufacturers; educators (teachers, school administrators, curriculum specialists), textbook publishers; trainers in business, industry and government; and research specialists representing linguitics, behavioural technology, men-machine communications, etc.

5. The obvious hardware improvements are needed in CAI as well as in other computer application areas: more reliable, less expensive components. Significant advances which promise to improve the performance and to reduce the cost of terminal displays have been demonstrated by the Plasma Display Group at the University of Illinois Coordinated Science Laboratory, and more recently by RCA. Work is also needed to provide CAI system hard copy output devices for graphic as well as alphanumeric information under both learner and programm control.

Clearly there is much work to be done. One can only hope that those involved in the work will heed Oettinger's articulate warning, "Whatever the setting for educational experimentation, it is vital in our still profound ignorance to shy away from rigid prescriptions of either goal or technique. There is too much rigidity even in the present innovation fad which, ironically, diverts human and financial resources from both basic research and sustained application and evaluation efforts into the most visible quickie approaches that can sustain the illusion of progress."

COMPUTER TECHNOLOGY AND THE FUTURE OF EDUCATION

Current applications of computers and related information-precessing techniques run the gamut in our society from the automatic control of factories to the scrutiny of sex returns. I have not seen any recent data, but we are certainly reaching the point at which a high percentage of regular employees in this country are paid by computerized payroll systems. As another example, every kind of complex experiment is beginning to be subject to computer assistance either in terms of the actual experimentation or in terms of extensive computations integral to the analysis of the experiment. These applications range from bubble-chamber data on elementary particles to the crystallography of protein molecules.

As yet, the use of computer technology in administration and management on the one hand, and scientific and engineering applications on the other, far exceed direct applications in education. However, if potentials are properly realized, the character and nature of education during the course of our lifetimes will be radically changed. Perhaps the most important aspect of computerized instructional devices is that the kind of individualized instruction once possible for only a few members of the aristocracy can be made available to all students at all levels of abilities.

Because some may not be familiar with how computers can be used to provide individualized instruction, let me briefly review the mode of operation. In the first place, because of its great speed of operation, a computer can handle simultaneously a large number of students for instance, 200 or more, and each of the 200 can be at a different point in the curriculum. In the simplest mode of operation, the terminal device at which the student sits is something like an electric typewriter. Messages can be typed out by the computer and the student in turn can enter his responses on the keyboard. The first and most important feature to add is the delivery of audio messages under computer control to the student. Not only children, but students of all ages learn by ear as much as by eye, and for tutorial ventures in individualized instruction it is essential that the computer system be able to talk to the student.

A simple example may make this idea more concrete. Practically no one learns mathematics simply by reading a book, except at a relatively advanced level. Hearing lectures and listening to someone else's talk seem to be almost psychologically essential to learning complex subjects, at least as far as ordinary learners are concerned. In addition to the typewriter and the earphones for audio messages, the next desirable feature is that graphical and pictorial displays be available under computer control. Such displays can be provided in a variety of formats. The simplest mode is to have colour slides that may be selected by computer control. More flexible, and therefore more desirable, devices are cathode-ray tubes that look very much like television sets. The beauty of cathode-ray tubes is that a graphical display may be shown to the student and then his own response, entered on a keyboard, can be made an integral part of the display itself.

This is not the place to review these matters in detail; but I mean to convey a visual image of a student sitting at a variety of terminal gear—as it is called in the computer world. These terminals are used to provide the student with individualized instruction. He receives information from audio messages, from typewritten messages, and also from visual displays ranging from graphics to complex photographs. In turn, he may respond to the system and give his own answers by using the keyboard on the typewriter. Other devices for student response are also available, but I shall not go into them now.

So, with such devices available, individualized instruction in a wide variety of subject matters may be offered students of all ages. The technology is already available, although it will continue to be improved. There are two main factors standing in our way. One is that currently it is expensive to prepare an individualized curriculum. The second factor, and even more important, is that as yet we have little operational experience in precisely how this should best be done. For some time to come, individualized instruction will have to depend on a basis of practical judgement and pedagogical intuition of the sort now used in constructing textbook materials for ordinary courses. One of the exciting potentialities of computer-assisted instruction is that for the first time we shall be able to get hard data to use as a basis for a more serious scientific investigation and evaluation of any given instructional programme.

To give a more concrete sense of the possibilities of individualized instruction, I would like to deseribe briefly three possible levels of interaction between the student and computer programme. Following a current usage, I shall refer to each of the instructional programmes as a particular system of instruction. At the simplest level there are *individualized drill-and-practice systems*, which are meant to supplement the regular curriculum taught by the teacher. The introduction of concepts and new ideas is handled in conventional fashion by the teacher. The role of the computer is to provide regular review and practice on basic concepts and skills. In the case of elementary mathematics, for example, each student would receive daily a certain number of exercises, which would be automatically presented, evaluated, and scored by the computer programme without any effort by the classroom teacher. Moreover, these exercises can be presented on an individualized basis, with the brighter students receiving exercises that are harder than the average, and the slower students receiving easier problemmes.

One important aspect of this kind of individualization should be emphasized. In using a computer in this fashion, it is not necessary to decide at the beginning of the school year in which track a student should be placed; for example, a student need not be classified as a slow student for the entire year. Individualized drill-and-practice work is suitable to all the elementary subjects which occupy a good part of the curriculum. Elementary mathematics, elementary science, and the beginning work in foreign language are typical parts of the curriculum which benefit from standardized and regularly presented drill-and-practice exercises. A large computer with 200 terminals can handle as many as 6,000 students on a daily basis in this instructional mode. In all likelihood, it will soon be feasible to increase these numbers to a thousand terminals and 30,000 students. Operational details of our 1965-66 drill-and-practice programme at Stanford are to be found in the forthcoming book by Suppes, Jerman, and Brian.

At the second and deeper level of interaction between student and computer programme there are *tutorial systems*, which take over the main responsibility both for presenting a concept and for developing skill in its use. The intention is to approximate the interaction a patient tutor would have with an individual student. An important aspect of the tutorial programmes in reading and elementary mathematics with which we have been concerned at Stanford in the past three years is that every effort is made to avoid an initial experience of failure on the part of the slower children. On the other hand, the programme has enough flexibility to avoid boring the brighter children with endlessly repetitive exercises. As soon as the student manifests a clear understanding of a concept on the basis of his handling of a number of exercises, he is moved on to a new concept and new exercises. (A detailed evaluation of the Stanford reading programme, which is under the direction of Richard C. Atkinson, may be found in the report by Wilson and Atkinson. A report on the tutorial mathematics programme will soon be available. The data show that the computer-based curriculum was particularly beneficial for the slower students.)

At the third and deepest level of interaction there are *dialogue systems* aimed at permitting the student to conduct a genuine dialogue with the computer. The dialogue systems at the present time exist primarily at the conceptual rather than the operational level, and I do want to emphasize that in the case of dialogue systems a number of difficult technical problems must first be solved. One problem is that of recognizing spoken speech. Especially in the case of young children, we would like the child to be able simply to ask the computer programme a question. To permit this interaction, we must be able to recognize the spoken speech of the child and also to recognize the meaning of the question he is asking. The problem of recognizing meaning is at least as difficult as that of recognizing the spoken speech. It will be some time before we will be able to do either one of these things with any efficiency and economy.

I would predict that within the next decade many children will use individualized drill-and-practice systems in elementary school; and by the time they reach high school, tutorial systems will be available on a broad basis. Their children may use dialogue systems throughout their school experience.

If these predictions are even approximately correct, they have far-reaching implications for education and society. As has been pointed out repeatedly by many people in many different ways, the role of education in our society is not simply the transmission of knowledge but also the transmission of culture, including the entire range of individual, political, and social values. Some recent studies—for example, the Coleman report—have attempted to show that the schools are not as effective in transmitting this culture as we might hope; but still there is little doubt that the schools play a major role, and the directions thay take have serious implications for the character of our society in the future. Now I hope it is evident from the very brief descriptions I have given that the widespread use of computer technology in education has an enormous potential for improving the quality of education, because the possibility of individualizing instruction at ever deeper levels of interaction can be realized in an economically feasible fashion. I take it that this potentiality is evident enough, and I would like to examine some of the problems it raises, problems now beginning to be widely discussed.

Three rather closely related issues are particularly prominent in this discussion. The first centers around the claim that the deep use of technology, especially computer technology, will impose a rigid regime of impersonalized teaching. In considering such a claim, it is important to say at once that indeed this is a possibility. Computer technology could be used this way, and in some instances it probably will. This is no different from saying that there are many kinds of teaching, some good and same bad. The important point to insist upon, however, is that it is certainly not a *necessary* aspect of the use of the technology. In fact, contrary to the expectations sometimes expressed in the popular press, I would claim that one of the computer's most important potentials is in making learning and teaching more personalized, rather than less so. Students will be subject to less regimentation and lockstepping, because computer systems will be able to offer highly individualized instruction. The routine that occupies a good part of the teacher's day can be taken over by the computer.

It is worth noting in this connection that the amount of paper work required of teachers is very much on the increase. The computer seems to offer the only possibility of decreasing the time spent in administrative routine by ordinary teachers. Let us examine briefly one or two aspects of instruction ranging from the elementary school to the college. At the elementary level, no one anticipates that students will spend most of their time at computer consoles. Only 20 to 30 per cent of the student's time would be spent in this fashion. Teachers would be able to work with classes reduced in size. Also, they could work more intensely with individual students, because some of the students will be at the console and, more importantly, because routine aspects of teaching will be handled by the computer system.

At the college level, the situation is somewhat different. At most colleges and universities, students do not now receive a great deal of individual attention from instructors. I think we can all recognize that the degree of personal attention is certainly not less in a computer programme deisgned to accommodate itself to the individual student's progress than in the lecture course that has more than 200 students in daily attendance. (In our tutorial Russian programme at Stanford, under the direction of Joseph Van Campen, all regular classroom instruction has been eliminated. Students receive 50 minutes daily of individualized instruction at a computer terminal consisting of a teletype with Cyrillic keyboard and earphones; the audio tapes are controlled by the computer.)

A second common claim is that the widespread use of computer technology will lead to excessive standardization of education. Again, it is important to admit at once that this is indeed a possibility. The sterility of standardization and what it implies for teaching used to be illustrated by a story about the French educational system. It was claimed that the French minister of education could look at his watch at any time of the school day and say at once what subject was being taught at each grade level throughout the country. The claim was not true, but such a situation could be brought about in the organization of computer-based instruction. It would technically be possible for a state department of education, for example, to require every fifth-grader at 11:03 in the morning to be subtracting one-fifth from three-tenths, or for every senior in high school to be reciting the virtues of a democratic society. The danger of the technology is that edicts can be enforced as well as issued, and many persons are rightly concerned at the spectre of the rigid standardization that could be imposed.

On the other hand, there is another meaning of standardization that holds great potential. This is the imposition of educational standards on schools and colleges throughout the land. Let me give one example of what I mean. A couple of years ago I consulted with one of the large city school systems in this country in connection with its mathematics programme. The curriculum outline of the mathematics programme running from kindergarten to high school was excellent. The curriculum as specified in the outline was about as good as any in the country. The real source of difficulty was the magnitude of the discrepancy between the actual performance of the students and the specified curriculum. At almost every grade level, students were performing far below the standard set in the curriculum guide. I do not mean to suggest that computer technology will, in one fell stroke, provide a solution to the difficult and complicated problems of raising the educational standards that now obtain among the poor and culturally deprived. I do say that the technoloy will provide us with unparalleled insight into the actual performance of students.

Yet I do not mean to suggest that this problem of standardization is not serious. It is, and it will take much wisdom to avoid its grosser aspects. But the point I would like to emphasize is that the wide use of computers permits the introduction of an almost unlimited diversity of curriculum and teaching. The very opposite of standardization *can* be achieved. I think we would all agree that the ever-increasing use of books from the sixteenth century to the present has deepened the varieties of educational and intellectual experience generally available. There is every reason to believe that the appropriate development of instructional programmes for computer systems will increase rather than decrease this variety of intellectual experience. The potential is there.

The real problem is that as yet we do not understand very well how to take advantage of this potential. If we examine the teaching of any subject in the curriculum, ranging from elementary mathematics to ancient history, what is striking is the great similarity between teachers and between textbooks dealing with the same subject, not the vast differences between them. It can even be argued that it is a subtle philosophical question of social policy to determine the extent to which we want to emphasize diversity in our teaching of standard subjects. Do we want a "cool" presentation of American history for some students and a fervent one for others? Do we want to emphasize geometric and perceptual aspects of mathematics more for some students, and symbolic and algebraic aspects more for others? Do we want to make the learning of language more oriented toward the ear for some students and more toward the eye for those who have a poor sense of auditory discrimination? These are issues that have as yet scarcely been explored in educational philosophy or in discussions of educational policy. With the advent of the new technology they will become practical questions of considerable moment.

The third and final issue I wish to discuss is the place of individuality and human freedom in the modern technology. The crudest from of opposition to widespread use of techology in education and in other parts of our society is to claim that we face the real danger of men becoming slaves of machines. I feel strongly that the threat to human individuality and freedom in our society does not come from technology at all, but from another source that was well described by John Stuart Mill more than a hundred years ago. In discussing precisely this matter in his famous essay *On Liberty*, he said,

> the greatest difficulty to be encountered does not lie in the appreciation of means towards an acknowledged end, but in the indifference of persons in general to the end itself. If it were felt that the free development of individuality is one of the leading essentials of well-being; that it is not only a co-ordinate element with all that is designated by the terms civilization, instruction, education, culture, but is itself a necessary part and condition of all those things; there would be no danger that liberty should be undervalued, and the adjustment of the boundaries between it and social control would present no extraordinary difficulty.

Just as books freed serious students from the tyranny of overly simple methods of oral recitation, so computers can free students from the drudgery of doing exactly similar tasks unadjusted and untailored to their individual needs. As in the case of other parts of our society, our new and wondrous technology is there for beneficial use. It is our problem to learn how to use it well. When a child of six begins to learn in school under the direction of a teacher, he hardly has a concept of a free intelligence able to reach objective knowledge of the world. He depends heavily upon every word and gesture of the teacher to guide his own reactions and responses.

This intellectual weaning of children is a complicated process that we do not yet manage or understand very well. There are too many adults among us who are not able to express their own feeling or to reach their own judgements. I would claim that the wise use of technology and science, particularly in education, presents a major opportunity and challenge. I do not want to claim that we know very much yet about how to realize the full potential of human beings; but I do not doubt that we can use our modern instruments to reduce the personal tyranny of one individual over another, wherever that tyranny depends upon ignorance.

9

NEW EDUCATION POLICY OF INDIA ON EDUCATIONAL TECHNOLOGY

I. PRESENT SITUATION

Several efforts have been made in the past to use technological aids for improving the quality of education. Audio-visual units and film libraries were set up at the Centre and in the States for promoting the use of educational films and projection/non-projection aids. Educational Technology cells were also established in 21 States/UTs in a phased manner and a Centre of Educational Technology was set up in the National Council of Educational Research and Training (NCERT) to stimulate the use of television and other instructional media. School radio broadcasts have been in vogue for more than 40 years. AIR's Educational Programme-Production units, set up in 44 of the network's 88 stations, produce radio programmes for primary and secondary schools, which are presently broadcast by 74 stations. General enrichment programmes of 15-20 minutes duration are relayed 3-5 school days per week for primary school children. Programmes for secondary school students are broadcast for 15-20 minutes on all school days. AIR stations at Delhi, Jalandhar, Hyderabad and all stations in Tamilnadu also broadcast programmes 5-7 days a week, in support of the correspondence courses conducted by

Universities. 3—4 adult-education programmes are broadcast per week by 14 AIR radio stations.

2. Curriculum-based school TV programmes for secondary school students are presently being telecast by 4 Doordarshan Kendras. Educational Television (ETV programmes) of general enrichment for children in the age group 5—11 years are being telecast in the respective regional languages through satellite, six days a week, in the 6 INSAT States, and are being relayed by all transmitters in the 4 other Hindi-speaking States. A 1-hour general enrichment programme for University/College students is also being telecast daily. 2,000 VHF and 2,000 Direct Reception Sets (DRS) have been provided for community viewing in selected village clusters in the 6 INSAT States, installed mostly in the village schools. Under the "INSAT for EDUCATION" project, launched in 1982, State Institutes of Educational project, launched in 1982, State Institutes of Educational Technology (SIETs) are being set up in the States of Andhra Pradesh, Bihar, Gujarat, Maharashtra, Orissa and Uttar Pradesh and a Central Institute of Educational Technology (CIET) has been established in the NCERT, with 100 per cent Central assistance, to generate educational software for children. Audio-visual Research Centres (AVRCs) and Educational Media Research Centres (EMRCs) have also been set up in 6 Universities to prepare educational TV programmes for University/College students. Some facilities for TV programme/production have also been developed in the Technical Teacher Training Institutions (TTTIs).

3. Video Technology has also appeared on the educational horizon. The Electronics Trade and Technology Development Corporation (ET&T) has formulated a "TELETEACH" project to prepare educational software on videotape. VCRs and viewing equipment would be provided in about 600 viewing centres to be established in schools this year. The Ministry has also identified certain subject areas in which educational software would be developed by ET&T.

4. Computer-education courses at the Master's level (NCA) are presently being offered in 25 Universities, in addition to the Ph.D., M.Tech. and B.Tech programmes conducted by the IITs and other technological institutions. Diploma level programmes are being run in 35 polytechnics. With the introduction of the Computer Literacy and Studies in Schools (CLASS) project, computers, for long the preserve of select research and technological institutions, have transcended these barriers and entered the schools. 750 secondary/higher secondary schools have been provided with micro-computers to familiarise students and teachers with the range of computer applications and their potential as a learning medium.

Targets Arising as an Implication of the NPE and Priority Measures During the VIIth Plan

5. The following tasks would emerge from the NPE statements:

(i) Expand the TV and Radio transmission network to:

Provide minimum ETV and Radio programme coverage for identified target groups in all major language zones by 1990.

establish Radio stations in teaching Universities/ Colleges during the VIIth Plan

provide a dedicated educational TV channel by 1991-92

create a dedicated satellite system for educational needs in the long-term;

(ii) Expansion of in-house programme-production facilities to generate adequate capacity in major Indian languages by 1990, and in other languages during the VIIIth Plan;

(iii) Development of facilities/organisations for production, duplication and dissemination of curricular support material using non-broadcast methods/graphic teaching aids during the VIIth Plan;

(iv) Development of training programmes/facilities for manpower generation for educational media during the VIIth Plan;

(v) Provide Radio receivers in all primary/elementary schools during the VIIth Plan and TV sets to all schools by 1995;

(vi) Eliminating elements of consumerism, violence etc. from media programmes without delay;

(vii) Expand existing/initiate new programmes for computer-manpower development during the VIIth Plan to reach desired levels by 1995;

(viii) Integration of computer-education modules in professional and general education courses at First-degree level and provision of computer facilities in these institutions—initiated in the VIIth Plan to be completed by 1995;

(ix) Introduction of elective computer-science courses at higher-secondary level during the VIIth Plan;

(x) Extension of computer literacy programmes to cover all higher-secondary schools by 1991, secondary schools by 1995 and elementary schools in the long-term:

(xi) Establish a national Centre of Educational Informatics during the VIIth Plan;

(xii) Mount a technology mission to develop a reliable source of electric supply to schools in remote areas by 1990.

III. STRATEGY ENVISAGED AND BASIC PRE-REQUISITES

6. The National Policy emphasises that "In order to avoid structural dualism, modern educational technology should out to the most distant areas and most deprived sections of beneficiaries simultaneously with the areas of comparative affluence and ready availability". This approach would intrinsically

favour the use of broadcast methods, with their inherent advantages of greater reach, convenience of management and cost-effectiveness, over thc non-broadcast methods largely oriented to individual learning. Because it is not possible to broadcast programmes for every class through Radio and TV, co-ordinated with their teaching schedule, these media can be utilised effectively only for enrichment of the learning process, and to transmit course material for distance education. However, the extent to which media like Radio and TV can be used in the service of education is, *inter alia*, dependent on the transmission capability of the network as well as the manner in which competing claims on broadcast time are sought to be rationalised. Large scale use of Audio and Video programmes in broadcast and non-broadcast modes would also generate enormous demand for qualified manpower to work in educational media set-ups. In the long-run, it would be desirable and probably essential that maintenance structures be decentralised, both organisationally and geographically, and local "technician-entrepreneurs" could be trained for such responsibilites. Education requires media support which is related to the curriculum as well as enrichment. Curriculum-based education also requires materials which the teacher can draw upon in the course of this teaching. This could be provided in the form of charts, slides, transparencies etc. Video technology offers considerable potential for improving the quality of education especially at higher levels.

7. Exposure and training in the use of computers in professional education implies intensified manpower-development programmes for computer professionals at different levels and integration of computer-education modules in all professionals disciplines, and even in the general education courses at the first-degree level; together with the provision of necessary staff and facilities in these institutions. Computers can play an important role in enhancing the efficiency of the teaching-learning process, to make children more creative and provide them with an individualised learning environment. Computer literacy will be crucial in preparing children to cope with the micro-computer explosion, which has the same potential for

social change as the industrial revolution. The demands of equity would, therefore, require that computer literacy programmes be progressively integrated with the school curriculum at lower-secondary and elementary levels.

8. Educational technology offers the means to reach large numbers in remote and inaccessible areas, remove disparity in educational facilities available to the disadvantaged and provide individualised instruction to learners conveniently suited to their needs and pace of learning. However, all technology requires supporting infrastructure, and unless that infrastruture, like trained manpower, competent and willing teachers, school buildings etc., exists, no technology—direct or distance—is likely to succeed. One of the major hurdles in the way of introducing modern technology in the rural hinterland is the availability of assured electric supply. Providing a source of assured electricity is a pre-requisite for using technological options in the service of education, and needs to be addressed on priority.

IV. ROLE OF VARIOUS ORGANISATIONS

9. The Ministry of Human Resource Development (MHRD) and the Ministry of Information and Broadcasting should jointly evolve a long-term perspective for media usage. The CIET and the UGC must continue to discharge a coordinating role, as well as provide the necessary leadership and guidance to the State agencies/Universities in setting up and managing production facilities, training of their staff, design of support material and tools for evaluation and programme research. The State Governments and their agencies would be responsible for the production of locally relevant programmes for the target audiences, supply and maintenance of receiving systems, production and distribution of support material, audience research and evaluation studies, and the recruitment and training of production staff and user custodians of receiving sets. Voluntary agencies and individual producers will be involved in all these activities to the extent possible. The Department of Electronics, as the policy-making body in the

field of computers, should be closely involved in the planning and development of various manpower programmes as at present, and in identifying the hardware needs of different educational institutions. The State Governments and their agencies, the UGC and other statutory bodies governing professional education at higher levels would share the responsibility for bringing about necessary changes in curriculum and admission requirements of various courses, accreditation and providing infrastrutural requirements. Since the measures suggested involve considerable investment in hardware facilities and would require expert guidance at all stages of implementation, the central government will have to continue to play a substantial role in the planning and implementation of this programme.

10

CONCLUSIONS

According to J.D. Finn technology is now making the future of instruction capricious and hazardous. But indoing so it has presented us with more opportunity and more choices than ever before. If the future is an adventure, it is an adventure because of technology. The cost of civilization is the fact that we can make wrong choices because of the alternatives technology presents. The reward of civilization is the freedom provided by technology and the opportunity to make the right choices. This cost and this reward we now face with the technology of the instructional process.

John W. Loughary has concluded that the most significant aspect of the student revolt is not their overtraining of appropriateness of subject matter or content. It is instead, their increasing rejection of traditional educational procedures.

B.F. Skinner has concluded that some promising advances have recently been made in the field of learning. Special tehniques have been designed to arrange what are called "contingencies of reinforcement" the relation which prevail between behaviour on the one hand and the consequences of that behaviour on the other—with the result that a much more effective control of behaviour has been achieved.

A large fraction of America's earlist textbooks had very long titles. The content of old textbooks in most fields, during any particular time varied more than is common today. Textbooks have been holding a very important place in the school programme in America.

C.R. Carpenter commenting on access to remote learning materials has observed that the problem that confronts us and which we shall attempt to resolve, is to show how the so called "mass media" and other associated and complemental technologies can be used in new patterns and varied configurations to provide some of the required conditions for formal instruction and the educational development of college students.

There is a discussion of spelling as a still that relates the sounds of speech to the written symbols that represent these sounds A.D. Leifer has said that it is nothing new when we state that television and film can teach and that they are capable of serving as substitutes for, or supplements to, more traditional modes of teaching.

Programmed instruction Bunduson and Faust have defined as a systematic development process rather than a product form, and computer assisted instruction is still too complex to be characterized as a kind of instructional medium.

Ainee Dorr Leifer has observed that scheduling of television and film differs in that television is most often broadcast at a specified time to a presumably large audience, while film is most often shown to a small audience at a time the teacher chooses. There is a growing recognition that television and film can also be explicitly used to convey visual and cognitive processes, that television and film programmes carry with them effective implicit as well as explicit content and that choosing either of these media as an educational agent communicates to students ideas about appropriate and useful modes of learning.

It will thus be seen that educational technology is a new and radical approach towards the achivement of educational objectives of an industrial society. More and more use of all the traditional as well as non-traditional modes of teaching like machines, films, radio, television and computers, is done for effective teaching.

BIBLIOGRAPHY

Allen, W. H., "Technology: Roles for men and Machines." *Britannica Review of American Education*, Vol. 1 (1969).

Angell, G. W., Effect of immediate knowledge of quiz results on final examination scores in freshman chemistry, *J. educ. Res.*, 1949.

Beck, J., On some methods of programming. Paper read at the Air Force Office of Scientific Research and the Univ. of Penna. Conference on the Automatic Teaching of Verbal and Symbolic Skills, Philadelphia, December, 1958.

Besnard, G. C., Briggs, L. J. and Walker, E. S., *The improved subject matter trainer.* Technical memorandum, Armament Systems Personnel Research Laboratory, Lowry Air Force Base, Colorado, April 1955.

Bloom, B. S., "Learning for Mastery," *Evaluation Comment.* University of California, Los Angeles, Center for the Study of Evaluation of Instructional Programmes. May 1968.

Briggs, L. J., The development and appraisal of special procedures for superior students and an analysis of the effects of "knowledge of results." *Abstr. Doctoral Disser.*, 1949.

———Intensive classes for superior students. J. *Educ. Psychol.*, 1947.

Briggs. L. J., Campeau, P. L , Gagne, R. M., and May, M. A., *Instructional Media: A procedure for the design of multi-media instruction, a critical review of research, and suggestions for future research.* Monograph No. 2. Palo Alto: American Institutes for Research. 1967.

Brinkman, E. H., Educability in visualization of objects in space: a programmed instruction approach. Unpublished doctoral dissertation, Univer. of Michigan, 1963.

Buckley, N., Programmed learning: return to reality. *Dun's Review*, 1964.

Bury, J. B., *The Idea of Prossess*, New York, Dover Publications 1955.

Carroll, J. B., Wanted: a research basis for educational policy on foreign language teaching. *Harvard educ. Rev.*, 1960, 30 (2), 128-140.

Coulson, J. E. (Ed.) *Programmed learning and computer-based instruction.* New York: Wiley, 1962.

Crowder, N. A., Intrinsically programmed materials for teaching complex skills and concepts. Paper read at the Amer. Psychol. Ass., Washington, D. C., August, 1958. (a)

——, Automatic tutoring by means of instrinsic programming. Paper read at the Air Force Office of Scientific Research and the Univ. of Penna. Conference on the Automatic Teaching of Verbal and Symbolic Skills, Philadelphia, December, 1958. (b)

——*An automatic tutoring book on number systems.* Vol. 1. Timonium Md.: Electronics Co., 1958.

Crutchfied, R. S. and M. V. Covington, Facilitation of creative thinking and problem solving in school children. Paper read at American Assn. for the Advancement of Science, Cleveland, December 29, 1963.

DeCecco, J. P., (Ed.) *Educational Technology.* New York; Holt, Rinehart and Winston, 1964.

Deese, J., *The Psychology of Learning.* New York: McGraw-Hill, 1958.

English, H. B , How psychology can facilitate military training —a concrete example. J. *Appl. Psychol.*, 1942.

Estes, W. K., Learning *Encyclopedia of educational research* (3rd ed.) New York: Macmillan, 1960.

Evans, J. L., Multiple-choice discrimination programming. Paper read at Amer. Psychol. Assn., New York, September, 1961.

Ferster, C. B., and Sapon, S. N., An application of recent developments in psychology to the teaching of German, *Harvard educ. Rev.*, 1958.

Finn, J. D., Technological development: its meaning for education. In R. T., Filep (Ed.), *Perspectivs in programming*. New York Macmillan, 1963.

Flanagan, J. C., "Individualizing Education." *Education*, Vol. 90(1970).

Gagne, R. M., *Conditions of Learning*. New York: Holt, Rinehart and Winston, Inc., 1965.

——, A *review of factors in learning efficiency*. AFOSRTN-58-294. Air Force Office of Scientific Research. Air Research and Development Command. U. S. Air Force. Washington 25, D. C., November 1958.

Gilbert, T. F., An early approximation to principles of programming continuous-discourse, self-instructional materials. A report to Bell Telephone Laboratories, Inc., Murray Hill, N. J., September 1958.

Glaser, R., (Ed.) *Training research and education*. Pittsburgh. Univ. of Pittsburgh Press, 1962.

———,(Ed.) *Teaching machines and programmed learning, II: data and directions*. Washington: Natl. Education Assn., 1965.

Some research problems in automated instruction: instructional programming and subject matter structure. In J. E. Coulson (Ed.), *Programmed learning and computer based instruction*. New York: Wiley, 1962.

Hoban, C. F., Jr., and Van Ormer, E. B. *Instructional Film Research, 1918-1950*. Technical Report No. SDC 269-7-19, Instructional Film Research Programme.

Homme, L., and Glaser, R., Relationships between the programmed textbook and teaching machines. Paper read at the Air Force Office of Scientific Research and the Univ. of Penna. Conference on the Automatic Teaching of Verbal and Symbolic Skills, Philadelphia, December 1958.

Kopstein, F. F. and Isabel J., Shillestad. *A survey of auto-instructional devices*. Wright-Patterson Air Force Base, Ohio: Aeronautical Systems Division, 1961. Technical Report 61-414.

Loushang, John W., (ed.) *Man Machine Systems in Education*, New York, Hamper and Row, 1966.

Lysaught, J. P., and C. M. Williams., *A guide to programmed instruction*. New York: Wiley, 1963.

Markle, Susan M. *Good frames and bad*. New York: Wiley, 1964.

Mechner, F , Science education and behavioural technology. In R. Glaser (Ed.), *Teaching machines and programmed learning, H: data and directions*: Washington, D. C.: National Education Assn., 1965.

Oliver, J. W., *History of American Technology*, New York Ronald Press, 1956.

Ramo, Simon, "A New Technique of Education," *Engineering and Science* 21: 17-22, Spring 1957.

Skinner, B. F., The Programming of verbal knowledge. In E. Galonter (Ed.), *Automatic teaching: the state of the art*. New York: Wiley, 1959.

Stolurow, L. M., *Teaching by machine*. Washington: U. S. Government Printing Office, 1961.

Stolurow, L. M. and D. Davis. Teaching machines and computer-based systems. In R. Glaser (E.d), *Teaching machines and programmed learning, II:data and directions*. Washington: National Education Association, 1965.

Taber, J. I., and R. Glaser. An exploratory evaluation of a discriminative transfer learning programme using literal prompts. *J. Educ. Res.*, 1962.

Index

INDEX